CCCC STUDIES IN WRITING & RHETORIC
Edited by Victor Villanueva, Washington State University

The aim of the CCCC Studies in Writing & Rhetoric Series is to influence how we think about language in action and especially how writing gets taught at the college level. The methods of studies vary from the critical to historical to linguistic to ethnographic, and their authors draw on work in various fields that inform composition—including rhetoric, communication, education, discourse analysis, psychology, cultural studies, and literature. Their focuses are similarly diverse—ranging from individual writers and teachers, to work on classrooms and communities and curricula, to analyses of the social, political, and material contexts of writing and its teaching.

SWR was one of the first scholarly book series to focus on the teaching of writing. It was established in 1980 by the Conference on College Composition and Communication (CCCC) in order to promote research in the emerging field of writing studies. As our field has grown, the research sponsored by SWR has continued to articulate the commitment of CCCC to supporting the work of writing teachers as reflective practitioners and intellectuals.

We are eager to identify influential work in writing and rhetoric as it emerges. We thus ask authors to send us project proposals that clearly situate their work in the field and show how they aim to redirect our ongoing conversations about writing and its teaching. Proposals should include an overview of the project, a brief annotated table of contents, and a sample chapter. They should not exceed 10,000 words.

To submit a proposal, please register as an author at www.editorialmanager.com/nctebp. Once registered, follow the steps to submit a proposal (be sure to choose SWR Book Proposal from the drop-down list of article submission types).

SWR Editorial Advisory Board

Victor Villanueva, SWR Editor, Washington State University
Anna Plemons, Associate Editor, Washington State University
Frances Condon, University of Waterloo
Ellen Cushman, Northeastern University
Deborah Holdstein, Columbia College Chicago
Asao Inoue, University of Washington Tacoma
Jay Jordan, University of Utah
Min-Zhan Lu, University of Louisville
Paula Mathieu, Boston College
Nedra Reynolds, University of Rhode Island
Jacqueline Rhodes, California State University, San Bernardino
Eileen Schell, Syracuse University
Jody Shipka, University of Maryland, Baltimore County
Vershawn Ashanti Young, University of Waterloo

Public Pedagogy in Composition Studies

Ashley J. Holmes
Georgia State University

Conference on College Composition and Communication

National Council of Teachers of English

Chapter 5 is a revised version of the article "Transformative Learning, Affect, and Reciprocal Care in Community Engagement" published in *Community Literacy Journal* 9.2 (2015).

Staff Editor: Bonny Graham
Series Editor: Victor Villanueva
Interior Design: Mary Rohrer
Cover Design: Mary Rohrer and Lynn Weckhorst

NCTE Stock Number: 38007; eStock Number: 38014
ISBN 978-0-8141-3800-7; eISBN 978-0-8141-3801-4

Copyright © 2016 by the Conference on College Composition and Communication of the National Council of Teachers of English.

All rights reserved. No part of this publication may be reproduced or transmitted in any form or by any means, electronic or mechanical, including photocopy, or any information storage and retrieval system, without permission from the copyright holder. Printed in the United States of America.

It is the policy of NCTE in its journals and other publications to provide a forum for the open discussion of ideas concerning the content and the teaching of English and the language arts. Publicity accorded to any particular point of view does not imply endorsement by the Executive Committee, the Board of Directors, or the membership at large, except in announcements of policy, where such endorsement is clearly specified.

NCTE provides equal employment opportunity (EEO) to all staff members and applicants for employment without regard to race, color, religion, sex, national origin, age, physical, mental or perceived handicap/disability, sexual orientation including gender identity or expression, ancestry, genetic information, marital status, military status, unfavorable discharge from military service, pregnancy, citizenship status, personal appearance, matriculation or political affiliation, or any other protected status under applicable federal, state, and local laws.

Every effort has been made to provide current URLs and email addresses, but because of the rapidly changing nature of the Web, some sites and addresses may no longer be accessible.

Publication partially funded by a subvention grant from the Conference on College Composition and Communication of the National Council of Teachers of English.

Library of Congress Cataloging-in-Publication Data

Names: Holmes, Ashley J., author.
Title: Public pedagogy in composition studies / by: Ashley J. Holmes.
Description: Urbana, IL : National Council of Teachers of English, [2016] | Series: Studies in Writing & Rhetoric | Includes bibliographical references and index.
Identifiers: LCCN 2016031374 (print) | LCCN 2016047693 (ebook) | ISBN 9780814138007 (pbk.) | ISBN 9780814138014 (eISBN) | ISBN 9780814138014
Subjects: LCSH: English language—Rhetoric—Study and teaching (Higher) | English language—Composition and exercises. | Academic writing—Social aspects.
Classification: LCC PE1404 .H75 2016 (print) | LCC PE1404 (ebook) | DDC 808/.0420711—dc23
LC record available at https://lccn.loc.gov/2016031374

CONTENTS

Preface   vii

Acknowledgments   xiii

1. Public Pedagogy in Composition Studies   1
2. Relocating the Composition Classroom: Going Public with Pedagogy   33
3. Productive Tensions: Administering Public Pedagogies   63
4. Constructing Institutional Histories for Going Public   96
5. Transformative Learning, Affect, and Reciprocal Care in Public Pedagogy   131

Conclusion   157

Appendixes   161

Notes   169

Works Cited   177

Index   193

Author   201

PREFACE

IN A RECENT WRITING ACROSS THE CURRICULUM session I attended at my university, a diverse group of faculty members were prompted to consider what, if anything, we remembered learning as undergraduate students. The room fell silent as geologists, historians, and psychologists strained to remember what it was they had learned in those first years of higher education before they became specialists in their fields. As the discussion progressed, it became clear that memories of our undergraduate educations were more impressionistic than specific. Many of us had trouble remembering the exact moments when we learned about Pavlov's dog or how to identify a comma splice, but we were able to recall a few powerful educational encounters.

What struck me as I reflected back on my own undergraduate education at North Carolina State University was that the memories that came to mind—the ones I believe had an impact on me in a lasting way—were ironically not in classrooms on my university's campus: they were in the halls of my state's General Assembly, in the teachers' lounge at Garner Senior High School, and in an unsteady canoe rowing down the Neuse River. For a social work course, I was assigned to visit the General Assembly to track a bill and meet face-to-face with my representatives to discuss potential legislation; walking the halls of my state legislature provided a context that activated my classroom-based learning and prompted me to apply my knowledge of social work to public policies. Similarly, during my semester-long student teaching experience at Garner High, I became immersed in the culture of public school teachers, which required me to begin bridging concepts I learned in the university course I took on teaching methods with my experiences as a student teacher and with the stories I heard in the teachers' lounge.

And finally, the canoeing course I took to fulfill a physical education requirement could have easily been forgettable, but the culminating full-day field trip down the Neuse River became compelling in the ways my teacher demonstrated—on location, physically and materially—an ethical approach to interacting with this environment, encouraging us to learn from and take care of resources that run through the backyards of our communities.

In each of these moments of learning, I was faced with the challenge of applying my classroom-based learning in public places. In these contexts, someone or something beyond the university became my teacher. Imbued with a sense of history and depth, unfamiliarity and wonder, these local, public sites for my learning resulted in a kind of disorientation that led to deep learning for me. In other words, school-initiated learning in nonschool places affected me in ways that moved beyond the courses in which my education was originally situated. I began to grasp the importance of understanding one's local surroundings by exploring the powerful synergies among education, social justice, activism, and civic responsibility. Today, as a reflective teacher, I realize my pedagogical values have emerged in part from the public aspects of my own educational development.

I start with these personal moments of learning because, at its core, this book is about public approaches to teaching writing that I believe will have an enduring impact on our students as learners—about how to invite students to apply school-based concepts of analysis, critical thinking, composition, and publication within local, public places in ways that are sometimes messy or disorienting but that are ultimately productive for their learning. As Henry A. Giroux and other scholars have argued, the rise of neoliberalism should cause teachers to question the way corporations surreptitiously educate students into an individualized and privatized model that risks the tenets of democratic citizenship within our communities. However, as composition teachers, I believe those of us who want to combat this neoliberal trend have an opportunity to do so by going public with our composition pedagogies, which starts with being transparent about the ways in which our institutions and classrooms are already steeped in neoliberal ideologies but also how we can choose to forge new pathways through public engagement that moves beyond armchair criticism from the classroom. *Public Pedagogy in Composition Studies* argues that an essential step in that process is designing assignments and creating administrative structures that relocate student experiences to new or unfamiliar publics outside the relative safety of the classroom, while still using the familiarity of the classroom for processing the sometimes affective responses that arise when going public. Without relocation, though, students are less likely to be confronted with the kind of dissonances that prompt transformative learning.

Since the start of my exploration of public pedagogy in composition studies, my goal has been to both document and more fully understand a growing trend in our field: going public with the work of teaching writing. From public and civic writing initiatives to service learning and community-based writing, composition studies already has a strong foundation in situating student writing and experiences in increasingly public spheres. The case studies highlighted throughout this book are meant to contribute to this base of scholarship by showing the diverse ways in which writing teachers and administrators within three writing programs across the United States are inviting their students to go public while building administrative and curricular supports for this public work. The book is also intended to initiate conversations about how our public pedagogies are having an impact on student learning experiences and about the importance of being mindful of affect and ethics through the processes of going public.

This is a *kairotic* moment within the academy for civic engagement and community-based projects. John M. Ackerman argues that terms such as *civic engagement, service, and outreach* have achieved "brand-name status," operating as "cornerstones of a liberal education . . . and as pathways between institutions of higher learning and their public constituencies" (77). Mirroring the public turn within composition studies, colleges and universities are incorporating civic and public engagement as "centerpiece[s] in strategic planning exercises" (77). I have witnessed this within my own institution, Georgia State University (GSU), whose strategic plan advocates for undergraduate "signature experiences" ("Goal 1"). These applied learning encounters—like the examples of public pedagogies in the coming pages—typically take students outside of the classroom and into the professional, urban, and public spaces of downtown Atlanta. GSU is not alone in valuing these kinds of public learning experiences; institutions such as Oberlin College, Syracuse University, and the University of Arizona—the three institutions I comparatively analyze throughout this book—have missions that encourage student engagement with communities beyond the campus. As the discourse of public outreach in higher education proliferates, composition teachers are presented with opportunities to ask critical questions about what it means to go public and how to best forge ethical alliances among students, teachers, publics, and institutions.

While our colleges and universities move toward increased public and civic engagement efforts, we are faced with the challenge of how to best support public pedagogies through administrative and institutional structures. Scholars in composition studies, particularly within discussions of service learning pedagogy, have been debating whether it is beneficial (for community members and programs, as well as students and universities) to institutionalize public outreach and service learning programs by creating stable centers and standardized curricula (see Mathieu; Feigenbaum). Paula Mathieu, employing terms by Michel de Certeau, has framed the institutionalization debate between strategic and tactical approaches, ultimately advocating for tactical approaches that are more responsive to the needs of community members in publics beyond the university. I respond to this debate in Chapter 3 by arguing for administering public pedagogies in ways that exploit the tensions between strategic and tactical approaches—seeking a balance between institutionalized programs and ones that are developed more organically from the publics outside of our institutions of higher education.

In a cultural context where colleges and universities are critiqued for increasing costs, staggering debt, and irrelevant instruction, we need to demonstrate our worth in material ways that positively impact our communities and that publicly document our efforts. One of the institutions in this study, Oberlin College, received quite a bit of negative media attention in February and March 2013 resulting from a series of hate-related incidents, including "racist, anti-Semitic, and antigay messages [being] left around campus" (Pérez-Peña and Gabriel). Amid the frenzy of the incidents, the college canceled classes, stating "we hope today will allow the entire community—students, faculty, and staff—to make a strong statement about the values we cherish here at Oberlin: inclusion, respect for others, and a strong and abiding faith in the worth of every individual" ("Classes Canceled"). This example corroborates why we need public pedagogies: to teach students methods for questioning and addressing injustices; to communicate through our actions our sense of respect for individuals locally and in communities beyond; and, to document the ways that our public pedagogies help address community problems. Making these moves helps us improve and enhance town-gown relations and publicize the contributions of our colleges and universities.

Many institutions, including the three within my study, have historical and contemporary divisions—both physical and perceived—between the school and the surrounding community, and public pedagogies represent an opportunity to begin bridging those divides. For example, I talked with graduate TAs and faculty members at Syracuse University about the historical roots of the spatial separation of the university at the top of a hill from the town below and how that spatial distance is maintained through, at times, strained relations today. However, the case studies from Syracuse in the coming pages highlight how partnering with new or unfamiliar on-campus publics—like A. V. Luce's pedagogies analyzed in Chapter 2—or administering ongoing, multisemester and multiyear partnerships with community groups—such as Steve Parks's projects analyzed in Chapter 3—can help students branch out of the familiarity and insularity of their comfort zones to engage with diverse public groups to enhance their learning. Similarly, in Chapter 4, I turn to historical accounts of how the University of Arizona barely achieved land grant status because of the unwillingness of local Tucson residents in the late nineteenth century to donate land; those historical tensions between the university and the surrounding community continue to ripple through outreach efforts more than 130 years later. In addition to modeling pedagogies and administrative approaches, *Public Pedagogy in Composition Studies* argues that it is essential for us to understand the historical divisions between town and gown and how those institutional histories manifest in our efforts to go public today. Many of the instructors and administrators I spoke with for my case studies articulated how their choice to have students go public was in part a means of addressing the historical and contemporary divides between their institution and their community. Indeed, despite the challenges of bridging the divides, these instructors mindfully prepare pedagogies that ask students to confront the realities and problems of the communities surrounding their institution by moving beyond the classroom into various publics.

As I prepare another set of syllabi for the coming semester, I think back to meaningful moments of learning in public places from my undergraduate studies, moments I have continued to revisit over the years. These experiences have at times caused me to consider my role as an academic citizen who can use the school-based skills I learned in my courses within nonacademic, everyday, and public spaces beyond the classroom. The case studies in this book suggest that part of what prompts the kind of transfer and application of course-based concepts is relocation through a public approach to pedagogy. Situating student learning within unfamiliar publics provides diverse contexts in which students may experience the kinds of dissonances that initiate transformation. Whether you are an administrator ready to redesign your program's goals to have a more public emphasis or a teacher interested in modifying your curriculum, I hope the following pages will offer some guidance as you go public with your composition pedagogies.

ACKNOWLEDGMENTS

I AM GRATEFUL TO SO MANY PEOPLE WHO contributed their time, knowledge, and resources to my research. This project would not have been possible without the support of nineteen writing teachers and administrators who graciously agreed to participate in an interview and share their pedagogical materials with me. Learning from their innovative ways of teaching and administering writing has been a pleasure. I am particularly indebted to the writing teachers who gave me permission to analyze their approaches in more detail and who, in many cases, took additional time to read my representation of their work and offer feedback: thank you to Jan Cooper, Crystal Fodrey, Anne-Marie Hall, Amy Kimme Hea, A. V. Luce, Steve Parks, Rebecca Richards, and Anne Trubek. Thank you also to Eileen Schell for organizing and hosting me for a three-day campus visit to Syracuse.

I want to thank Victor Villanueva for seeing potential in my research; I have appreciated your kindness, candor, and understanding throughout this process. Thank you also to the two reviewers of my initial proposal and the two external reviewers of my complete manuscript; your thorough and thoughtful feedback helped me enhance the book. Thank you to my production editor, Bonny Graham; copy editor, Joshua Rosenberg; and the other staff and designers at NCTE and CCCC who worked to prepare the book for publication.

The first iteration of this project became my dissertation for the PhD in rhetoric, composition, and the teaching of English I earned at the University of Arizona, and I would like to thank my committee for providing me with indispensable feedback that helped shape my research. Thank you to Amy Kimme Hea, my dissertation chair, for being a supportive mentor, encouraging me in the early stages of my research, challenging my assumptions, and celebrating victories along the way. Thank you to Anne-Marie Hall for balancing sincere praise with tough questions. Many thanks also to Maritza Cardenas for helping advance my work. I am grateful for friends from the University of Arizona who read early drafts of my writing and/or listened supportively as I worked through the ideas for this book, especially Jenna Vinson, Rebecca Richards, Crystal Fodrey, Elise Verzosa Hurley, Jennifer Haley-Brown, Amanda Wray, Erica Cirillo-McCarthy, Faith Kurtyka, Londie Martin, and Rachael Wendler Shah.

Thank you to my colleagues at Georgia State University—Lynée Gaillet and George Pullman for reading late drafts of the manuscript, and Mary Hocks and Michael Harker for your mentorship. Thank you also to current department chair Lynée and former chair Randy Malamud for your ongoing support of this project, and I am grateful to GSU for awarding me a PAWS Junior Faculty Research Funding Award, which provided the sabbatical that allowed me to complete the writing and final revision of this book.

I am lucky to have had incredible professors and colleagues who, over the years and still today, contribute to my development as a teacher and scholar; thank you to Chris Anson and Nancy Penrose at North Carolina State University, and to Jessie Moore, Paula Rosinski, Tim Peeples, Michael Strickland, Rebecca Pope-Ruark, and Peter Felten at Elon University.

I want to thank my mother, Debra Martin, for pushing me to dream big and to set manageable parameters for achieving my goals. Thank you to Walter and Graham for sharing your first years with my first book. Dan, thank you for everything—for believing in me, for keeping me afloat, for supporting my career choices, and for being an amazing partner and father. I am forever grateful.

1

Public Pedagogy in Composition Studies

> In our journals and at our conferences, one finds repeated again and again the assertion that our work—our teaching, researching, and theorizing—can clarify and even improve the prospects of literacy in democratic culture. If we really believe this, we must acknowledge our obligation to air that work in the most expansive, inclusive forums possible. . . . We must go public. And we can.
>
> —Peter Mortensen, "Going Public"

IN THE NEARLY TWO DECADES SINCE PETER MORTENSEN emphatically asserted "we must go public," writing teachers, administrators, and students have answered his call. The prevalence of publications and conference presentations related to public engagement and public writing show that composition specialists have raised and begun addressing important pedagogical and administrative questions related to the public turn in composition studies. While the 2013 Conference on College Composition and Communication (CCCC) theme, "The Public Work of Composition," highlighted the ongoing and strengthening connections between composition studies and public outreach, there is still more work to be done. When I began designing my study of public pedagogy, I found myself agreeing with the tenor of Mortensen's mandate that "we must go public. And we can" (182), but I also wanted to know: How does public pedagogy impact student learning? How might composition courses employing public pedagogies fit within the broader structure of a writing program? In what ways might administrators gain institutional support for public pedagogy in composition? I valued the knowledge students gained from going public with their experiences and writing in my courses, but I sought an approach to composition pedagogy that accounted for and critiqued the diverse public sites where I chose to (re)locate my pedagogy and that acknowledged the significance of those publics as locations—places with histories and rhetorically positioned within broader spheres.

Works like Paula Mathieu's *Tactics of Hope*, Christian Weisser's *Beyond Academic Discourse*, and Eli Goldblatt's *Because We Live Here*—among many others—have been essential source books, guiding my own sense of the public turn in composition studies and the possibilities for how I might design pedagogies to support students in going public. In more recent publications, I began to see that phrase—"go public"—repeated more often. For example, Linda Flower's *Community Literacy and the Rhetoric of Public Engagement* addresses significant questions about how and where "ordinary people go public" (5), and Nancy Welch's *Living Room* translates lessons from the past about "what it means, and what it takes, for most people to try to go public" into specific pedagogies for composition and rhetoric classrooms (9). And, Shirley K Rose and Irwin Weiser's edited collection *Going Public* considers community-based and pedagogical concerns by addressing publics related to writing program administration. My hope is that *Public Pedagogy in Composition Studies* contributes meaningfully to these discussions of the public turn by (1) offering a series of comparative case studies that highlight pedagogical examples and administrative approaches for how many practitioners in our field are going public with pedagogy, (2) arguing for the significance of understanding our institutional histories in contemporary efforts to go public, and (3) prompting critical questions about how teachers should ethically attend to students' affective responses that may arise from public pedagogies, while acknowledging the power of disorienting dilemmas in students' learning.

Given the strong base of scholarship in public writing within the field, it was not surprising for me to find—through the interviews I conducted with writing teachers and administrators at Oberlin College, Syracuse University, and the University of Arizona—that many compositionists are already going public. What I did not fully anticipate were the diverse terminologies being used by study participants to name, define, and discuss quite similar pedagogical approaches:

> "The terms I tend to graft onto are *community partnership, civic,* . . . [and] *social change.*"
>
> "My word is usually *community*, and I kind of think of that and use it in contrast to academic writing."
>
> "I think the term that has come up quite a bit . . . is *community engagement.*"
>
> "The term that I used . . . was *client project*, but *service learning* became more easily index-able [at my institution]."
>
> "I find myself leaning more towards *service learning* because to me it imbues that sense of public."
>
> "*Service learning* is a term that I use just because people know what it means."
>
> "I gravitate toward *real world* mostly . . . because the way that I envision public is students going to areas outside of the university."

The sampling of quotes from teachers in my study showcases just a few examples within the broad range of terms composition teachers are using to describe pedagogical practices that have a common interest in going public. Words such as *civic* and *social change* suggest pedagogies for democratic or activist purposes, whereas words like *service learning, community engagement,* and *community partnership* suggest pedagogies that require students to directly serve their local communities; moreover, *client project* and *real world* suggest a professional writing or internship-style approach to the public work of composition. And, of course, each of the quoted teachers had a particular rhetorical purpose for naming their pedagogies as they did—whether because of the value and understanding within one's particular institutional or professional context or because of one's personal conception of what it means to go public. While the teachers I interviewed represented this variety in terminology, I also found this multiplicity echoed within our field's professional conferences.

For instance, when I presented at the inaugural Conference on Community Writing in October 2015, I attended panels that demonstrated the range of ways teacher-scholars are interpreting the public work of "community writing"—from service learning, to place-based ecocomposition, to the use of Twitter in local business communities. Likewise, the submission category for CCCC, "Community, Civic, & Public," represents an assortment of names; no other CCCC category has quite this level of catchall. While an array of terms can be advantageous in representing a polyvocality that captures the shades of difference in our approaches, I want to make the case for *publics* as a useful umbrella term for composition pedagogies that have a common interest in relocating student writing and experiences to places beyond the classroom to enhance student learning. One of the risks in using different terminologies is the potential for missed connections and neglected conversations. While I am not advocating for losing these terms—terms that I use throughout my scholarship, too—I hope that we might also form stronger alliances around our common goals of going public.

Based on the case studies I feature in the coming pages, I define public pedagogy in composition studies as an approach to the teaching of writing that values the educative potential for public sites, communities, and persons beyond the boundaries of the traditional classroom and/or campus community; these values initiate moves to go public with composition pedagogies by relocating composition teaching and learning within increasingly public spheres. Public pedagogies often require students to encounter new or unfamiliar places (or to approach familiar publics from a new perspective) and, because they are situated within public contexts beyond the teacher's control, students sometimes experience spatially prompted disorienting dilemmas that can ultimately be productive for their learning. My usage of the term *public pedagogy* draws on theories from curriculum studies, as I advocate for the umbrella concept of publics to both represent a common language for the public work we do within composition studies and to expand our sense of what it means (and where) to go public. Indeed, while my own way into public pedagogy began with service learning (a pedagogy that I continue to value and implement), I advocate for public pedagogy as an approach that does not limit public engagement to service. Public pedagogy has allowed me to envision teaching and administering writing in ways that broaden the scope of possible locations for writing, to relocate learning to public sites outside of formal schools, and critically attend to place-based issues while going public. For me, as for many of the teachers I interviewed for this study, asking students to engage with new or unfamiliar public locations—sometimes through service learning or for civic purposes, though not always—became a central value for students' learning in composition courses with a public pedagogy.

Public pedagogy, like other community-based and critical pedagogies, attempts to break down the perceived and actual barriers between town and gown. Taking a public approach to composition pedagogy means facilitating students' understanding of the significance of learning that happens in public spaces that may be marked as nonschool, unacademic, or everyday. For composition teachers and administrators, public pedagogy may result in a radical shifting of authority from traditional fonts of academic knowledge—the credentialed professor and the stacks in the campus library—to public sources of knowledge—the director of a local nonprofit organization and the streets and neighborhoods in our surrounding communities. Scholars such as Henry A. Giroux have raised important concerns about the powerfully negative educative potential of corporations, and I argue that public pedagogy in composition studies counters this neoliberal agenda by assigning students to study and/or serve their communities and to learn from the diverse publics around them, despite the risks that these experiences may involve participation in neoliberal forces.

While public pedagogy in composition studies connects with many of the goals of cultural studies, critical analysis, and writing for civic purposes, my analysis of the case studies demonstrates how it can differ from those approaches in the pedagogical methods used. While cultural critique and civic writing can happen wholly inside of formal school spaces, public pedagogy, drawing on community-based commitments of service learning and place-based approaches to teaching writing, involves students *going* public—through, for instance, community service, observing or gardening in a nearby park, or participating in an in-person protest.[1] Indeed, it is the act of *going* public that imbues this pedagogical approach with so much potential. Teachers who go public with pedagogy recognize that, even though critique and analysis within the classroom are valuable approaches, they ultimately cannot replicate the visceral experiences of engaging with new or unfamiliar spaces on or off campus, experiences that can spark deeply meaningful learning for students. The examples from composition teachers I interviewed suggest that relocation is a key feature in public pedagogy—relocating both the sites of composition teaching and learning, and, by extension, re-envisioning writing program administration and work within our institutions through a more public lens.

The comparative, cross-institutional study I conducted takes a snapshot of how composition teachers and writing program administrators in three different institutions across the United States are currently going public with their pedagogy. Through analyzing best practices of programs and instructors, *Public Pedagogy in Composition Studies* documents model programs and pedagogies. The book considers public pedagogy at a number of levels: within composition pedagogy (Chapter 2), as part of writing program administration (Chapter 3), in the context of contemporary institutional conversations and historical trajectories (Chapter 4), and in tandem with students' transformative and affective learning (Chapter 5). Before delving into the findings of my case studies, though, I provide in this chapter background information on the study I conducted, a review of public pedagogy theorizations within curriculum studies, and a rationale for relocating composition pedagogies.

CASE STUDIES OF PUBLIC PEDAGOGIES

In 2011, I set out to study the ways writing teachers and program administrators were going public with their pedagogies and how they were supporting that work administratively. My research from that time has resulted in the case studies of public pedagogies within the Rhetoric and Writing Program at Oberlin College, the Syracuse University Writing Program,[2] and the Writing Program at University of Arizona, on which I draw in the coming chapters. Bearing some similarity to Carol P. Hartzog's 1986 study *Composition and the Academy*, the project I designed approached writing programs—including their administrators and instructors, their goals and objectives, their histories and future plans, their institutional and geographical contexts—as significant sites of scholarly study. I selected the three sites for comparative study in this project because each has an explicitly public approach to the teaching of writing through coursework, outreach initiatives, and/or an institutional history of public engagement. Drawing on the wealth of knowledge of the practitioners within those writing programs, my comparative study relies on nineteen interviews I conducted with graduate teaching assistants, faculty, and administrators; program and teaching documents I collected from study participants, such as syllabi, assignment sheets, and program mission statements; and notes and observations I made from campus visits to two of the three research sites.[3] Through the IRB-approved consent process, all participants chose to be named in the study; participants whose interviews and course or administrative materials I drew on heavily were also given an opportunity to read and give me feedback on the drafts of the chapters in which they are referenced.[4]

In addition to selecting institutions based on existing public initiatives, I also sought diversity in terms of institution location, type, and size, as well as the kind of program or department and the courses, majors, or minors each oversees. Because of the comparative nature of this study, differences across institutions inform the analysis of how public pedagogies function within local contexts. In "Institutional Differences in Pursuing the Public Good," Barbara A. Holland argues that the growing engagement movement in higher education is making it "more important than ever to understand the distinctions among institution types and to consider why engagement seems to take root in some institutional contexts more readily than others" (235–36). Holland contends that the general public and media too often look to research universities as the measuring stick for engagement efforts, when her analysis finds that these institutions are often the least likely to involve themselves in a civic mission or engaged scholarship. According to Holland, different institutional types and missions result from the different ways administrators assess risk, value, and profitability. As I considered institutions for my study, I wanted to make sure research and liberal arts institutions were represented, as well as public and private, among other differences.

Table 1 summarizes some of these key distinctions among the three research sites in my study. The University of Arizona and Oberlin College represent two different ends of the spectrum in terms of size and differences in institutional type, with Syracuse University falling in the middle in terms of size and being a private, research institution.

My selection of a range of institutions and programs was meant, in part, to address some of the limitations that might emerge from focusing on a case study of only one program. However, the small number of study sites is not representative of the diverse programs and schools where composition is taught. Two of the three institutions are private, and all three institutions are fairly highly ranked within the *U.S. News & World Report* College Rankings: Oberlin College is ranked #23 of National Liberal Arts Colleges, Syracuse University is #61 of National Universities, and the University of Arizona is #121 of National Universities ("*U.S. News*"). In other words, these are institutions with national reputations, a degree of prestige, and well-established institutional histories. Even though there are a number of colleges and universities that may not share characteristics with the three sites in my study, the data I collected has applicability in a range of institutional contexts. Like Hartzog explained in her study of writing programs, my study "is not, nor does it pretend to be, a comprehensive study of writing programs in the country today," nor a comprehensive consideration of public composition pedagogies within the full range of institution types (x). For the scope of this study, though, the three selected institu-

Table 1. Comparative Data for Three Research Sites

	Oberlin College	Syracuse University	University of Arizona
Geographical Location	Midwest Oberlin, OH	Northeast Syracuse, NY	Southwest Tucson, AZ
Institution Type	Private Liberal Arts College	Private Research University	Public Research I University
Institution Size (Number of Students)[5]	2,912	21,789	39,086
Program or Department's Institutional Affiliation	Department of Rhetoric and Composition, stand-alone department	Department of Writing Studies, Rhetoric, and Composition (formerly the Syracuse University Writing Program), stand-alone department	Writing Program, within the Department of English
Level and/or Type of Courses Overseen	General education writing; First-year seminars; Undergraduate minor	General education writing; Undergraduate major and minor; Graduate program	General education writing (lower and upper division)

tions offered me the chance to delve deeply into a close analysis of how each program was going public and then make comparative claims about how public pedagogies function in different institutional and programmatic contexts, even though those institutional contexts were localized and narrowly defined.

My method of comparative analysis involved "access[ing] different levels"—e.g., curricular, programmatic, departmental, institutional, historical—in order to "examine how they relate to each other and inform the discourse of pedagogy and the act of teaching" (Alexander 513). As Robin Alexander argues, comparativists have tended to ignore pedagogy, and her claims guided my attempt to account for the ways in which "local values, ideas, and debates are part of a much wider educational discourse" (513). The case studies, when taken together through a comparative lens, demonstrate how accessing different levels for comparison allows us to "teas[e] out what is universal in pedagogy from what is unique or site/culture specific; informing the development of pedagogy theory; and extending the vocabulary and repertoire of pedagogic practice" (Alexander 513). For example, my analysis in Chapter 2 shows how a common feature of public pedagogies across institutional contexts, and even within different kinds of composition courses, involves asking students to engage with unfamiliar publics, or to approach familiar publics from a new perspective; however, the comparison also suggests that some of the administrative methods I highlight in Chapter 3—such as next step course sequencing—may be challenging within departments or programs that do not have enough writing courses to create an extended series. In sum, while these three case studies are not wholly representative of the diverse contexts in which compositionists teach and administer programs, I believe they offer a sense of what may translate easily within similar or different kinds of courses and programs. Before delving further into how teachers are going public with composition pedagogy, the next section highlights some of the early conceptions of public pedagogy as the term has been defined within curriculum studies and cultural critique, as well as how the theory's foundations connect with values in the field of composition.

THE "FABULOUS HAZE" SURROUNDING THE TERM *PUBLIC PEDAGOGY*

Educational researchers Jennifer A. Sandlin, Michael P. O'Malley, and Jake Burdick identify the first appearance of *public pedagogy* in 1894, and they trace how the term "has been widely deployed as a theoretical construct in education research to focus on processes and sites of education beyond formal schooling" (338). Sandlin,

O'Malley, and Burdick also note that the term's usage proliferated in the mid-1990s, resulting in part from the work of cultural studies theorist Henry A. Giroux. Giroux's early work on public pedagogy, such as his 1999 article "Public Pedagogy and Rodent Politics," critiques the educative, neoliberal influences of corporations. Giroux argues that corporations, like the Walt Disney Corporation, function as "teaching machines" espousing ideologies that "rewrite memory" and "influence how young people are educated" ("Mouse Power" 222–23). However, since Giroux's conception of the term, scholars from fields such as education and curriculum studies, anthropology, and language and literacy studies have sought to build on and extend theories of critical public pedagogy. Editors of the *Handbook of Public Pedagogy*—the first comprehensive collection published on the concept—note that public pedagogy has been defined in a variety of ways and within a range of contexts (Sandlin, Schultz, and Burdick 2). Indeed, as Glenn C. Savage notes, "there appears to be a fabulous haze surrounding the term [public pedagogy] . . . which renders it both exciting and problematic to consider" (103). Other scholars similarly note that "multiple and distinct articulations of public pedagogy exist within the literature" (O'Malley, Sandlin, and Burdick). While the fabulous haze presents challenges to researchers of public pedagogies, defining what public pedagogy means for composition specialists can help clarify the usage for our particular discipline, while still maintaining its interdisciplinary roots.

Within their contribution to the *Encyclopedia of Curriculum Studies*, O'Malley, Sandlin, and Burdick offer their definition of *public pedagogy* for curriculum studies:

> Public pedagogy is a theoretical construct focusing on various forms and sites of education and learning occurring beyond formal schooling practices; in institutions other than schools, such as museums, zoos, libraries, and public parks; in informal educational sites such as popular culture, media, commercial spaces, and the Internet, and in or through figures and sites of activism, including "public intellectuals," grassroots social activism, and various social movements. (697)

Definitions from curriculum studies, like the one quoted here, focus on how public locations beyond schools have the potential to be educative; this definition is rooted in the way Giroux theorized public pedagogy in his critique of the Disney Corporation.

Giroux's scholarship emphasizes the importance of cultural studies and critical pedagogy, and composition specialists who already value these approaches to the teaching of writing will find many commonalities between those and his conception of public pedagogy. Giroux's definition of *public pedagogy* hinges on his belief that the cultural is pedagogical, and he sees culture as a "powerful educational force" that shapes individuals through the narratives, metaphors, and images that it produces ("Cultural Studies, Public Pedagogy" 62). Therefore, Giroux is particularly concerned with how corporations and neoliberal forces espouse a public pedagogy that educates young people to value consumerism and individualism, and he advocates for educators to engage students in critical analysis of public media and mass culture ("Cultural Studies, Public Pedagogy" 62). In a recent study of Stephen Colbert's *The Colbert Report*, Sophia A. McClennen extends Giroux's conception of public pedagogy and mass media to argue that "post-9/11 satire" communicated through cable television is "one of the most significant forms of critical pedagogy in operation today" (73). For Giroux, though, cultural studies and critique serve as pedagogical tactics for combating the powerful messages targeted toward young people: in other words, he advocates for countering the corporate-driven public pedagogy of consumer culture with critical pedagogy in the classroom. Of course, cultural studies and critique of mass media have a strong tradition in composition studies. As James Berlin argued in *Rhetorics, Poetics, and Cultures*, compositionists should instruct students "to see not only the rhetoric of the college essay, but also the rhetoric of the institution of schooling, of politics, and of the media," providing "students with the heuristics to penetrate [semiotic] codes" (93). Like Giroux, Berlin's work conveys powerful commitments to critical and cultural analysis within composition studies; the public pedagogies I highlight in the coming pages invite students to move beyond the classroom, though not abandoning the classroom entirely, to engage public spaces as a method of analysis and critique.

Giroux's public pedagogy also aligns with composition teaching that emphasizes the civic purposes for public writing. Because the health of democracy is tied in with the system of education in the United States, corporate-driven public pedagogy is particularly dangerous because it risks jeopardizing the foundations of our democratic society—public citizenship and agency—by replacing them with increasingly privatized and commodified notions of citizenship and agency (Giroux, "Mouse Power"). Like John Dewey and many other educational theorists, Giroux values the symbiotic relationship between education and democracy, and he critiques neoliberal corporations for "teach[ing] an utterly privatized notion of citizenship and democracy" ("Mouse Power" 222). In this way, corporations pose a unique and serious threat to our nation's democracy by valuing consumption and individualism as models of citizenship and by de-emphasizing the importance of "non-commodified public spheres" ("Mouse Power" 222). Neoliberalism, as one of the most powerful "anti-democratic ideologies," is therefore threatening "a critically informed citizenry, a viable notion of social agency, and the idea of the university as a democratic public sphere" (Giroux, "Cultural Studies in Dark Times"). The commercialization and privatization of citizenship limits the sense of agency young people might envision for themselves in public spheres. In *Living Room*, Nancy Welch identifies how the social turn in composition studies is at odds with the growth of privatization resulting from neoliberalism: "Even as our field has increasingly focused on the public dimensions of students' writing and writing pedagogy, the national turn has been in the opposite direction, toward increasing privatization" (7). Welch goes on to examine neoliberal logic and to highlight models and lessons from historical case studies of effective rhetorical action. While Welch's work is more interested in how writing and rhetoric can address some of these problems, she shares many of Giroux's concerns with the proliferation of neoliberalism and its impact on students as citizens and writers.

In addition to Welch's consideration of neoliberalism and the privatization of public writing, other scholars in composition studies have addressed neoliberalism, often via Giroux, and in some cases these scholars have explicitly engaged with his theory of public pedagogy. In their 2004 article "Cultural Studies, Rhetorical Studies, and Composition," Ryan Claycomb and Rachel Riedner briefly mention "neoliberal public pedagogy" as a component of "disciplinarity that governs intellectual production." Claycomb and Riedner contend that disciplinarity "reduces much intellectual labor to budgetary line items," which suggests a "neoliberal public pedagogy that focuses on the production of workers and consumers for the newest phase of the capitalist economy." In Riedner's more recent collaboration with Kevin Mahoney, *Democracies to Come*, they work more in-depth with Giroux's theories of neoliberal public pedagogy. Riedner and Mahoney highlight the struggle between neoliberalism and cultural studies and how the tensions in this struggle produce pressures that "can be seen as pedagogical, what Giroux calls an educational force of the larger culture, in the sense that they seek to define, instruct, or even discipline us in the possibilities for social life, public ideas, and identity formations" (32). Ultimately, Riedner and Mahoney call for a cultural studies model that works "with communities both inside and outside of the classroom" (33); however, they highlight that "critical pedagogical practices that focus on the classroom as the primary, if not sole, site of pedagogy [eschew] broader theoretical implications . . . and de-prioritiz[e] non-classroom cultural spaces" (11). Riedner and Mahoney propose that educators bridge the theory/practice divide—and by extension the inside/outside classroom divide—in cultural studies by "considering pedagogy as a contingent, situated practice that brings theory and practice together" (11). Public pedagogy in composition courses invites students to engage with and critically study public locations beyond the classroom, offering an approach to teaching writing that helps students see the power of rhetoric in breaking down neoliberal agendas within their everyday lives. Moreover, a public pedagogy that invites students to see the educative potential of locations beyond the classroom models that publics are not meant to be feared but can be sites of meaningful learning and social advocacy.

Giroux's conception of corporate public pedagogy has been critiqued for being overly negative and limiting the possibilities for agency. Glenn Savage argues that, too often, public pedagogies are "posited as negative ideological forces that are largely seen to *act upon* and *corrupt* individuals" (emphasis in original, 109). Part of the problem Savage identifies is that public pedagogy expressed in this manner serves to "silence the counter hegemonic possibilities . . . of subaltern resistance" (109). Glenn raises a fair concern with Giroux's conception of public pedagogy as being a powerful ideological tool used by neoliberal corporations. How, then, can students resist corporate public pedagogy, and what will our role as composition teachers be in facilitating this resistance? While I agree that Giroux's work tends to emphasize problems rather than solutions, I believe he does provide insight into the possibilities for subverting or, at the least, redirecting neoliberal public pedagogy. As previously mentioned, Giroux advocates for the study and critique of culture and mass media, primary outlets for the spread of neoliberal public pedagogies. Additionally, in defining civic education, Giroux highlights the importance of "developing democratic public spheres both within and outside the schools"; doing so, contends Giroux, allows us to "reclaim the notions of struggle, solidarity, and hope around forms of social action that expand rather than restrict the notion of civic courage and public life" (*Schooling* 35). Unlike Savage's critique of the limitations in a neoliberal view of public pedagogy, Giroux suggests expanded possibilities for hope and social action. Even though Giroux is not directly addressing public pedagogy in this context, his recommendations certainly have implications for a pedagogy that is increasingly turning toward public engagement:

> As teachers, we can help make the political more pedagogical by joining with social groups and movements outside the schools that are struggling in order to address a number of important social problems and issues. . . . As critical educators, we can move beyond our social function as public/university/

private school teachers so that we can apply and enrich our knowledge and skills through practical engagements in oppositional public spheres outside the schools. (*Schooling* 35)

In other words, while much of Giroux's scholarship on public pedagogy may leave educators wary of engaging with publics beyond the classroom because of the neoliberal risks they pose, placing this work in the broader context of Giroux's views on the purposes of education for the development of civil society indicates the power he sees in forming alliances to address social problems. Giroux proposes partnerships with "social groups" and engagement within "oppositional public spheres outside the schools," again indicating the value and importance of going public. Even within one of his seminal essays on public pedagogy, Giroux makes the case that preserving democracy and our roles as active, engaged citizens means paying attention to "how we educate our youth" through "the stories that are told in the noncommodified spheres of our public culture" ("Mouse Power" 228).

The potential Giroux highlights for oppositional and noncommodified public spheres outside of schools provides a pathway for composition specialists interested in public pedagogy. Giroux's conception of public pedagogy led me at first to be concerned about the negative, neoliberal forces students might encounter if I situated my teaching within public spheres: Would students learn anything valuable within a context dominated by corporations that promote privatization, capitalism, and individuality? Indeed, I believe this is why many scholars who have critiqued Giroux's approach are left feeling frustrated, with few options for combating what is portrayed as a powerfully negative public pedagogy that our students encounter constantly in their everyday lives—perhaps school should be a location where these forces are not dominating the agenda. However, ideologies of neoliberalism are so pervasive, we cannot claim that school-based experiences are free of them, especially as institutions of higher education are increasingly run like corporations (Bousquet). In *Rhetorics for Community Action*, Phyllis Ryder argues that "the university operates in a space saturated with neoliberal justifications for its purpose: to boost the economy, to create good workers, and to create its 'products' efficiently" (241). Moreover, from my experiences of collaborating with nonprofit organizations, engaging with activist public street art (Holmes, "Street Art as Public Pedagogy"), and partnering with local schools, I have found that not all public pedagogies are inherently corrupt—that publics beyond the university also have valuable lessons to teach my composition students, especially when those publics are representative of the kinds of noncommodified public spheres Giroux writes about.

Even though publics beyond the classroom can and do expose students to negative forces of neoliberalism, publics and counterpublics can also powerfully teach students in different and positive ways. In her critique of the Habermasian conception of the bourgeois public sphere, Nancy Fraser argues that subaltern counterpublics are "parallel discursive arenas where members of subordinated social groups [women, workers, peoples of color, and gays and lesbians] invent and circulate counterdiscourses, which in turn permit them to formulate oppositional interpretations of their identities, interests, and needs" (67). Similarly, Michael Warner has conceived of a counterpublic as a group "in conflict not only with the dominant social group but with the norms that constitute the dominant culture as a public" (112). Thus, counterpublics invite the kind of critique and resistance of dominant practices, and in some cases the practices of neoliberal corporations. Going public may be one way to help students see a multiplicity of (counter) publics and to become critical of how each can serve in a pedagogical capacity, for good or for bad.

Warner argues that "counterpublics are publics, too," and that they function similarly (113). Extending this claim, we can see how both publics and counterpublics have educative power as public pedagogies; in other words, corporations are not the only publics educating young people into what it means to be a citizen, even if corporations as dominant structures tend to be powerfully persuasive. Fraser's rethinking of the public sphere, though, reminds us that there are multiple and competing publics and counterpublics, and this multiplicity and competition gives me hope as an educator who believes that students can meaningfully learn from publics beyond the classroom. While corporate sites and messages cannot be ignored, I ultimately believe that the value of public sites for student writing and learning outweigh the risks of moving beyond the classroom. We should guide students to critically consider the way ideologies function in all spaces, academic or public. As editors of the collection *Rural Literacies* contend, "to engage in public pedagogy . . . means both to teach beyond the classroom and to analyze the pedagogies of those other institutions and groups who shape the public's understanding of social and political issues" (Donehower, Hogg, and Schell 7). The both/and of teaching beyond the classroom while also analyzing is important: going public with composition pedagogy involves, first, relocation to increasingly public sites but, subsequently, requires critical engagement with and critique of those locations, as well as the social and political implications of that public work.

RELOCATING COMPOSITION PEDAGOGY

In my analysis of the case studies of public pedagogy, I found that relocation—from traditional school classroom spaces to increasingly public, unfamiliar, and/or everyday places—became an important component for going public in composition courses. Researchers have called for teachers to come to a better understanding of how the locations or sites of our pedagogies affect teaching and learning. Jeffrey R. Di Leo, Walter R. Jacobs, and Amy Lee argue that we need to expand our thinking of educational sites beyond traditional spaces of the four-walled classroom. Doing so, they believe, will help students continue to apply their course-based learning and transfer school-based concepts to a range of nonschool experiences. "If students expect that learning can only occur against the backdrop of a blackboard," Di Leo, Jacobs, and Lee maintain, "then . . . they will *turn off* their learning expectations" when they leave those traditional classroom spaces (8). In the same ways we prepare for courses by selecting course readings and crafting writing assignments, Di Leo, Jacobs, and Lee ask us to also take time to carefully select public sites of pedagogy.

Relocating our sites of education requires a belief that student experiences in locations beyond formal schools and classrooms can have a powerful impact on their learning. As editors of the *Handbook of Public Pedagogy* note, "schools are not the sole sites of teaching, learning, and curricula, and that perhaps they are not even the most influential" (Sandlin, Schultz, and Burdick 2). The concept of valuing the educative potential of nonschool places and people has its roots in experiential education. For instance, in *Democracy and Education*, John Dewey clearly makes a distinction between "schooling" and "education," arguing that education can happen in a number of places that are not necessarily schools (76). Similarly, in *Deschooling Society*, Ivan Illich argues that "we have all learned most of what we know outside of school" (28). Echoing Dewey and Illich in "Outside Curricula and Public Pedagogy," William H. Schubert contends that focusing only on school-based curricula "presents a myopic view of what shapes human beings" (16). When teachers relocate their pedagogies in public locations beyond the classroom, they are contesting the traditional assumption that the teacher and the school are the only arbiters of meaningful knowledge.

Relocating composition teaching and learning to public sites also means critically attending to issues of space, place, and the geographies of writing. Composition researchers, such as Nedra Reynolds and Johnathon Mauk, have called for teachers of writing to further explore the relationship between place and the teaching of composition. In "Location, Location, Location" for instance, Mauk suggests that the "physical geography of an institution, and the human geography which surrounds and constitutes it, have an impact on the topography of composition courses—and ultimately influence the success (or failure) of pedagogical strategies" (374). Mauk's attention to both physical and human geography calls composition specialists to be mindful of the places in which we situate our teaching and students' learning, as well as the educative potential for public places that surround our institutions. Mauk advocates for assignments that invite students to excavate their everyday lives, again, aligning with the idea that public pedagogies value everyday sites of learning and public knowledge. Part of what is compelling about this conception of public pedagogy, as opposed to conceptions that suggest subjects have little agency in neoliberal forces of public pedagogy, is how Mauk frames students as "agents of academic work" who are "using academic tools within their nonacademic lives," moving them "beyond the academic/nonacademic dichotomy" (362). Mauk's claims suggest that students can act as agents within their lives by valuing public sources of knowledge that emerge from engaging with public sites.

Other composition scholars have called for a relocation of teaching and writing to another public site: the streets. In *Tactics of Hope*, Paula Mathieu argues for writing in the streets, bringing street life into the writing classroom, as well as getting students, teachers, writers, and scholars in the streets (2). Mathieu grounds her turn to the streets in spatial and temporal politics, arguing that the public turn in composition "represents a significant redrawing of geographic boundaries that define sites for composition teaching and research" (14). Similarly, Nedra Reynolds argues for "streetwork" in *Geographies of Writing*. She uses examples from student projects at the University of Leeds to show how "streetwork begins from geographic assumptions that places and senses of place are complicated, difficult to access, and constantly in flux" (117). The work of Mathieu and Reynolds highlights the importance of physically and spatially going public by moving from traditional classroom spaces into the streets, suggesting that the sights, sounds, people, and spaces within these publics offer students a valuable and realistic context for their use of writing and rhetoric.

Movement from traditional academic spaces to increasingly public spaces is also being discussed by scholars of public and civic rhetoric. "The public work of rhetoric," argue editors John M. Ackerman and David J. Coogan, "is not shaped in our treatises and classrooms alone but in the material and discursive histories of communities outside of academe" (1–2). While Ackerman and Coogan note that communities can benefit from rhetoricians, they also emphasize that "rhetoric can also benefit from community partnerships premised on a negotiated search for the common good" (1–2). However, central to the task of studying rhetoric "out there" is "a shedding of academic adornments . . . and a more grounded conception of public need" (1). For Ackerman and Coogan, academics must step out of the ivory tower and into public spaces "out there" in order to study realistic and everyday examples of rhetoric. However, framing publics as "out there" constructs a binary relationship between the academy and spaces beyond.

"REAL WORLD" PUBLICS "OUT THERE"

With an emphasis on relocation, the way I have defined public pedagogy based on the case studies from my research implies a number of binaries, such as school/nonschool, on-campus/off-campus, four-walled classroom/no-walled public spaces, academic world/real world, in here/out there. Nedra Reynolds critiques moves to construct "a problematic separation between classrooms and the real world," arguing that seeing writing classes as "mere rehearsal for the 'real world out there' reproduces a binary relationship between the world and the academy that geographers and many spatial theorists would reject" (44). While I agree with Reynolds's critique of constructing a binary relationship between academic and real world spaces, or even academic and public spaces, my position is that the historical privileging of the academy—the ivory tower—already puts nonacademic spaces at risk for being perceived as not worthy of academic study and engagement. Thus, part of the importance of going public by physically and spatially moving beyond traditional classroom spaces means tilting the scales to imbue nonacademic publics and counterpublics with the kind of scholarly respect that traditional academic spaces—campus libraries, faculty offices, classrooms—already inherently have.

Traditional classroom spaces are no less "real" than publics beyond and the classroom often replicates the real world; however, I do see these spaces as different. According to Reynolds, a binary construction of academic space versus real world space "makes us think . . . that borders just need to be stepped over," which she suggests as a limiting or reductive perspective (45). In my experience, however, stepping over boundaries is precisely what needs to happen—at least as a first step—in many cases. For example, when

I taught as a lecturer at a private liberal arts university that was primarily a residential campus, students rarely left the boundaries of campus and often knew little about the surrounding town; in fact, in the years I was there, both students and faculty often referred to this phenomenon as "the bubble." When I began asking students on that campus to go public through service learning, my motives were first to have students step over the border—to burst the bubble. In this context, stepping over the border became the first move in valuing public sites for pedagogy, seeing them as valuable contexts for student writing and learning and communicating those values to students.

Reynolds suggests that we should resist "containerized conceptions of space" by focusing on "spatial practices of the everyday" (45). While our arguments align here, I wonder how students will be able to engage with diverse spaces and people if their everyday spatial practices are confined to the campus boundaries. Even at the institution where I now teach—a largely commuter campus in downtown Atlanta—students still experience somewhat of a bubble effect, rarely venturing beyond the few city blocks where their classes are held and their car is parked. In this case, students live far away but are equally unfamiliar with the community surrounding campus: many students live in the greater metro Atlanta area, commuting miles on interstates to come to campus, and know little about the local, public context in which their school is situated. I use public pedagogies in this urban environment to invite students to study public street art or to serve as mentors at a nearby middle school. When I designed a service learning partnership with a local middle school three miles from campus, I learned that the majority of students in my course had never even heard of the school, even though it was just around the corner. In other words, while I do not want to construct a problematic binary relationship, public pedagogy in composition studies calls us to be mindful of the spatial differences (as well as similarities) between traditional academic spaces and public spaces in order to help students see the interconnections among their academics, their everyday life experiences, *and* the experiences of local public and counterpublic groups with which they may rarely interact or study.

Many arguments that tend to construct boundaries between the "real" world and the academic world hinge on the idea that the work in classrooms is inauthentic, or at least less authentic than what happens in nonclassroom spaces. For example Paul Heilker, who Reynolds critiques, contends that "the classroom does not and can not offer students real rhetorical situations in which to understand writing and social action," primarily because of a lack of "real audiences and purposes" (71). Heilker, making similar arguments to the ones I have forwarded for public pedagogy, contends that "writing teachers need to relocate the *where* of composition instruction outside the academic classroom" (71). Likewise, Ellen Cushman and Challon Emmons advocate for "real world contact zones," as opposed to Mary Louise Pratt's classroom-based contact zones, because they afford opportunities for "multicultural and literacy issues [to] be negotiated through face-to-face interaction and experiential learning," rather than the "superficial interactions" that may occur in a classroom "where students have little stake in expanding their conceptions of others or in negotiating interpretations with those who are represented" (205). For Heilker, as well as Cushman and Emmons, the traditional academic classroom space does not fully represent the diversity and rhetorical complexities—in terms of civic issues, multiculturalism, and literacy—that students may (or may not) encounter in their everyday lives. I value students going public—physically and spatially—in composition pedagogies not because I conceive of the classroom as any less real than public spaces beyond but because the classroom can feel like a somewhat protected environment. Inviting students to go public welcomes riskiness and messiness in the processes of composing and community engagement: possibilities that I see as potentially productive for student learning.

RISKY PUBLICS

A line of inquiry I explore in more detail in Chapter 5 is the way public pedagogies situate student learning within public spaces over which teachers have less control; the risk and unknowns of working within publics beyond the relative safety of the classroom can be both disorienting and transformative for students. Relocating the context and space for student learning experiences introduces a kind of spatial shock—a discomfort from engaging with unfamiliar public places that, with teacher and classroom-based support, can provoke students to confront their assumptions about people and places that are different from them.

Part of what initiates risky public experiences is when we situate student learning in what Donald Schön calls the "swampy lowlands." As Patty Wharton-Michael et al. argue, learning that occurs in strictly academic environments, the authors argue, is limited to "manageable problems," whereas "the swampy lowlands" require students to address messy complexities of problems (Schön qtd. in Wharton-Michael et al. 68). In this way, public scholarship "draws knowledge out of disciplinary boxes ensconced in the ivory tower into the swampy lowlands that require multiple perspectives for diverse and complex audiences" (Wharton-Michael et al. 69). They argue that public scholarship promotes "transference of discipline knowledge," which encourages "adaptation, abstraction, and flexibility" in student learning (Wharton-Michael et al. 68). The distinction that is significant for public pedagogy, in my opinion, is not between real and unreal spaces but between low risk and somewhat higher risk pedagogical contexts—between pedagogies that are nicely planned or manageably accepted and pedagogies that are messy, complex, and often unexpected, despite teachers' best laid plans for going public. As I argue in Chapter 5, the challenge for students, teachers, and the publics with which we partner is to try to strike a balance between the risks and messiness of publics beyond the classroom and the disorientation, affective responses, and transformative learning that may occur as a result.

I believe the kind of disorientation students may experience as a result of relocating our pedagogies to local, public spheres is deeply connected to students' physical and material experiences in new places. Jenna Vinson describes these visceral experiences as "spatial shock": "students' feelings of discomfort, uneasiness, or alarm that surface in the moment of crossing a material boundary and visiting an unfamiliar place." Like Vinson, I see moments of spatial shock—sometimes personal and emotive—as productive for student learning; spatial shock can bring "both recognition of socially-produced assumptions and, potentially, reflection on one's own subject-position as an outsider to that place" (Vinson). Learning and growth in this context typically results from students' physical engagement with places in their local communities, often locations that are new to them, or approaching familiar places with an unfamiliar or critical perspective. Students in a 3000-level course I recently taught titled Literacy, Community, and Public Schools experienced spatial shock when I relocated their course experiences to our partnering local middle school. Students in my course immediately reacted to the locked school doors, complex buzz-in and sign-in procedures, visible video cameras around the school, and school codes that did not allow students to carry backpacks between classes.

Students in the Literacy, Community, and Public Schools course also experienced the frustrations associated with public pedagogies situated in contexts beyond the teacher's control. For example, as a required service learning component students in my course served as mentors for middle school students who were defined by administrators as on the cusp of being at risk. Students in my course became frustrated when they would show up to our partnering middle school and their student mentee was absent or unable to leave class that day to meet with their mentor. These were situations that were unexpected and beyond my control. As a class, we talked through my students' understandable frustration at having made a special trip to the middle school and not having the opportunity to complete their mentorship assignment. Through our discussions, it became clear to me that some students in my course were privileging our project over what they perceived as less important tasks in the middle school, suggesting that the middle school students could simply make up a test at a different time or take their school picture on another day. Sometimes, the tone of the discussion shifted to the point where students in my course were nearly demanding the opportunity to serve, instead of seeing the opportunity as a privilege in itself. We spent much of the semester talking through the challenges of partnering with publics, the demands placed on public school administrators' time, and our purposes and goals for being in the middle school. And, by the end of the semester, I believe many students began to learn from these unexpected challenges we faced in our partnership, seeing them as opportunities for inquiry and as a chance to move toward mutual understanding between their goals and expectations and those of the public community group with which we partnered. The messiness that came with unexpected challenges in going public represented some of the most valuable lessons students learned in the course.

Another major benefit I see in relocating student experience in increasingly public, nonclassroom spaces is the possibility for decentering authority in ways that are different from what is often possible solely in the classroom. In the same course on Literacy, Community, and Public Schools, I scheduled six of our two-and-a-half-hour seminars as onsite meetings at our partnering middle school. After direct interaction with middle school students for one hour, we used the remaining class time to debrief and reflect on students' experiences and learning for the day. In one of these debriefing sessions, I asked if one of the school administrators had a few minutes to join our class to answer questions. Students in my course asked about the home lives of the middle school students, the challenges the students and their families faced, and the demands of being a school administrator. The school administrator gave students in my course valuable information that I simply could not have given them; his firsthand knowledge and experience in this particular school and with these particular middle school students was also not something we could find in a library book. This impromptu forty-five-minute discussion became one of the most meaningful learning experiences in the course, and students referenced it repeatedly in their journals and in their final research papers. In this context, I saw my pedagogical role as liaison between local publics that offered essential knowledge and the students in my course who needed the kinds of direct experiences in the local public community in order to gain this knowledge. Of course, I could have invited a local school administrator to speak to students in our college classroom or even used Skype to virtually bring him to class. However, I believe the experience would have been less meaningful taken out of the local middle school context and location. If students in my course had not been observing and experiencing middle school students within that specific local public, their questions would not have been the same and would not have had the same exigencies. Because I chose to go public with pedagogy in this course, the school administrator became the teacher of students in my course momentarily; I was able to offer the class time for what I saw as a valuable spur of the moment discussion, even though I had other plans on my course agenda. This example, though, underscores the importance of traditional classroom spaces, too.

I see the traditional on-campus classroom space as equally important to an effective public pedagogy. While we cannot pretend that the classroom offers any more safety than publics beyond the classroom, I believe it offers an important space for regrouping, debriefing, and contextualizing public knowledge through an academic lens. The traditional classroom space is, not surprisingly, what separates our courses from everyday life, and thus, we need traditional classrooms as places to make sense of our public experiences. The traditional classroom provides a context for discussing theories and readings, exchanging essays for peer review, and reconnecting in ways that are not always possible in local public contexts. To use the Literacy, Community, and Public Schools course as an example again, we used our traditional classroom time to address students' concerns or questions that may have been too risky to communicate within our partnering middle school—questions about an observation of a teacher speaking harshly to a student in the hallway or about the ethics of video cameras in the school. Additionally, the traditional classroom provided a somewhat more controlled context to balance the messiness of what we could not control in the middle school; I could plan an agenda for our class that usually resulted in fewer disruptions and unexpected changes. Because the messiness of our public engagement days was demanding for some students (and, quite honestly, for me as their instructor), I believe our in-class days provided some relief—a chance to engage pedagogically in a manageable, typical, and expected way.

Therefore, my arguments for relocation are not to suggest that we abandon traditional classrooms as sites for learning, because I believe it is within these spaces that we can offer the kind of support—or reciprocal care, as I explain in Chapter 5—that helps students make sense of their public experiences.

The reciprocity and transparency for which I advocate in an ethical approach to public pedagogies aligns with core tenets of service learning. The growth of service learning is evident in our journals, at our conferences, and on our campuses, and compositionists have been exploring best methods for incorporating public service within a context of teaching writing. Part of my interest in going public with pedagogy emerged from my experimentation with service learning pedagogies. In the examples throughout this book, and in scholarly conversations I reference, there are a number of ways in which public pedagogy and service learning overlap. Because public pedagogy sees the educative potential in sites beyond the composition classroom, the community partnerships that arise from service learning suggest a similar pedagogical relationship, especially when those partnerships are founded on reciprocity with an expectation that all participants have something to learn and gain from the engagement. Throughout this chapter I have advocated for the language of public pedagogy and the lens of publics, as opposed to service learning or other terms for similar approaches, for two main reasons: (1) I find the broader lens of publics invites a range of public engagements, many of which may not involve direct service to an organization, and (2) I believe the emphasis on relocation to public, often nonschool, sites in public pedagogy highlights what I find to be particularly valuable about the approach, an aspect of service learning that is certainly present but not always accentuated. In other words, most service learning projects would fall under the umbrella of public pedagogy in composition studies, but I see the concept of public pedagogy as allowing for public engagement that is not limited to service. Whether through service learning or another approach to public pedagogy, the proliferation of digital and social media provides yet another method for studying and engaging with publics beyond the classroom.

DIGITAL PUBLICS AS PEDAGOGICAL

Two recent studies of social media and public pedagogy demonstrate the great potential of this approach in composition studies. In his contribution to the *Handbook of Public Pedagogy*, Alex Reid examines how social media "destabilizes the conventions that have allowed us to consider a 'public pedagogy' separated from formal schooling and other sites of learning" (195). Reid notes how social media transform conventional public spaces, like a mall food court, into sites of formal schooling "when a student accesses an online course" at that location; conversely, "the traditional classroom becomes a site of public pedagogy when students use mobile phones and laptops to check their Facebook accounts" (195). Reid's work highlights the continued blurring of boundaries between public/private, school/nonschool. Moreover, responding to Giroux's calls for intervention in public pedagogy, Reid concludes that "social media have the potential to bring critical-pedagogical work into public spaces" (199); this resonates with a view of public pedagogy in composition studies that values the positive educational potential for public sites of student writing and learning. In a more recent article on social media and public pedagogy, Joannah Portman-Daley interviewed members of the "net generation" to examine the use of social media for civic purposes. When Portman-Daley asked student activists in her study about the digital democratic learning that happened in nonschool spaces, she found respondents were "hesitant to admit that it was 'real' learning or teaching—precisely because, for them, it wasn't related to a traditional, classroom-based agenda." Portman-Daley goes on to critique the "informal/formal learning binary" for "failing to recognize the more progressive roles and implications of pedagogy." If composition teachers can use public pedagogies to help communicate a value for learning in spaces beyond the classroom, students will see the value in studying and engaging with these nontraditional sites of schooling.

Other scholars in computers and composition have explored the ways in which digital, social, and mobile media intersect with an increasingly public and/or civically engaged pedagogy. For example in *Writing Community Change*, Jeffrey T. Grabill analyzes "the practices of ordinary people making [and using] technologies to solve local problems" (1). In discussing pedagogical approaches, Grabill advocates for "locating the civic" and developing ways to "locate civic rhetorical performances," rather than working with abstract notions of civic. Grabill's attention to location here aligns with how I have defined public pedagogy based on the case studies I conducted; as with locating the civic, an abstract notion of public will also not be useful unless we locate and more specifically define that public.

As a teacher of digital writing, I often ask students to engage with digital publics; however, I also have some concerns about how student learning may differ in a wholly digital experience with publics. The case studies in *Public Pedagogy in Composition Studies* show the significance of relocating student learning through powerful, in-person student experiences in public places beyond the classroom; the physical and material experience of being in diverse publics is part of what I believe makes public pedagogy a transformative learning tool. In other words, I am unsure if reinterpreting students' public experiences to a mediated rather than a physical experience would result in the same kind of learning. I see this as an area ripe for more research. Admittedly, the case studies in the coming pages deal only tangentially with digital publics and, in some cases, not at all. The schema I suggest at the end of Chapter 2 leaves room for future research into how physical and digital locations intersect with public purposes for composition pedagogies. As I suggest in the conclusion, though, my own approaches to bridging the digital and material through public pedagogies has recently drawn me to incorporate more mobile technologies into my instruction; in mobile composition, students have the potential to physically be in public locations while also engaging with digital, online technologies.

PREVIEW OF THE CHAPTERS

Drawing on the interviews, teaching and program materials, and historical documents I collected and analyzed, the following chapters offer composition teachers and administrators examples and models for going public with pedagogy and administration. Beginning with a narrowed scope, Chapter 2 analyzes three case studies of public pedagogies from specific composition courses. In the first example, I analyze an interdisciplinary first-year seminar from Oberlin College that invites students to go public by visiting surrounding watersheds and gathering oral histories from local residents. Next, I examine a writing assignment from Syracuse University that asks students to engage with on-campus communities that represent new or unfamiliar publics to them, resulting in a partnership with the student-led HIV/AIDS organization. I then review a project from the University of Arizona that prompts students to visit local, public spaces to observe and critique spatial inequalities. Throughout the analysis, I apply and extend Elenore Long's pedagogical schema for students going public. I conclude this chapter by offering a heuristic on which to plot intersections between the locations and rhetorical purposes of public pedagogies.

Chapter 3 broadens the scope to writing programs by focusing on the administrative strategy of curriculum design and how, when approached from the perspective of morphing, it can exploit tensions between stasis and change, creating a productive method for administering public pedagogies. At Oberlin College, I look at how their community-based writing program initiative evolved over time and how part of its strength and sustainability arose from its curricular ties. I then examine a course sequencing strategy that employs a series of "next step" courses within the undergraduate writing and rhetoric major at Syracuse University. The final administrative example is from the University of Arizona's public events and pedagogy, showing how they are supported through the curriculum, custom publications, public events, and assessment.

Broadening further to an institutional level, Chapter 4 analyzes the mission statements of Oberlin College, Syracuse University, and the University of Arizona, showing how they function ideologically and rhetorically to construct an identity for members of their institutional communities—an identity that often values public engagement and service. Because these mission statements are framed within the storied histories of each institution, historical narratives represent an economy of literacy that carries weight within institutions, particularly in the language of upper-level administration. Drawing on the histories of my three research sites, I demonstrate how composition specialists might construct partial institutional histories to help support public pedagogies by, in these cases, tracing an institution's roots in religion, morality, coeducation, and/or African American education, as well as land-grant founding and ties to local Native populations.

The final chapter shifts back to a narrowed snapshot of a moment in a composition course by highlighting some of the affective responses that may arise for students, public partners, and teachers when we situate our pedagogies in public sites beyond the classroom. I analyze a teacher-narrated moment of student distress to demonstrate how theories of transformative learning might help us theorize affect in public pedagogies. To conclude, I offer a reciprocal model of care that employs tenets of feminist pedagogy, such as transparency and decentering of authority, and that acknowledges the valid emotions students, teachers, and members of local publics may experience. I call for composition specialists who employ public pedagogies to see the power of all participants to both give and receive care in transformative education.

2

Relocating the Composition Classroom: Going Public with Pedagogy

IN THE PREVIOUS CHAPTER, I DEFINED PUBLIC PEDAGOGY in composition studies as an approach to the teaching of writing that values the educative potential for public sites, communities, and persons beyond the boundaries of the traditional classroom and/or campus community. Drawing on the work of scholars in curriculum studies, I advocated for a more expansive view of education that posits schools as "not the sole sites of teaching, learning, and curricula," and, by extension, teachers as not the only arbiters of important knowledge (Sandlin, Schultz, and Burdick 2). When we ask students to engage with public places to gather information for their writing and when we assign them to write for public audiences, we are demonstrating how schools are not the only places for instruction and teachers are not the only readers of student writing. The phraseology of going public suggests movement and action; and, in this chapter, I argue for the significance of relocation in public pedagogy—movement away from traditional or formal places of learning (i.e., the classroom, the academy) toward more public locations for education, while still maintaining important ties to classroom and campus spaces. The examples in this chapter answer Riedner and Mahoney's call in *Democracies to Come* for models that work with communities "both inside and outside of the classroom" (33). However, I agree with Riedner and Mahoney's claim that pedagogies focusing on "the classroom as the primary, if not sole, site of pedagogy . . . de-prioritiz[e] non-classroom cultural spaces," and I see public pedagogy in composition as the kind of "contingent, situated practice that brings theory and practice together" (11).

In the interviews I conducted for this study, composition teachers indicated that going somewhere new, different, and/or unfamiliar became an important part of the learning experience for students. In this chapter, I document the similarities and differences in how three instructors approach going public with their composition pedagogy: (1) in Field-Based Writing at Oberlin College, Jan Cooper and Mary Garvin ask students to go public by visiting rural locations, collecting ecological data, and interviewing local residents in a nearby watershed; (2) in Critical Research and Inquiry at Syracuse University, A. V. Luce partners students with an unfamiliar public on campus: a newly developed student HIV/AIDS organization; and (3), in first-year and advanced composition courses at the University of Arizona, Crystal Fodrey prompts students to spatially critique a local place of their choosing, resulting in analyses of tattoo parlors, classrooms, and neighborhoods. The composition pedagogies I analyze come from courses that vary in level (first-year, second-year, upper-division) and type (interdisciplinary, themed, advanced).

The assignments in this chapter are united as examples of public pedagogy in composition by (1) a common value in the public knowledge of community members not traditionally associated with academia and (2) a provocation of students' insularity such that they must go public by venturing to unfamiliar places. Thus, these examples value public knowledge and public sites for learning, inviting students to cross boundaries and move in and through increasingly public spaces for writing and analysis. Assigning students to engage with publics beyond the classroom helps "connect critical ideas, traditions, and values to the public realm of everyday life" (Giroux, "Is There a Role" 185). In this way, the teachers highlighted in the chapter engage in a pedagogy of responsibility that Giroux has argued is so essential to combating privatization and ideological propaganda. Moreover, what makes these examples compelling as public pedagogies is the way they critically attend to issues of place as central to students' learning. Giroux claims that educational work must be addressed "within many kinds of public spaces" in order to both "critique existing institutions and struggle to work towards fulfilling the promise of a radical global democracy" ("Is There a Role" 189). Going public with composition pedagogy by working within diverse places beyond the classroom offers students the opportunity to consider where and how power circulates within society, how it impacts democracy, and what possibilities there are for using writing and rhetoric to move toward social change and positively contribute to one's surrounding community. I begin my analysis by examining Elenore Long's schema for students taking public action to identify the ways in which it intersects with the public pedagogies in my study.

PEDAGOGIES FOR PUBLIC ACTION

Within the growing area of composition scholarship that theorizes the public turn, Elenore Long's *Community Literacy and the Rhetoric of Local Publics* represents a significant perspective that encourages scholars to focus on the local and to see local publics as the "community within community literacy" (5). One of the sections within Long's book that I found particularly useful in corroborating public pedagogy was the way she describes five pedagogical approaches for supporting students' public action: interpretative, institutional, tactical, inquiry-driven, and performative. In the public pedagogies I analyze in the coming pages, I found examples that connected with Long's interpretative, institutional, and inquiry-driven pedagogies. I ultimately argue that while Long's schema provides a productive framework for public pedagogies more can be done to attend to issues of place, space, and relocation. Building on her work, I offer a model at the end of this chapter that invites teachers to critically consider issues of place as they relocate their pedagogies to increasingly public spheres.

Table 2 displays Long's schema that identifies public actions students might take within each of the five types of pedagogy she names.[1] Though these pedagogies are described separately, Long notes that many of the pedagogies overlap, and, thus, are not discrete. Long's interpretative pedagogies draw on literacy skills familiar to students and teachers in English departments: reading, analyzing, writing, and interpreting texts. However, as Long explains, students go public with interpretation by visiting new places and forging new relationships with community members. As a result of these public experiences, students gain insights that prompt them to interrogate and revise their assumptions (Long 158–63). In each of the coming examples, I highlight the significance of "going somewhere new" and how the act of going public by leaving the traditional classroom space might impact how we teach and how students write and learn.

Long describes institutional pedagogies as being similar to interpretative, except that they focus on students' futures and they use professional roles as a means for students to go public (163–64). Institutional pedagogies prompt students to challenge norms and confront inequities caused by institutions. By working with local community members, students recognize the agency and expertise of diverse stakeholders and begin to incorporate this local public knowledge into the decision-making processes of institutions to promote social change. All three examples from my study employ institutional pedagogies by teaching students methods for conduct-

Table 2. Elenore Long's Pedagogical Practices for Students' Public Action

Pedagogies:	Interpretative	Institutional	Tactical	Inquiry-Driven	Performative
Students take public action by . . .	. . . going somewhere new, building relationships, confronting and revising familiar stereotypes.	. . . learning professional methods for recognizing the expertise and agency of others.	. . . learning to circulate their own public writing that challenges the status quo.	. . . deliberating pressing social issues with community partners; circulating documents that serve as catalysts for social change.	. . . engaging as rhetors with others to gain the practical wisdom required to build inclusive communities for effective problem solving.

From *Community Literacy and the Rhetoric of Local Publics* (155) by Elenore Long. ©2008 by Parlor Press and the WAC Clearinghouse. Used by permission.

ing research (e.g., collecting interviews, distributing surveys, conducting observations) that can result in social change and by asking students to write for public and professional contexts. Additionally, institutional pedagogies invite students to recognize the knowledge and expertise of local public community members; in this way, they align with public pedagogy by acknowledging that schools and academic experts are not the only arbiters of knowledge. Institutional approaches to going public retain ties to traditional purposes of higher education (preparing students for their future lives and careers) while also prompting students to question institutional protocols, contest injustices, and work within systems to move toward social change.

Whereas institutional pedagogies are firmly situated within formal public institutions, Long defines tactical pedagogies as ones that upset the status quo. Tactical pedagogies teach students to "circulate counterpublic discourses," situating this social and political work within larger historical narratives of radical social movements (Long 171). Because students are encouraged to "find their own venues for going public," tactical pedagogies tend to result in short-term "public bursts" (Long 175). In the interviews I conducted with teachers in my study, I did not find examples that fit easily into Long's category of tactical pedagogies. One reason for this may be the risks associated with going public in ways that disrupt the status quo, especially given the fact that many of the writing teachers I interviewed were graduate teaching assistants with little job security.

Short-term tactical pedagogies can lead to a fourth pedagogy identified by Long: inquiry-driven pedagogies, which involve students going public by constructing venues for extended, focused, and deliberative dialogue (175). Within these discursive spaces, students position themselves as members of a local public and work with intercultural partners to "deliberate about pressing social problems, working toward both personal and public change" (175). While similar to institutional pedagogies, inquiry-driven pedagogies engage students in public action here and now, whereas institutional pedagogies provide preparation for students' futures (Long). In the pedagogical examples I analyze in this chapter, two of the three instructors incorporate inquiry-driven pedagogies when going public. In both cases, I focus on how the instructors assign projects that ask students to work with community members (on or off campus) to deliberate social issues and work toward addressing them through the circulation of student-generated public writing.

The final pedagogy Long posits is performative, which uses the drama of public performance to "call a public into being" (189). While the examples I examine in this chapter do not align with this approach, performative pedagogies are valuable in helping students see the connections among inquiry and performance, and, through public performances and teacher guidance, students develop "reflective, rhetorical agency" (Long 192). Performative pedagogies tend to overlap with others—most often tactical and inquiry-driven pedagogies.

To preview the pedagogies I examine in more detail in the next sections, Table 3 offers a brief comparative overview of the three courses. The public pedagogies these instructors employ in their courses share similarities in how they value public, and sometimes nonschool, sites for student learning. However, they also demonstrate different approaches in how they define the scope and range of publics and in where they locate their public pedagogy.

Table 3. Overview of Composition Courses for Comparative Analysis

Institution	Instructor(s)	Course(s)	Type of Course & Level
Oberlin College	Jan Cooper & Mary Garvin[2]	FYSP 116: Field-Based Writing	Interdisciplinary first-year seminar
Syracuse University	A. V. Luce	WRT 205: Critical Research and Inquiry	Second course in required writing series, typically taken in second year
University of Arizona	Crystal Fodrey	ENG 102: First-Year Writing	Second course in required first-year writing series, typically taken in second semester
		ENG 306: Advanced Composition	Elective for students who have completed the first-year writing requirement

GOING PUBLIC BY INVESTIGATING LOCAL LANDS AND PEOPLE

In a Field-Based Writing course at Oberlin College, students went public by venturing off campus to investigate local lands and to interview and write for local populations. These approaches represent a public pedagogy that values local public places as important sites of learning and nonschool members of the community as significant contributors to and stakeholders of students' learning and writing. Students continued to learn important course-based concepts, such as ethnographic research methods, and they composed documents that they circulated to local public audiences. This pedagogical example highlights how public pedagogies represent valuable border crossing by engaging with publics beyond campus, but it also demonstrates how these moves, while bearing similarities to service learning, are not limited to public service. Cooper and Garvin's pedagogy highlights how having students physically go to new places can be a valuable teaching and learning approach.

At Oberlin College, I interviewed rhetoric and composition department faculty member Jan Cooper, and she told me about a first-year seminar course, Field-Based Writing: Ecology of the Vermilion River Watershed, she co-taught with biology professor Mary Garvin in 2003 and 2008. As a first-year seminar course, all of the students enrolled were in their first year at Oberlin, and many of them partially fulfilled their Writing Requirement through the course. Cooper explained in our interview that she and Garvin conceived of the course when they realized that ecology and the teaching of writing both share an "emphasis on developing observational skills" and on "visual recording or visual learning" (Cooper). From the Fall 2008 syllabus that Cooper shared with me, the teachers describe the course as follows:

> This is a course about observing the natural world around us by using the tools of ecology, the study of the interactions between organisms and their environment. Through field studies on the Vermilion River and its tributaries, we will have the opportunity to watch an ecosystem near Oberlin progress through autumn. We will also explore a variety of ways to

communicate our observations, from field notes to lab reports to science writing for general audiences. In the process, you will gain information literacy skills and work toward earning certification for the Writing Proficiency Requirement through weekly writing assignments. Students' writing will be discussed in class and with the instructors in individual appointments.

As the course description indicates, Field-Based Writing was an interdisciplinary course that combined instruction in ecology with practice in writing. The field-based component of the course required students to go public by visiting off-campus locations, and these field experiences were related to both the scientific and composition goals of the course. For example, students took trips to Lake Erie and surrounding watersheds to conduct ecological experiments. Students also engaged with "human ecology" by talking to farmers along the Vermilion River and by ultimately composing and publishing a text, *Living in the Vermilion Watershed*, which had a target audience of local residents (Cooper).

Table 4 summarizes aspects from Long's schema that correspond to practices within Field-Based Writing; these include interpretative, institutional, and inquiry-driven pedagogies. In each case, I translate a specific component of Long's schema (the second horizontal line) into its specific action within the course (the third horizontal line).

In Field-Based Writing, students engaged in Long's interpretative pedagogies by going somewhere new and building new relationships with the local environment, land, and people; the course assignments also encouraged students to confront stereotypes and circulate their new knowledge in public forums. As Long explains, there are a number of pedagogical benefits to getting students off campus: venturing to a new context "stirs things up" in students' minds and provides the "critical distance" needed to identify, interrogate, and revise their understanding of social issues (158–59). Field-Based Writing assigned students to conduct biological labs in the field along the Vermilion River, and students also talked to

Table 4. Students' Public Actions in Jan Cooper and Mary Garvin's Field-Based Writing Course at Oberlin College

	Interpretative Pedagogies			Institutional Pedagogies		Inquiry-Driven Pedagogies
Students take public action by...	going somewhere new:	building new relationships	confronting and revising stereotypes	learning professional methods for local research,	recognizing the expertise and agency of others,	circulating documents that serve as catalysts for social change,
Student actions in Field-Based Writing	the Vermilion River and rural farmlands of the Midwest.	with the Vermilion River Watershed, farmers, and rural residents.	about farmers and rural residents.	including field-based research, writing, and ethnography.	such as farmers and rural residents.	through the publication *Living in the Vermilion River Watershed*.

people who farm along the river (Cooper). By relying on observational skills—as both scientific researchers and field-based writers—students were able to closely examine local places and people to confront and address the social and political ramifications of environmental issues and their impact on local publics.

Through field-based experiences, students built new relationships with the local land and residents, and these new relationships encouraged students to confront stereotypes. For example, in my interview with Cooper, she explained how many of her students "had never lived in the Midwest," "had never lived near farming country," "and didn't know that much about farmers . . . or rural residents as an audience." Because students interviewed local farmers and ultimately composed documents for them as an audience, they were confronting stereotypes they had about farmers. Cooper expounded that some of her students "had this notion of farmers as people who had never heard of environmentalism, when actually the farmers in our area have to preserve their soil; they have to preserve their ecology, and they are not all big agri-business people." Through assignments and discussions in the course, Cooper said they had to "unpack" students' experiences and confront their assumptions and stereotypes—talk about "who farmers are as an audience" and about people who "move out into the country because they don't want to live in a town or a city." As a result of their experiences in the course, students gained "different perspectives on the biological ecology but also the human ecology of the area" (Cooper).

Cooper and Garvin's course also involved students learning field-based and ethnographic research methods; enacting these methods also helped students recognize the expertise and agency of local community residents. This kind of learning might fall under what Long identifies as an institutional pedagogy because it teaches students professional methods of research that may be useful to them in their academic futures and/or careers. In addition, an institutional pedagogy invites students to see public locations and people beyond the academy as significant for academic study—all while employing traditional academic methods of research. Similar to the projects Long reviews from Pittsburgh's Community Literacy Center, students in Cooper and Garvin's course listened to the "perspectives of local residents" and drew on that expertise "to build more robust representations" of community-based problems (Long 168). The final, public result of this research and consultation was a student-generated publication intended for a local audience.

The publication *Living in the Vermilion River Watershed*, edited by Cooper and Garvin and composed primarily by students in Field-Based Writing, became a significant public component of the course. I see this publication as what Long calls an inquiry-driven pedagogy because it exemplifies how students circulate documents that demonstrate their new knowledge. In our interview, Cooper explained that she and Garvin applied for and received an Ohio Environmental Protection Agency grant "to create a book out of some of the materials that we were collecting . . . and some of the materials that students were writing for the class." The book that resulted from this class and grant project is now available on the Western Reserve Land Conservancy's website (Garvin and Cooper). Throughout the course, Cooper framed students' writing assignments within the possibility of publication in this book: "Your intended audience for [this assignment] is that of *Living in the Vermilion River Watershed*—residents of the watershed. If the final draft of this piece meets the standards of the book, we may post it online for the book's actual readers" (Cooper and Garvin). Cooper's assignment sheets stress the importance of students "using simple and clear language appropriate to audience," and she explained in our interview how much of the course involved students exploring and coming to a better understanding of the intended audience, which involved confronting assumptions (Cooper and Garvin). Cooper told me that she and Garvin hoped the publication would help local residents "learn more about their own area and hopefully increase their interest in preserving the river that served as the basis of the area" (Cooper). The collection features articles that range from historical accounts of the geology of the watershed area, to explanations of bacteria in the river, to analyses of the first Native peoples to settle the watershed area; many articles also include a list of additional resources that readers could consult for more information (Garvin and Cooper).

Cooper and Garvin's course also prompted students to critically attend to issues of place by asking students to keep field journals and take photographs as a method of "paying attention in a particular way to a particular place" (Cooper). Indeed, going public by physically being and writing in the local watershed area had a positive impact on student learning. Going public is intriguing in part because it is "something different from what [students] are doing in . . . other classes" (Cooper); however, more importantly, Cooper noted that going public in her course gave students an "imperative . . . [and] a level of immediacy that engaged them more thoroughly." In fact, this attention to public place is central to public pedagogies in composition studies, generating an emphasis on relocation of student writing and experience to publics beyond the classroom.

Cooper and Garvin's course demonstrates what Giroux argues is necessary in public pedagogy: "to link knowing with action" ("Neoliberalism as Public Pedagogy" 497). The public actions Cooper and Garvin's students took—visiting local places, interviewing community members, and publishing for a local audience—helped develop students' sense of local community needs and knowledge and engender a sense of responsibility in using writing to help address community problems. Their public pedagogy fits with the responsibilities Giroux says educators have to teach students to "fight for an inclusive and radical democracy," not just by understanding but also by "providing the conditions for assuming the responsibilities we have as citizens" to expose and eliminate injustices ("Neoliberalism as Public Pedagogy" 497). Inviting students to go public can help provide the conditions necessary for assuming these responsibilities. While the publication students ultimately produced could be seen as a service to the local community, the methods Cooper and Garvin took in the course were not explicitly through a service learning model; the attention to place and getting students out into their communities to investigate and learn, though, became central to their public pedagogy.

GOING PUBLIC BY PARTNERING WITH UNFAMILIAR ON-CAMPUS ORGANIZATIONS

Whereas Cooper and Garvin's course brought students off campus to conduct field-based research on the biological and human ecology of the Vermilion River Watershed, the next course I examine invited students to explore a new or unfamiliar community without necessarily leaving the bounds of campus. Interestingly, because the on-campus experience was unfamiliar, this instructor's version of the Critical Research and Inquiry course at Syracuse University prompted students to interrogate assumptions and circulate public documents in ways that resulted in a level of engagement similar to what Cooper described emerging from her course. Despite these similarities, instructor A. V. Luce framed students' work of going public through a service learning approach. Here is a prime example of how Cooper and Luce might productively align their pedagogies through a common lens of publics and a theoretical approach of public pedagogy that values knowledge outside the classroom and that critically attends to issues of place. When I visited Syracuse University in March 2011, I interviewed graduate teaching assistant (TA) A. V. Luce, who, at the time, was teaching Writing 205: Critical Research and Inquiry.[3] On his Writing 205 syllabus, Luce explained to students that the course focused on issues related to HIV/AIDS and included a service learning component:

> As the course develops, we'll begin to connect our rhetorical frame with the readings, research methods, and service projects that we undertake. These projects will explore issues of sexuality, specifically regarding HIV/AIDS. . . . The more we understand, analyze and research this issue, the more we will be in a position to offer help developing appropriate materials, critique projects and programs as well as challenge the way we thought about HIV/AIDS and sexuality. Further, we have the opportunity through service learning to apply what we read, discuss and write to real situations, with real people. ("Syllabus WRT205")

Luce's syllabus included readings and class discussions that helped students gain a fuller understanding of some of the issues related to HIV/AIDS; he paired these assignments with a semester-long service learning project that partnered his class with a new student organization on campus called OrangeAID. In our interview, Luce explained that through the partnership with OrangeAID he wanted to prompt students to explore questions such as "how do you begin social programs about issues?" and "how do you . . . creat[e] and sustain programs and organizations that are supposed to benefit . . . students?" (Luce). Luce designed the course so that small groups of students would work on pieces of a larger campus-based project related to HIV/AIDS awareness, specifically supporting the efforts of the burgeoning OrangeAID group. At the time of our interview, around mid-semester, Luce suggested some student projects that he thought might unfold as the semester progressed; these included obtaining funding for OrangeAID to help sustain it beyond the year, connecting OrangeAID with other organizations on campus related to other student identities, developing a survey to assess students' awareness of HIV/AIDS on campus, and connecting OrangeAID to Greek organizations with service components.

Table 5 pairs components of Luce's pedagogy with what I see as corresponding parts of Long's schema, specifically interpretative, institutional, and inquiry-driven pedagogies. Again, the second horizontal line lists Long's schema for how students take public action, and the third horizontal line represents the specific public actions taken by students in Luce's Critical Research and Inquiry course.

Much like Cooper and Garvin's course at Oberlin College, Luce's course at Syracuse involved students going somewhere new, building new relationships, and confronting/revising stereotypes. I see each of these public actions as aligning with how Long defines

Table 5. Students' Public Actions in A. V. Luce's Critical Research and Inquiry Writing Course at Syracuse University

	Interpretative Pedagogies			Institutional Pedagogies	Inquiry-Driven Pedagogies	
Students take public action by . . .	going somewhere new	building new relationships	confronting and revising stereotypes	learning professional methods for local research,	deliberating pressing social issues with community partners,	circulating documents that serve as catalysts for social change
Student actions in Critical Research and Inquiry	within the likely unfamiliar experience of HIV/AIDS campus communities.	with key stakeholders in new HIV/AIDS campus communities.	about persons with HIV/AIDS.	such as methods for designing and distributing surveys.	including issues related to HIV/AIDS with new campus-community partners.	through the student survey on HIV/AIDS on campus.

interpretative pedagogies. Luce's approach differed somewhat from Cooper and Garvin's in that students did not leave campus for field-based experiences. However, in our interview, Luce explained his belief that students approach HIV/AIDS on campus as a "foreign land": "students' unfamiliarity with engaging HIV on campus . . . does make campus potentially a 'foreign land,' much like Syracuse the community would be" (Luce). In other words, comparing these pedagogies across institutional contexts, Luce, in my estimation, sees student engagement with HIV/AIDS on campus as the equivalent of going somewhere new, like the Vermilion River Watershed in Field-Based Writing at Oberlin College. This is an interesting and significant reinterpretation of what it means to go public. When I asked about Luce's choice to partner with a group on campus rather than off, he admitted that this form of going public is "what some people would consider very safe" because students are not partnering with a community group or nonprofit organization off campus (Luce). However, he defended his choice to partner with OrangeAID, explaining that such a partnership prompted students to confront their campus community through a new, and for many students unfamiliar, lens focused on issues related to HIV/AIDS. This form of going public provided an opportunity for students to explore highly charged social issues within a somewhat familiar context of the school's campus. Moreover, Luce's public pedagogy asked students to critically examine a place with which they assume familiarity (the campus) and to re-envision their everyday campus context from a new positionality.

To complete course assignments, students in Luce's course built new relationships with key stakeholders in the student-led OrangeAID organization. I see this component of Luce's pedagogy corresponding to Long's interpretative pedagogies because it involves students confronting and revising stereotypes because of newly established relationships that cause them to question those misrepresentations. For example, students in Luce's course were assigned to conduct a "needs assessment" for OrangeAID and worked closely with the undergraduate student who founded the organization. Because students worked alongside the founders of the organization hearing their values and beliefs about HIV/AIDS on campus, Luce's students were prompted to confront and revise stereotypes they may have previously held. In preparation for their service projects, Luce assigned students to read Elizabeth Pisani's *The Wisdom of Whores*, and he prompted students to pay "close attention" to "how writing is used to depict HIV/AIDS." Through a combination of the on-campus partnership and course readings, Luce's public pedagogy asked students to confront their assumptions and revise stereotypes they have held in the past.

Luce's course also introduced students to professional research methods—a component of Long's institutional pedagogies. Luce's assignments taught students research skills that directly had an impact on their service work with OrangeAID but which could also be easily transferred to other kinds of academic and community-based research. Some of Luce's course assignments that explicitly addressed research methods included the following: a research method profile, a service journal entry that involved students observing community spaces and writing thick descriptions, a web or diagram illustrating stakeholder relationships, and a journal entry he called an "honesty box" that prompts students to foreground their assumptions (Luce).[4] Mirroring the project-based work that many students will experience in their professional careers, Luce organized students to work in small groups, each taking on different pieces of the larger class service project. One group, for instance, designed and implemented a survey to collect data for the OrangeAID organization; another group prepared an IRB application for student research, and yet another group sought grant-funding opportunities for potential community projects. If we read these pedagogies through Long's institutional lens, we see how Luce is preparing students for their futures by teaching them important skills of research and collaboration. Additionally, Luce's pedagogies prompt students to work within the institutional system of the university to, for instance, obtain IRB approval and secure grant funding. While discussions in class may have prompted students to question or disrupt the status quo (a tactical pedagogy, as defined by Long), the public actions students ultimately took seem to fall within an institutional approach toward social change.

A final aspect of Luce's course that I believe is representative of public pedagogy is the survey his students designed, tested, and distributed on campus; this survey became one of the major collaborative projects of Luce's course, and it was also an important contribution to their on-campus partner. The public action of distributing the student-generated survey aligns with some aspects of Long's inquiry-driven pedagogies. First, students deliberated social issues related to HIV/AIDS—such as what level of involvement the government should have in researching and caring for persons with HIV/AIDS and their sense of a general lack of awareness about HIV/AIDS issues on Syracuse University's campus—with their classmates and with peers in OrangeAID. However, Long's analysis frames this deliberation as happening with "community partners," typically off-campus nonprofit organizations rather than on-campus student organizations. This is where Luce's public pedagogy offers a different interpretation of what it means to go public, because students, in terms of time and space, are not going far to experience that public. Yet, what is important for public pedagogy is that students were confronted with a new public experience, even if the public was located within a familiar campus context. Despite some of the differences in Luce's course compared to Long's explanation, the student survey from Luce's course functions as an inquiry-driven pedagogy because it involved circulating documents for social change. Results from the survey, for instance, could initiate changes in policies about and awareness of HIV/AIDS issues on Syracuse's campus. While Luce's assignments correlate to some aspects of Long's inquiry-driven pedagogies, I must also note that the project seemed to be contained within the one-semester course; thus, it may not represent the kinds of long-term inquiry that Long associates with this approach in her analysis of multiyear, ongoing projects such as the Community Literacy Center in Pittsburgh.

This example from Luce's course at Syracuse University demonstrates how instructors can incorporate public pedagogies in ways that value public knowledge and that situate students in unfamiliar contexts without even leaving the bounds of the campus community. Luce's pedagogy helps combat what Giroux has theorized as a neoliberal public pedagogy that engenders a "belief in the power of . . . self-interest" that "replaces any notion of shared responsibility or social justice" ("Cultural Studies in Dark Times"). Students working together to address social justice issues around HIV/AIDS on campus disrupts neoliberal agendas by developing alternate pathways of student engagement and the use of public writing for social action. When I compare Luce's on-campus partnership with Cooper and Garvin's off-campus field-based experiences, I see similarities in how the instructors valued the pedagogy of publics beyond the classroom, beyond the teacher, and beyond a static, ivory-tower curriculum. Both courses represent a public pedagogy in the ways they: (1) prompted students to engage with important public issues (the environment or HIV/AIDS) that had an impact on students' local communities (whether defined as local region or campus community), (2) taught students how to conduct research and collect data (through scientific labs, interviews, and surveys) that would equip them to serve as agents of social change, (3) assigned them to employ that data to address public issues through writing (through a student publication for local residents or survey results for an on-campus organization), and (4) invited students to critically engage with new or unfamiliar places, whether on or off campus. In the final pedagogical example I analyze, the instructor's pedagogy shares these values in students investigating local public issues, conducting research, and using writing to move toward social change.

GOING PUBLIC THROUGH SPATIAL ANALYSIS OF LOCAL PUBLIC SITES

The last example of going public in composition comes from Crystal Fodrey, who, at the time of our interview, was a graduate TA at the University of Arizona. Fodrey asked students to spatially analyze local public places and, in some cases, to write about these spaces in forms of public writing. Fodrey's public pedagogy values public knowledge beyond the classroom by prompting students to see everyday places as sites for inquiry and investigation; her public pedagogy also critically attends to place by instructing students in spatial analysis, drawing their attention to the spatial impact of going public, and prompting them to incorporate their experiences of going public into their writing. Fodrey's course also demonstrates how students can address public issues and go public without necessarily having a service learning component (like Cooper and Garvin's course at Oberlin College) and without necessarily leaving campus (like Luce's course at Syracuse University). I analyze two similar spatial analysis assignments that Fodrey taught in two different composition courses—English 102, the second of a two-course first-year writing sequence, and English 306, an advanced composition course that Fodrey designed as a creative nonfiction course.

In English 102, Fodrey taught a rhetorical analysis assignment in which students analyze spaces of personal importance. On the assignment sheet, Fodrey asked students to "write an essay in which you explore the significance of the ideologies that exist in one of the public spaces you explored in your Unit 1 short assignment"; one of the stated goals was for students to "become more aware of how the very spaces that surround [them] are rhetorically situated (i.e., persuasive, powerful, political, endowed with meaning, and productive of meaning)" ("Unit 1"). Fodrey suggested that students might explore spaces on the university's campus, spaces represented on their maps of personally significant places (an in-class invention activity), or an online space, and she asked students to examine spaces that "exhibit inequalities of race, class, gender, sexuality, ability, etc." ("Unit 1").

Fodrey taught a similar spatial analysis assignment in English 306, but the goals were for students to learn about public forms of research, like investigative journalism, and to write public creative nonfiction essays (Fodrey). Fodrey asked students to "select, define, and research a space that you're curious about so that you can add your voice to the conversation regarding the space" ("Unit 2"). As with the rhetorical analysis assignment in English 102, Fodrey encouraged students to examine issues of inequality within the spaces they analyze and research. She gave students a variety of options for considering audience, including a reader who would be interested but (1) "unaware of the inequality in the space you've chosen," (2) "does not realize the extent of the inequality," (3) "has a misconception about this space," or (4) "does not know this space exists at all" ("Unit 2").

Table 6 summarizes the intersections I see among the public actions Fodrey's students took in her courses and various pedagogical approaches outlined by Long, including aspects of interpretative and institutional pedagogies.

A significant component of Fodrey's spatial analysis assignments involved students visiting spaces and locations of their choice; in relationship to Long's schema, this often means students take public action by going somewhere new. However, similar to Luce's on-campus service learning work at Syracuse University, not all of Fodrey's students left the boundaries of campus, and, in some cases, students visited places that were seemingly familiar to them. Interestingly, students are invited to see a space from a new or unfamiliar perspective in order to produce a fresh analysis. On her assignment

Table 6. Students' Public Actions in Crystal Fodrey's First-Year and Advanced Composition Courses at the University of Arizona

	Interpretative Pedagogies				Institutional Pedagogies
Students take public action by...	going somewhere new:	confronting and revising stereotypes	composing personal narratives and public writing	circulating new knowledge	learning professional methods for local research,
Student actions in First-Year and Advanced Composition	a local place of their choice.	about local spaces, places, and locations.	through their analytical essay assignment.	within targeted public publications.	including investigative journalism, observation, and writing on location.

sheet, Fodrey quotes from geographer and spatial theorist Edward Soja's work to explain her intentions for their assignment:

> My objective . . . is to encourage you . . . to think differently about the meanings and significance of space and those related concepts that "compose and comprise the inherent spatiality of human life." . . . I am not suggesting that you discard your old and familiar ways of thinking about space and spatiality, but rather that you question them in new ways that are aimed at opening up and expanding the scope and critical sensibility of your already established spatial or geographical imaginations. (Soja qtd. in "Unit 2")

Thus, students go public by visiting local public spaces and then analyzing spatial inequalities. As Fodrey explained in our interview, this sometimes involved students analyzing on-campus spaces, like classrooms, but at other times it involved students visiting new or unfamiliar spaces, like tattoo parlors. Even though Fodrey noted that students do not necessarily have to leave campus to go public and learn from that spatial experience, she commented that part of what makes the assignment so valuable is that students

> go out into the community, they [step] out of the spaces where they feel comfortable . . . , [and] they become an outsider somewhere else looking in to that kind of other space that they may not understand—or maybe they do understand but they don't think other people see it quite the way that they do. (Fodrey)

According to Fodrey, students ultimately came to new realizations that were revealed in their writing. In Chapter 5, I explore the affective responses that may arise when students step out of their comfort zones but also how discomfort and affect, when balanced with an ethics of care, can be productive and transformative for students' learning.

Both of Fodrey's spatial analysis assignments prompt students to confront and revise stereotypes, in part because of the way she frames the assignment around issues of inequality and misperception of space. Fodrey explained in our interview that a number of her students selected spaces in South Tucson—an area that some students think is unsafe and that also happens to include a number of Tucson's Hispanic, particularly Mexican and Mexican American, neighborhood communities. Because some students enrolled in Fodrey's courses are from South Tucson, she told me that they selected those spaces, in part, to make arguments that "South Tucson is not this scary, gang-infested space that people should avoid in Tucson" (Fodrey). Fodrey also described a student project that involved analysis of inequalities in classroom spaces on the University of Arizona's campus, specifically desk spaces for students who are obese. The student, who self-identified as obese, examined how in many of the classrooms on campus there is nowhere for her to sit, and, in her public creative nonfiction essay, she used narrative of her personal experience to illustrate that injustice and advocate for the rights of obese students. Seeing public spaces through the lens of inequality helped Fodrey's students reassess stereotypes about different geographies and populations.

Fodrey's pedagogy also involved students approaching spatial analysis by examining the intersections of the personal and the public. Fodrey's course taught students the skills of investigative journalism and creative nonfiction—both of which serve the personal and public, an aspect of Long's interpretative pedagogies, through the process of research and the result of public writing. Fodrey's course, however, offers a model that differs from other examples of interpretative pedagogies examined by Long because it does not have a service learning component (Long 160). Fodrey's public pedagogy demonstrates a new model for how instructors might ask students to go public—break down perceived barriers between private and public, confront stereotypes and inequality, write for public audiences—without necessarily situating this approach in a service learning frame.

Another important component of public pedagogy in Fodrey's courses involved students circulating their writing and new knowledge through publication. I read this pedagogical approach as bearing similarity to Long's interpretative pedagogies. In her advanced composition course, Fodrey encouraged students to identify a specific publication—such as *TIME*, *Newsweek*, or the campus newspaper, *The Daily Wildcat*—for their writing. While some students chose not to move forward with publication, Fodrey explained how she used this component of the assignment to discuss rhetorical concerns related to audience. Her explanation is reminiscent of Cooper and Garvin's Field-Based Writing assignment that asked students to write for a very specific local audience; in Fodrey's case, she explained the significance of audience: "if you're writing for a local, Tucson-based audience you don't have to explain what the University of Arizona is, but if you're writing for a national audience, you imagine this is going to get published in *TIME*, you have to frame it completely differently." Because Fodrey asked her students to write for a realistic public audience, her students' writing had the potential to be circulated broadly and to move toward addressing social issues through publication.

Like the examples from Syracuse University and Oberlin College, Fodrey's course also involved instruction in research methods, which I see as aligning with the way Long defines institutional pedagogies. In Fodrey's courses, students learned to collect data through site observations, and she prompted them to write on location (i.e., handwrite or type while they are physically visiting a site) during these observations. She also incorporated instruction in literary and investigative journalism so that the course had "a rich research-based portion to it" (Fodrey). As she explained in our interview, Fodrey's students were "doing ethnographic research; they're going out and talking to people; they're immersing themselves in the spaces." Thus, Fodrey's public pedagogy invites students to visit local sites and to see these public, typically nonschool, locations as places for research, sites for investigating social issues, and inspiration for their public writing. I see this as falling under what Long identifies as an institutional pedagogical approach to public action because students are learning methodological research skills that will be useful in their futures as academics and professionals.

Public pedagogies exist at the intersections of the public and the academic, the institutional and the activist. Pedagogy is no longer restricted to schools; as Giroux has argued, it is our responsibility as educators to theorize "the role that pedagogy might play in linking learning to social change outside of traditional sites of schooling" ("Cultural Studies, Public Pedagogy" 61). Fodrey's moves to relocate her pedagogy and students' learning to public sites outside of the traditional classroom helps students build the ties between learning, writing, and social change.

In my application of Long's schema, I have argued that the pedagogies of Cooper, Luce, and Fodrey correspond to the categories of interpretative, institutional, and inquiry-driven pedagogies. My analysis demonstrates how composition instructors across different institutional and course contexts are implementing similar methods for going public, even if they are using different terminology for naming their pedagogical approaches. Long's categories offer instructors a useful model for considering the various ways in which their students might engage in public action and how they might offer instructional support for students in that endeavor. While I advocate for Long's schema, I also see some limitations in its framing, and, in the final section, I argue for extending one component of Long's schema to more fully emphasize (re)location in public pedagogy.

LOCATING THE PUBLIC SITES AND PURPOSES OF COMPOSITION PEDAGOGY

Over the last decade, composition scholars have drawn on spatial theories from cultural geography to help composition teachers consider the significance of place, space, and location in relationship to the teaching of writing (see Keller and Weisser; Mauk; Reynolds). When considering a public pedagogy, I believe it is essential for teachers to consider *where*—to locate student experiences in publics that will help them learn what it means to be an effective writer and rhetor in the academy and in their everyday lives. I advocate for a public location because I believe it affords the greatest opportunity for students to engage, learn from, and possibly serve their local community. As I consider my own pedagogical values, I want to teach composition in ways that prompt students to interact with unfamiliar publics, to write about issues that are meaningful within their local public context, and to circulate their writing in publics beyond the academy; to do this work effectively, we must be mindful of location, relocating and re-envisioning our classroom spaces in more public ways.

If we look comparatively across the examples in this chapter, a point of similarity is the significance each teacher placed on the public location of their pedagogy. In other words, going public for these composition courses meant interacting with and experiencing unfamiliar places—regardless of whether those places were on or off campus and whether or not they involved interaction with a community organization through a service learning partnership. In some cases, the locations were likely familiar but students had to approach and analyze them from a new and unfamiliar perspective.

During our interview, each composition teacher articulated the importance of having students experience unfamiliar places and how doing so led to a deeper level of engagement. For example, Cooper explained that the labs in her Field-Based Writing course "were so wonderful because they got [students] off campus and out into natural areas"; moreover, she stated her belief that students were "engaged more . . . thoroughly" because of these site visits. Similarly, Fodrey commented that "leaving the classroom wakes [students] up in a way that they become more engaged. They're like, 'wow, we're going on a field trip!'" Framing important pedagogical work as a field trip may seem elementary on the one hand, but on the other hand there are a number of studies, particularly related to video games, that emphasize the importance of play in enhancing student engagement and increasing the possibility of students seeing themselves as change agents in the world (see, among others, Gee; McAllister). In short, we should not underestimate the venturing and going—the "field trip"—aspects of public pedagogy; going somewhere new breaks the monotony of traditional classroom spaces and can provoke a deeper level of engagement.

Going public by encountering unfamiliar places is also a way for students to see connections among the diverse spaces they move through on a daily basis. Part of Luce's reasoning for having students investigate issues related to sexuality was to help them see that "their dorm life is their classroom life" and vice versa; for Luce, "public [became] a way to bridge the town and gown." Indeed, as Mauk argues, when students "excavate knowledge" from their everyday lives by interviewing friends, family, and coworkers, "students are agents of academic work . . . using academic tools within their non-academic lives . . . enabl[ing] them to imagine themselves as public intellectuals who bring together the activities of various spaces and systems" (362). By having students conduct research within the familiar space of campus but through a new lens of HIV/AIDS, Luce invited students to bring the knowledge that they were learning in the classroom into public spaces and to also bring public knowledge from the field back into their academic work in the classroom. Again, I see this reciprocal value of public and academic knowledge as a primary goal of public pedagogy in composition studies; blurring the lines between public and academy, community and institution, and town and gown helps us forward that agenda.

While I see Long's schema as a valuable tool, I believe it ultimately misses the significance of place that is central to public pedagogy in composition studies. Even though the final chapter of Long's book focuses on pedagogy, the majority of *Community Literacy and the Rhetoric of Local Publics* introduces and applies Long's five-point heuristic for local public work, which provides a framework for her comparison of how everyday citizens (not necessarily students) go public. The components of her heuristic for local public work include metaphor, context, tenor of discourse, literacy practices, and rhetorical invention (16). Part of what I found most intriguing about Long's work was the focus on context—what defines the "local" in her rhetoric of "local publics," the *where* of literate practices, and "the community in community literacy" (207). Long argues that local publics are "at once discursive and material"; they are the "sites that people devise to address distinct rhetorical agendas," and local publics are "the sites where ordinary people tend to develop their voices and repertoires for going public" (207). Despite her initial attention to site and location in defining local publics, Long ultimately de-emphasizes location in her final chapter on pedagogical practices, suggesting that "it is probably not enough for students to go to new places or to work with others in new ways—as important as these moves may be" (199).

While I agree that students going to new places will not, by itself, necessarily result in more meaningful learning, I contend that it is of considerable import when designing and implementing public pedagogies in composition curricula. As the examples from Oberlin College, Syracuse University, and the University of Arizona demonstrate, venturing to new places was integral to the way composition teachers designed their assignments and to the way students learned about writing. Without site visits to Lake Erie, for instance, students would have learned about field-based writing in very different, arguably less effective, ways. However, Long's suggestion that it is not enough to simply go to new places calls us to be mindful of the kinds of public learning experiences we are planning for students. Indeed, haphazardly positioning students in local publics will not successfully serve our pedagogical ends.

To facilitate a more carefully constructed and located public pedagogy, I offer composition teachers the following tentative model. As we consider the public, new, and/or unfamiliar places for our composition pedagogies, I believe it is also important to align location with the educational purposes we have for students going public. Figure 1 is a graphic representation of the intersections between possible locations (x axis) and educational purposes (y axis) of public pedagogies. The x axis of Figure 1 suggests that instructors consider the locations of public pedagogy on a continuum that may range from physical and/or local public places to digital and/or global public spaces. The y axis is organized on a continuum ranging from more traditional educational purposes (e.g., to learn or critique) and moves toward more civic and activist purposes (e.g., to affect social change or forward an activist agenda). As the quadrant summaries indicate, the graph moves from the upper, right first quadrant, with traditional educational purposes in locations that could be removed (spatially and materially) from the proximity of campus, to the upper, left second quadrant with traditional purposes in locations that are in close proximity to campus; then, in the third quadrant, the close proximity to campus remains the same, but the educational purposes turn toward the civic, social, and activist, and the final quadrant pairs these more public purposes with locations that are digital and/or global. Often the location of one's pedagogy could align with multiple educational purposes, and, in such a case, plotting these along a vertical line could be a useful approach (see Figure 2). Certainly Figure 1 does not encompass all of the many locations and diverse educational purposes one could include in a public pedagogy. However, I hope that it might represent a start, a tentative model, that could serve as a planning tool to help composition teachers design and locate their public pedagogies.

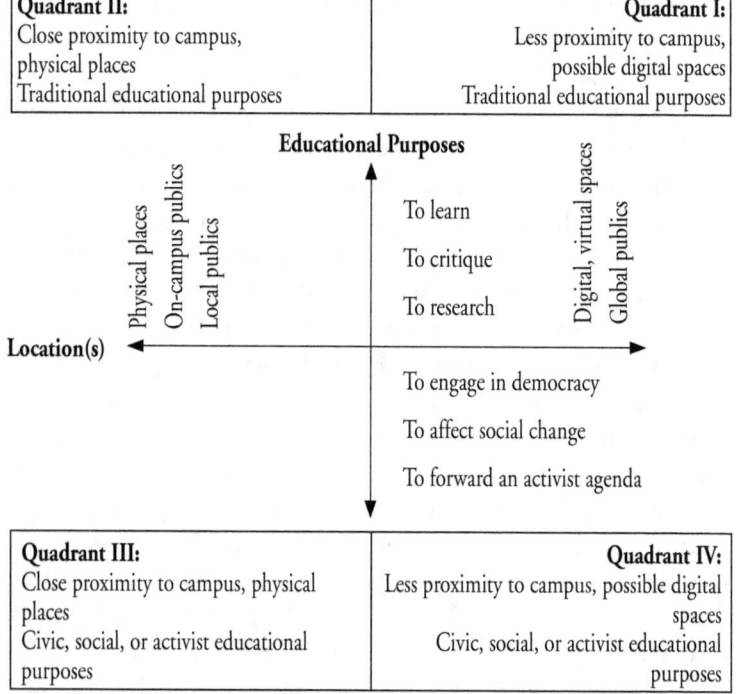

Figure 1. Graphic representation of the intersections between the locations and educational purposes of public pedagogy.

To see how this model might be used to plan for public pedagogy in a composition course, in Figure 2 I have plotted some components of the Field-Based Writing course that Cooper and Garvin taught at Oberlin College. I want to be clear that Cooper and Garvin did not use this graphic to plan the public components of their course. However, for the sake of demonstrating the graphic in use, I am working backwards to show how the pedagogy that was enacted might have been located and purposed using Figure 2.[5]

In Figure 2, I have located the public pedagogy in Cooper and Garvin's course in the second and third quadrants, which means

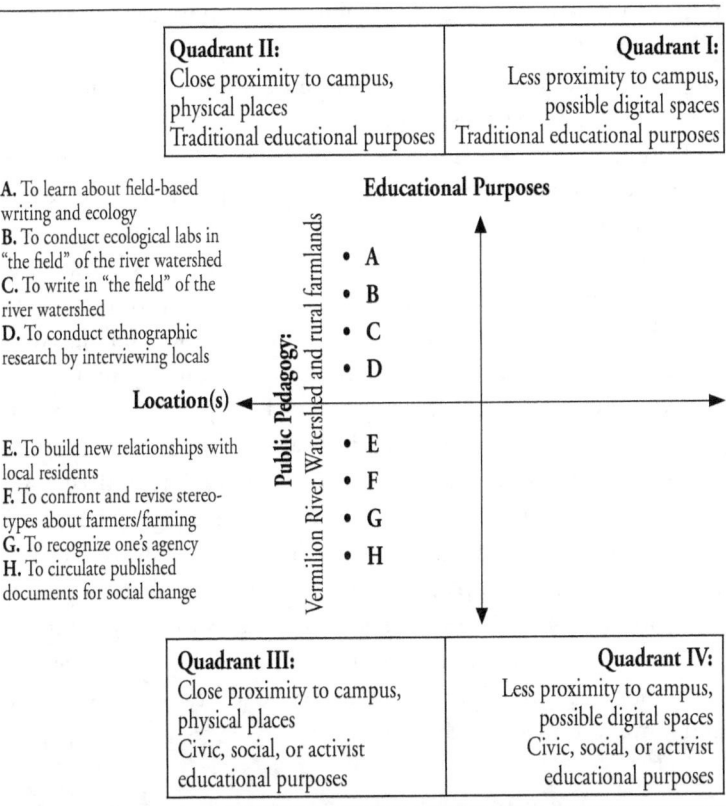

Figure 2. An example of Cooper and Garvin's Field-Based Writing course at Oberlin College using the graphic for plotting public pedagogy.

that the location is a physical and local site (in this case, the Vermilion River Watershed and rural farmlands) and the educational purposes range from fairly traditional academic goals (in quadrant II, upper left) to more public, social, and activist goals (in quadrant III, lower left). Part of what I see as compelling about this example is how the educational goals of Cooper and Garvin's course do not abandon traditional academic goals of teaching students to write and conduct research. As Long's previously quoted comment highlights, simply going to a new location will not lead to better learning, and we must keep our goals grounded in these traditional purposes. However, we can also see how Cooper and Garvin go public with their pedagogy by moving toward more civic and social goals in the third quadrant. It is this set of goals that I believe is enhanced by a public pedagogy that does not confine students to the four walls of the classroom.

Planning where and for what purposes students will go public is an essential component of forwarding the public work of composition pedagogy. The pedagogical examples discussed in this chapter emphasize the importance of location. In each case, the definition and location of local publics varies—the Vermilion River Watershed, on-campus (but "foreign") organization OrangeAID, student-selected sites such as classrooms and local neighborhoods. However, composition teachers use these local public sites to teach students about the importance of engaging the local community and campus for research and the power of writing and rhetoric within these public contexts. These public pedagogies show how composition teachers have taken up the ethical challenges of addressing increasingly privatized and neoliberal messages students face within public spheres by assigning students to engage with local public places and to use writing and publishing to circulate alternate messages that question stereotypes, address local problems, and move toward social change.

3

Productive Tensions: Administering Public Pedagogies

HOW TO GO PUBLIC WITH PEDAGOGY WITHIN a specific composition course is often influenced by the policies and values of a writing program. Building on the innovative pedagogies discussed in Chapter 2, this chapter considers public pedagogy from the perspective of the Writing Program Administrator (WPA), drawing on specific strategies of WPAs I interviewed for my study. In the following pages, I identify replicable administrative methods that WPAs at other institutions might use to organize and structure a more public focus within their programs. My impetus for this work comes from my belief in the possibility of designing sustainable, strategic, and institutionalized public programs that anticipate unsustainability as inevitable, employ tactics to remain responsive to public concerns, and that remain mindful of and open to the bottom-up, organic, and community-based needs that are often positioned in opposition to institutions of higher education. I argue that it is indeed possible (and perhaps preferable) to strike a productive tension between sustainability and unsustainability, strategies and tactics, and institutionalized and community-based approaches. By comparatively analyzing techniques from WPAs I interviewed, I identify an administrative approach—curriculum design that allows for morphing—which offers the possibility of exploiting dichotomous tensions between stasis and change, creating a productive method for administering pedagogies that invite students to go public.

Relocating the sites of composition teaching and learning to increasingly public spheres beyond the classroom has direct implications for writing program administration, and a number of scholars have argued for the value of extending the public role of the WPA and writing programs. For example, Kelly Ritter suggests reconsidering administrative service to a "truly public authority, which works for a public, student-centered good" (57). Recounting her collaborations with WPAs at four other institutions to create a system-wide rubric for basic writing, Ritter contends that extra-institutional partnerships are often an untapped potential source of power and agency for WPAs (57). She concludes by recommending that WPAs "make [their] program truly 'public'" and "start [thinking] of [their] program as one that serves a larger community beyond [their] home institution" (Ritter 60–61). Making similar claims in the introduction to *Going Public*, Shirley K Rose and Irwin Weiser contend that "public engagement initiatives have the potential to transform our understanding of the 'service' role of writing courses from that of 'serving' other academic programs to 'serving' a much more broadly defined public" (4). Beyond a few published examples, though—notably Eli Goldblatt's *Because We Live Here* (2007), Jeffrey T. Grabill and Lynée Lewis Gaillet's "Writing Program Design in the Metropolitan University" (2002), Anne-Marie Hall's "Expanding the Community" (2002), Steve Parks and Eli Goldblatt's "Writing Beyond the Curriculum" (2000), and Shirley K Rose and Irwin Weiser's *Going Public* (2010)—administrators have very few models for how to develop writing programs with civic, public, and service-oriented goals and objectives.[1] As the number of writing programs and WPAs interested in going public with pedagogy and administration grows, administrators have a range of course development and sequencing issues to consider. The administrative examples in this chapter help reinforce the kind of pedagogies that value public knowledge beyond the academy and support the relocation of our composition pedagogies beyond traditional classroom spaces through community-based writing centers, partnerships with public community groups, and the creation of on-campus public spaces for sharing student writing.

EXPLOITING DICHOTOMIES

In her conclusion to the edited collection *Unsustainable: Re-imagining Community Literacy, Public Writing, Service-Learning, and the University*, Jessica Restaino argues for scholars and teachers working on university/community partnerships to reject binaries and rethink relationships. Because public pedagogies invite students to critically attend to and often cross boundaries between the university and surrounding public communities, or between familiar places and unfamiliar places, scholarship that examines partnerships and dichotomies between public/academic, inside/outside, us/them can help practitioners productively theorize public pedagogy in composition studies. In *Unsustainable*, Restaino characterizes the trend within scholarship on community outreach to construct binaries between the university and the community and aptly notes that teachers attempting to serve both "community and university standards find themselves quickly ensnarled in a dichotomous spider's web" (256). Indeed, Restaino and Laurie JC Cella's collection is premised on a critique of these binaries as they invite readers to reconsider the value of both long-term and short-term public projects and redefine "standard definition[s] of success" and assessment (Cella 3).

Table 7 lists some of the common binaries that tend to emerge in scholarship on service learning, public writing, and community/university partnerships. The first of these binaries (academic/public) lies at the heart of public pedagogies because it demonstrates the historical divide between what has been considered valuable academic knowledge within institutions of higher education (i.e., what is important to learn in classrooms) and what has been considered less valuable community-based public knowledge (i.e., learning that happens outside of classrooms). Theories of public pedagogy collapse this binary and overturn the dynamics by situating traditional academic learning within public, nonschool locations and by valuing public and community-based sources of knowledge by respecting the knowledge of academic "outsiders."

Table 7. Common Binaries in Scholarship on University/Community Partnerships

Academic	Public
Institutional	Community-Based
"Us"/Insiders	"Them"/Outsiders
Strategies	Tactics
Sustainable/Long-Term	Unsustainable/Short-Term
Top-Down	Bottom-Up
Stable/Static	Unstable/Changing

One of the major problems with binaries, however, is that practitioners tend to, whether explicitly or implicitly, assign value or preference to one over the other. For example, Paula Mathieu has advocated so fervently for tactics over strategies—and, at times, other approaches in the right column instead of the left—because of the historical precedence of universities primarily initiating projects for their own purposes and those institutions ignoring community needs and/or exploiting community-based projects. Because scholarship on community literacy, public outreach, and civic engagement often works to break down barriers between the ivory tower and the surrounding community, the left side of the column is often vilified; our progressive and liberatory goals often seek to subvert traditional power structures that are represented within institutions of higher education. However, knowing that projects shift and sometimes fail, Restaino cautions practitioners against the tendency to "mark one 'side' or the other as a winner or loser" (258). Restaino and Cella, as well as the authors in their collection, suggest that we avoid or at least rethink reductive binaries that fracture and divide our attempts to productively partner university and community interests: Restaino questions, "how can we destabilize our oversimplified dividing walls and discover more complex means of owning and making meaningful that which rests somewhere in between?" (257). I agree with Restaino and Cella's claim that we must find a balance—somewhere in between. Rather than outright rejecting binaries, though, I argue that writing program administrators can use the tensions between these dichotomies to their advantage, taking a both/and approach to help move public pedagogies forward and design effective programmatic infrastructures. Before exploring how WPAs might exploit dichotomous tensions, I provide a more in-depth look at debates within composition studies about institutionalized models of service learning (Feigenbaum; Mathieu) that undergird our understanding of the traditional dynamics between colleges/universities and the publics with which they sometimes partner.

Institutionalized versus Community-Based Models

Institutions of higher education in the United States are increasingly moving toward institutionalized systems for supporting service learning, public outreach, and/or civic engagement—approaches that overlap with the goals of public pedagogies in composition studies. More and more campuses are devoting spaces, funding, and staffing to the creation of campuswide centers, the alignment of mission statements and student learning outcomes, and the development of course designations and curricular requirements—all with the explicit goal of connecting students with public communities beyond the classroom or campus. Organizations like Campus Compact were created to help institutionalize public engagement by providing supporting infrastructure.[2] They offer staff to coordinate projects, training for faculty, scholarships, and other incentives for students, and "the institutional will to make civic and community engagement a priority" ("Who We Are"). Moreover, publications targeted at college and university leaders and administrators, such as *Educating Citizens* (Colby, Elrich, Beaumont, and Stephens 2003), *Educating for Democracy* (Colby, Beaumont, Elrich, and Corngold 2007), and *Becoming an Engaged Campus* (Beere, Votruba, and Wells 2011), indicate the growing interest in finding effective institutional exemplars to further support public outreach.

Some models call for a complete realignment of an institution's goals and mission toward the goals of going public. The authors of *Becoming an Engaged Campus*, for instance, advocate for a change strategy called an "alignment process" that they argue will "cause all of the elements within [an institution] to function in a way that promotes public engagement" (Beere, Votruba, and Wells 2). This process, drawn from the practices of high-performance companies, involves aligning everything from an institution's vision and mission to promotion and tenure within a frame that values and rewards public engagement initiatives until the work is "deeply embedded in the institution, and support and commitment for public engagement permeate the organization" (33). While supporting and rewarding faculty who go public with pedagogy is certainly important, moves to institutionalize through alignment represent a top-down approach that often values macro-level statistics and public recognition for the institution at the expense of the micro-level needs of community organizations.[3]

Within composition studies, Paula Mathieu has been one of the most vocal critics of institutionalized service learning programs because she argues this movement typically benefits the university's public image without actually serving the needs of the community. Mathieu critiques the push to institutionalize by claiming that it relies on strategic and mandated methods, seeking to create stable spaces—like campus service learning centers—and required student volunteerism that resist the "local rhetorical responsiveness" of more tactical approaches to community engagement (*Tactics* 96). Even the potential advantages of institutionalized service learning, "measurable success, broad institutional presence, and sustainability," are problematic because they create a generic set of needs derived by the institution, rather than community partners, that result in benign tasks for students and/or unnecessary (even potentially harmful) service projects for the community (Mathieu, *Tactics* 99). Mathieu makes the case for a bottom-up, tactical approach to service learning that consults the expertise of community partners and works rhetorically within local space and time (*Tactics* 106).

Mathieu's important critique of institutionalization of community-based projects has prompted composition specialists to ask tough questions about efforts to create stable, sustainable, goal-oriented programs that mandate service requirements in composition courses. However, Mathieu's stance has also been critiqued for presenting a problematic binary, leaving administrators with limited options for responsive public collaborations within institutional frameworks. Paul Feigenbaum, for example, argues for the incorporation of "relationship-centered practice" and advocates for scholars to use tactics that "ultimately have strategic consequences" (49). In a recent chapter within the edited collection *Unsustainable*, Mathieu clarifies and further reflects on her previous arguments: she explains that projects should begin from a tactical approach, but she also acknowledges that institutional structures can be useful in helping build sustainable projects. However, Mathieu remains skeptical of movements to institutionalize and, citing the ending of one of her community-based projects (Kids' 2 Cents) as an example, she disrupts the common claim that institutionalization necessarily leads to long-term sustainability in projects. Ultimately, Mathieu advocates for a "deeper and richer understanding of the vast network of complexities"—institutional entanglements—"that frame, work toward, and pull apart community projects" ("After Tactics" 23). In her conclusion to *Unsustainable*, Restaino arrives at the crux of the problem:

> despite Mathieu's justified distrust of institutions and their strategic approaches to [community] partnership, the university continues to initiate and . . . support [community] projects. . . . In other words, whether or not we might be "bad" for each other, in fact we continue to have something to do with each other. (255)

Knowing that partnerships between universities and publics beyond academia will continue to exist for one reason or another, the question shifts to how administrators might design and implement programs that provide supporting and sustaining infrastructures while also remaining responsive to community interests and the need for projects to evolve.

When I consider the way in which I began to incorporate public pedagogies into the teaching of writing in my courses, I am reminded of the very institutionalized model through which I first came to value these pedagogical approaches. For me, going public began with incorporating service learning into first-year composition, and I began this approach largely because of a faculty development workshop and a "meet and greet" luncheon with community partners during my second year as a lecturer at a private liberal arts university. The workshops were part of an interdisciplinary, year-long program intended to introduce theories and best practices for teaching service learning, and the luncheon was organized through the campus service learning center, affiliated with Campus Compact,[4] offering an opportunity for faculty members to meet with leaders of local nonprofit organizations to talk about potential projects. Both of these events significantly affected my teaching and scholarship: I met a number of community partners in a city where I was a newcomer; I began integrating community-based writing and service learning projects in my curricula; and I applied for and received an internal grant to fund a service learning curriculum redesign project. As I reflect back on these experiences nearly ten years later, they seem rather ordinary as institutional practices—workshops, luncheons, and internal grants advertised on faculty listservs. I certainly had an interest in public engagement that I developed as an undergraduate (see Preface), and I was curious about pedagogies that invited students to go public. In thinking back, though, I realize that much of the reason I became involved with public pedagogies in the first place was because of the institutional culture within which I was working—a culture that rewarded public outreach and community engagement while providing its faculty with a great deal of administrative support to incorporate innovative teaching methods.

Given the recent debates within composition studies about institutionalized models of service learning, I struggle with where WPAs should draw the line, in part because my own experiences suggest that institutional models can be effective, even if flawed. I often wonder if I would have had the courage to go public with pedagogy without institutional constructs that invited me to study service learning theories, valued my participation in civic engagement faculty development programs, and supported me in the challenging and risky work of reaching out to community partners in an unfamiliar local context. On the other hand, I continue to question whether this institutionalized model might have contributed to some of the complications I encountered. For example, instead of arriving at partnerships organically and from the ground up, I worked through the campus service learning center to initiate partnerships with six local nonprofit organizations, and this institutionalized model of having partnerships made for me, even though I was consulted during that process, led me to take a more passive role in sustaining those partnerships.[5] Having a central office easily set up the partnership took the labor out of finding my own community partners, making my own connections, and building strong relationships. While this institutionalized support saved me time, I never felt that the partnerships were mine to foster in the same way I might have if I had found the partners on my own. In other words, the somewhat contrived and constructed relationship, perhaps because of the institutionalized model through which we came to be partnered, made communication issues more challenging. My motivations for studying administrative approaches to going public stem from the benefits and challenges of my past experiences with institutionalized models for going public. How can WPAs more effectively support instructors in relocating their composition pedagogies within publics beyond the classroom or campus? How can administrators design composition curricula that support a critical approach to public places and that value public knowledge and learning?

Curriculum Design That Allows for Morphing

Based on the interviews I conducted with WPAs, I found that one of the best methods for supporting public pedagogy within a writing program is curriculum design—more specifically, an approach to curricular development that allows for morphing and that draws on the productive tensions between stasis and change. Considering the common binaries from Table 7, if we were to position curriculum design and morphing on the table, the former would roughly align with the left column and the latter with the right column. Overlapping with concepts on the left side of Table 7, curriculum design is a practice that most often happens within institutional contexts and for fairly strategic purposes, often resulting from top-down mandates (e.g., accreditation agencies or legislative bodies). The curriculum, once designed, can represent a static piece of the writing program, though I intend to trouble that notion by pairing curriculum design with morphing. Curriculum design can, on the surface, seem like a mundane and ordinary institutionalized practice—much like the email on a faculty listserv that led to my first encounter with service learning pedagogies—but, as the administrative examples in this chapter demonstrate, using the curriculum as a stable but changing component within one's administration can help scaffold public pedagogy.

When paired with morphing, curriculum design can be a powerful, even liberatory tool. Bearing similarities to tactics and change, morphing more closely aligns with the right column of Table 7. As an administrative strategy, designing a curriculum that also morphs means allowing projects to evolve, even if those changing public projects risk instability or unsustainability. My choice to use the term *morphing* came specifically from my interview with Anne Trubek, chair of the Department of Rhetoric and Composition at Oberlin College at the time of our interview, as she described the changes that happened in the Community-Based Writing Program she helped initiate, which I examine in more detail in the coming pages. Morphing was an appealing concept for me; it captured the sentiment Paula Mathieu suggests in her reflection on unsustainable public projects: "sometimes projects that end can begin again" ("After Tactics" 29). Moreover, as I considered how morphing fit the examples at Syracuse University and the University of Arizona, I began to see that part of the success for all of these projects was in their ability to be agile, to respond to the exigencies of multiple and often competing agendas between publics and institutions of higher education. The need for flexibility and recognizing that projects evolve is also emphasized in Cella's introduction to *Unsustainable*. Community needs change and universities may not be able to support ongoing projects; the important point that Cella underscores is that practitioners should "not lose hope when projects seem to shift, evolve, and/or end unexpectedly. We believe these endings can often provide the seeds for a renewed project, though one with a new purpose or new partners" (3).

Cella and Restaino question the tendency to value long-term sustainability in public partnerships and projects. Coinciding with some components of the ecocomposition movement (see, for example, Dobrin and Weisser; Owens), the importance of sustainability emerged in service learning scholarship as a response to problematic models of teachers, scholars, and students swooping in for one-time, short-term projects, in some cases leaving community partners with more problems than assistance (Cushman, "Sustainable"; Mathieu, *Tactics*). In an often-cited essay advocating for sustainability in service learning—one that helped build a strong narrative of sustainability within service learning scholarship—Ellen Cushman suggests the significance of capacity building to ensure turnover does not mean that a project ends; Cushman offers research-based service learning as a model that "does not rely on any one person but that allows for turnover as collaborators inevitably leave and new ones come on board" ("Sustainable" 61).[6] Writing about university and public school partnerships, Anne-Marie Hall makes similar arguments: "do not rely on one leader for everything . . . develop programs that are flexible. . . . One person cannot sustain a program" ("Expanding" 325). Conversations about sustainability in partnerships represent an important foundation for public pedagogies within composition studies. However, as Peter Goggin argues in the collection *Rhetorics, Literacies, and Narratives of Sustainability*, terms like "sustainability" and "green" have become "buzzwords" that must be examined "critically, if not cynically" (7). Translating this critical work into practices for WPAs may mean exploiting binaries such as sustainability and unsustainability, acknowledging the strengths and shortcomings of each, and finding a productive balance to support public pedagogy through curriculum design that morphs.

Finding the balance, or, perhaps more precisely, harnessing the productive tensions between sustainability/unsustainability and stasis/change can help administrators institutionalize public pedagogies in ways that remain responsive to public interests. One model of how to harness these tensions to support institutionally sustainable work is represented in Thia Wolf, Jill Swiencicki, and Chris Fosen's critique of "business as usual" (BAU). These three WPAs align common sustainability arguments for maintenance and endurance with a problematic model of BAU within research on climate change. They draw similarities between the experiences of climate scientists who battle with "'normal' but harmful environmental practices" and WPAs who battle with "normal but harmful institutional practices" (Wolf et al. 140). They suggest that wedge theory—a model coming out of the environmental sciences—offers a means by which WPAs can combat the unsustainable practices of BAU by using "stabilization wedges" to respond purposefully to changes in the short-term while seeking "more radical, structural and bureaucratic changes for the long term" (143). Wolf and colleagues offer an example from their first-year composition program: the Town Hall Meeting as a wedge to revise curriculum and move toward "more institutionally-sustainable WPA work" (143). Their example of using institutional constructs to move toward curriculum revision has much in common with the examples I analyze from the institutions in my study. The work of Wolf, Swiencicki, and Fosen calls us to be mindful of the tension between sustainability (maintenance and endurance) and complacency (business as usual). Similarly, curriculum design that allows for morphing resists complacency in meaningful ways—representing strategies of change that should be responsive to the needs of student learners and publics beyond the classroom.

Another example of how writing program administrators can use institutionalized structures like the curriculum in ways that remain responsive and tactical is by creating what E. Shelley Reid calls a "culture of changing" within the writing program (21). Reid calls for administrators to focus on the process of *changing*, rather than the stasis product of *change*, defining "*changing* as an expectation rather than an imposition" (12). While she identifies a number of advantages to creating a culture of curriculum change such as opportunities for collaboration, leadership, and reflection, Reid also acknowledges the risks of building a program around constant change, which can read/feel like instability. Knowing that WPAs face instability on nearly a daily basis, though, Reid advocates for "directed, purposeful changing" in order to avoid the frustrating cycle of "only reactive change" (24). Reid's culture of changing within writing programs mirrors the kind of balanced approach to curriculum design that allows for morphing—an approach that can help administrators effectively initiate and support public pedagogies. WPAs need strategic, purposeful approaches—which often means anchoring the work in stable, institutionalized infrastructures like the curriculum—but Reid's examples and arguments support the idea that the move toward institutionalization can be done within a model of morphing by ascribing to a culture of changing.

In the following pages, I highlight administrative approaches for each of the institutions and programs in my study; Table 8 summarizes and previews how program administrators use a combination of curriculum design and morphing to support public pedagogy within their writing centers, undergraduate writing majors, and first-year writing courses.

Table 8. Summary of Program Initiatives and Administrative Approaches

Institution	Program Initiative	Administrative Approach of Curriculum Design That Allows for Morphing
Oberlin College	Community-Based Writing Program	Tutor training attached to Rhetoric and Composition course. Morphed into Ninde Scholars Program.
Syracuse University	First-Year and Undergraduate Major Courses in the Writing Program	Used existing set of undergraduate courses to create a series of "next step" courses. Morphed components of public projects to fit with course goals, and vice versa, across several semesters.
University of Arizona	Revision of the First-Year Writing Curriculum	Revised the second-semester first-year writing course to include more public components. Supported the revised curriculum by morphing a public showcase of student writing, changing a custom inhouse textbook publication, and continually assessing the revised curriculum.

"IT KEPT MORPHING": A COMMUNITY-BASED WRITING PROGRAM AT OBERLIN COLLEGE

The Community-Based Writing Program (CBWP) at Oberlin College began as an off-campus public extension of a traditional on-campus writing center. By relocating students' experiences of writing tutoring to public sites beyond the campus, this approach valued public knowledge and helped Oberlin students critically engage with public places and persons beyond campus. The CBWP is an excellent example of how a project can evolve and shift over time; in this case, morphing from a short-term, ad hoc program to a more centrally institutionalized program with a broader set of goals. Part of what is significant, though, is that through these changes the CBWP was able to keep ongoing connections to the Rhetoric and Composition curriculum. For these reasons, the example of the CBWP at Oberlin demonstrates the potential of an administrative approach to going public that utilizes the productive tensions between curriculum design and morphing, between strategies and tactics that Mathieu has written about, and between models of sustainability and unsustainability that Restaino, Cella, and others have explored.

I learned about the beginnings and evolution of Oberlin College's CBWP when I interviewed Anne Trubek in the spring of 2011. When I selected the Department of Rhetoric and Composition as one of three research sites for my study, the CBWP was one of the main reasons why. However, when I first contacted Trubek, she explained that the CBWP was no longer part of the department. My first thought was to consider another research site, but then I became curious about what happened to the program, assuming this could be an interesting example of unsustainability. I soon learned that the program did not end per se; rather it morphed into a new program (the Ninde Scholars program) that still exists with some financial and pedagogical ties to the Department of Rhetoric and Composition. The CBWP began as a side project for an already well-established and institutionalized program, the Writing Associates Program, that offers "free and student-staffed writing tutor service based at Oberlin College" ("Writing Associates").

Oberlin students who are interested in serving as writing associates must first take RHET 401: Teaching and Tutoring Writing Across the Curriculum. Trubek was teaching RHET 401 in 2003, and, because the on-campus writing center did not receive a "huge amount of traffic," she and the writing associates came up with the idea to offer writing tutoring at the local high school. With the assistance of a grant from SCALE/LAN (Student Coalition for Action in Literacy Education/Literacy Action Network), the CBWP was piloted in Spring 2003 ("Community-Based"). In the following years, the CBWP expanded to include four sites: Oberlin High School, Adult Basic Literacy Education at the Joint Vocational School, ACCESS Lorain County, and Grafton Correctional Institute ("Community-Based"). Situating student learning in public schools, adult education sites, and prisons, the CBWP's approach valued the public experiences and knowledge students gained from a relocated pedagogy that critically attended to the intersections of community literacy in local publics. From the way Trubek described the program in our interview, it seems that its creation would align more with how Mathieu describes tactical public projects than strategic projects; RHET 401 students wanted to tutor a broader and more present population, and Trubek knew that the surrounding community would likely benefit from the tutoring students had to offer. The moment was right, and the grant funding helped support the program's expansion.

However, as with many programs that begin from a tactical approach, issues with sustainability began to arise. Trubek explained that while the initial program was very successful, the CBWP continued running into the same problems within the community as they had on campus: "nobody was showing up" to the drop-in writing center. However, rather than abandoning the idea and ultimately having an unsustainable program, Trubek explained how the CBWP "kept morphing":

> We got a lot of buy-in from the community, and I went in with a couple of other people in town, the local school district and the urban league, to create a college access program for low-income students at the local high school, Oberlin High

School. We created what was called the Ninde Scholars program. (Trubek)

The resulting Ninde Scholars Program is a college-access and college-readiness program that "targets [in the Oberlin city area] under-represented and low-income students and those who would be the first in their families to attend college" ("Ninde Scholars"). While the program that grew out of the CBWP initially emphasized writing instruction, Trubek noted that "it just got much larger," expanding to include helping "students with the college application process and search." Trubek handed over the directorship of the Ninde Scholars program to Bo Arbogast in 2006, an administrator who is not affiliated with the Department of Rhetoric and Composition. Figure 3 illustrates the ways in which the Ninde Scholars Program continues to overlap in significant ways with the Department of Rhetoric and Composition and the Writing Associates Program out of which it initially grew.

Trubek's collaboration with others to envision a new program and her interest in allowing the CBWP to morph into the most pressing needs for the community represent, I argue, strategic moves toward sustainability and institutionalization that also maintain some of the tactical roots that helped start the original pro-

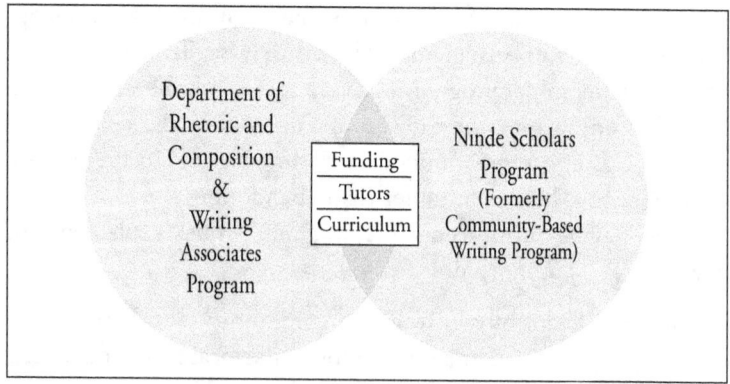

Figure 3. Oberlin College Department of Rhetoric and Composition and Ninde Scholars Program.

gram—an approach that models how other administrators might support public pedagogy in their own writing programs. In the case of the CBWP, sustainability became important because it allowed for an extended and more in-depth partnership with one community partner (Oberlin High School). As Cushman, Hall, and other scholars have written about, community outreach projects often begin with the work of one devoted faculty member and/or a small group of students, any of whom may not be in the picture after a few years' time. The advantage of finding more sustainable options for projects like the CBWP is that the community continues to be served and the partnership is preserved, even if the people involved or the goals of the project shift. In this case, what led to increased sustainability resulted from a more institutionalized program that benefited from full-time administrative staff and long-term funding. While these can be seen as strategic moves, I also see them as balanced with the tactical approach of morphing: being ready for constant change and knowing that unsustainability is never too far away, but neither is rebirth: "projects that end can begin again" (Mathieu, "After Tactics" 29).

Even though the Ninde Scholars Program is a separate program not officially affiliated with the Department of Rhetoric and Composition, Bo Arbogast, Director of Ninde Scholars at the time of our interview, emphasized how the program and the department are "still linked." One major link is represented in the students who are trained as writing associates and who also serve as tutors for the Ninde Scholars. "In the beginning," explained Arbogast, "I would say all of the tutors were writing associates from the Rhet/Comp Department, and, now, a portion of them [still] are . . . there's a sizable contingent of writing associates . . . in our cadre of tutors." In part this link remains for financial reasons; the Department of Rhetoric and Composition pays for Ninde Scholars tutors who have gone through the RHET 401 training.[7] Beyond the financial ties, the curriculum also represents a significant way in which the Ninde Scholars Program continues to thrive from its roots in the CBWP.

In my assessment of how the CBWP morphed into the Ninde Scholars Program, I contend one of the pieces that allowed for a successful transition was the grounding of both projects in the curriculum design of Rhetoric and Composition coursework. As Arbogast explained in our interview, the contingent of tutors who have also taken the RHET 401 course are often better prepared than other tutors in the Ninde Scholars Program: "I definitely feel that the tutors from the Rhet/Comp Department [who] have taken [RHET 401] really have a stronger understanding of how to work with students in terms of writing," and they are "generally more advanced in their thinking about how to help students approach academic tasks, not just writing, but social studies, history, [even] math" (Arbogast). And, while RHET 401 is not a requirement for all Ninde Scholars tutors, the pedagogical theory behind the course still finds its way into the teacher training and preparation for a majority of tutors. For example, Arbogast piloted a training program in which tutors shared relevant readings and then discussed and applied the theories to their tutoring experiences with the Ninde Scholars; Arbogast noted that "some of those readings actually came from the Rhetoric 401 course about teaching and tutoring writing." The Ninde Scholars Program's public pedagogy succeeded, in part, because of the curriculum that it grew out of (the RHET 401 course) and the curricular components that continue to ripple through the program today.

As a program developed out of Oberlin's campus writing center, the CBWP was perhaps uniquely suited for experimentation with public engagement and for morphing into the kind of program that was most needed in the community. As Linda S. Bergmann has argued, writing centers are "sometimes seen (or see themselves) as marginal or marginalized," but "life on the margins can offer opportunities to experiment and change . . . and can foster engagement with institutions outside the university" (160). The program that Trubek and students in RHET 401 were able to pilot in 2003 and that Trubek helped shepherd through expansion and ultimately evolution into the Ninde Scholars Program likely benefited from being on the margins. In this case, the margins provided an opportunity for experimentation with relocating pedagogy into more public locations. But the move from a pilot program on the margins—one class, one faculty member, and a small group of students with an idea for going public with their writing center—to an institutionalized, interdisciplinary program on Oberlin's campus did not happen by accident. Trubek strategically sought ways to make the program sustainable because "the college has an unfortunate history of starting community projects and abandoning them" (Trubek). Trubek did not want to fall into the trap of starting with "really great ideas and high ambitions" for going public, only for the ideas to "get too large, or [for us to] get bored and they stop." Trubek's claims here represent an imperative for institutions and WPAs to follow through with the public projects they initiate. Trubek's work to institutionalize the CBWP could be read as strategic in ways that could lead to the "predetermined goals" and "generic and benign" tasks for community service that Mathieu has argued against (*Tactics* 99). However, Trubek's administrative approach of allowing and encouraging the CBWP to morph, while keeping its foundational ties within the RHET 401 curriculum, represents the kind of sustainable institutionalization that remains responsive to community needs and that retains some of the tactical approach that led to its inception. The Ninde Scholars Program's public pedagogy, originated in the CBWP, continues to challenge Oberlin students by relocating their experiences and learning within increasingly public spheres; administrators support this public pedagogy by allowing the program and curricula to morph.

"NEXT STEP" COURSES: SEQUENCING WITH AN UNDERGRADUATE MAJOR

The CBWP at Oberlin morphed in ways that led to its administration ultimately being located outside of the department, even though curricular ties remain; this next example from Syracuse University's Writing Program shows how administrators might work within their own department or program's curricula to support public pedagogies that also remain responsive to the exigencies of local publics. This example of creating a sequence of "next step" courses demonstrates how allowing projects to morph while grounding them in curriculum design draws on the productive tensions between strategies/tactics and sustainability/unsustainability to effectively support a public pedagogy. Moreover, the course sequencing at Syracuse suggests that having an undergraduate writing major may allow for more options in how to design and develop course curricula that support public pedagogy.

In my spring 2011 visit to Syracuse University, I had the opportunity to interview Steve Parks, associate professor of writing and rhetoric, who has a wealth of experience with implementing public projects that partner the university with surrounding community groups in both Syracuse and Philadelphia. Parks employs a public pedagogy in the way he designs courses that situate student learning and experiences within local public places and by valuing the public knowledge of community members beyond the academy and traditional classroom. For example, during my visit, I was scheduled to observe one of Parks's classes that was meeting off campus with a local community group as part of the Near West Side project; unfortunately, a snowstorm and canceled classes prevented my observation, but Parks met with me to discuss how he approaches community partnerships as a "sustained, multiyear commitment." Just as Trubek at Oberlin College was concerned about sustainability in implementing community projects, Parks told me of his engagement in long-term projects that move toward "social change," rather than "one-time events" that serve public needs in the short-term without addressing the larger social, economic, and political issues. Parks explained that what he has tried to do with his courses is "to think about how students can be in dialogue with an existing project in the community, or in a set of communities, . . . that relate to how writing can speak to issues of economic and social justice." Students in Parks's courses often write for public audiences, collaborate with public community members beyond the campus community, and go public by meeting, writing, and researching in public locations off campus. One of the advantages of Parks's approach is that sequencing multiple courses over several semesters results in public projects already being in place at the start of the semester, which allows students to jump in with a focused set of goals rather than spending much of their time building a solid partnership with a local public group.

The administrative method Parks uses for engaging students in existing projects and for keeping public projects sustained over multiple semesters and academic years is what he calls "next step courses." The process involves initiating an extended public partnership and organizing a series of "next step" courses that help support and sustain his public pedagogy over multiple semesters and even academic years. A version of this process is illustrated in Figure 4, which shows a series of three undergraduate courses Parks taught over the course of three semesters that each related to a different part of an ongoing public project ("Current and Recent Course Offerings").

In my interview with Parks, he explained how he sequences "next step" courses:

> I usually have some type of project that I know when I step into it it's going to be two to three to four years. I work with Eileen [Schell, who was chair of the Writing Program at the time] to set up a set of classes that I know every semester for that period of time I'm going to have classes that are connected to it. And sometimes the projects begin in first-year writing and then move to the second course, then they move to our gateway course into the major, and then they move

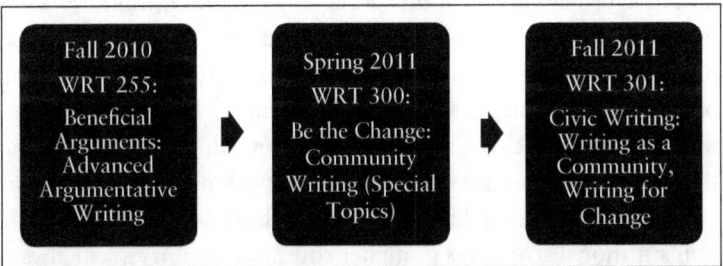

Figure 4. Steve Parks's "next step" course sequencing in Syracuse University's Writing Program.

up to civic writing. . . . Sometimes you just begin within the major. . . . Sometimes it begins in independent studies that coalesce and show the need for a new course and that new course is then coupled with other courses. But usually, there's anywhere—over the course of that period—[from] four to five courses that I advertise as the "next step course."

Because Parks initiates public projects that are multiyear and ongoing, students tend to follow projects through to the next step course, and Parks often seeks out specific students to encourage their continued participation. The effect of this is that, as his course sequences progress, "anywhere from five to ten students" have been ongoing participants in the community project, and these students "supply the knowledge base" for the course by drawing on their experiences with and knowledge of the community project in the previous courses. Because of their ongoing participation in the public project, these students "are really linked to the community" and "they know everybody" associated with the project. In other words, they've made the kinds of community connections and built the kinds of trust needed to move beyond short-term projects, and, in this way, Parks suggests that these students have "transcended the student label" because they do not only pop into community projects for one semester but are engaging in multisemester or multiyear community work (Parks, Personal Interview).

Part of what is so compelling about Parks's model of using next step courses is that it creates a productive tension between sustainability and unsustainability, using an approach to curriculum design that allows for morphing to keep the community work fresh and responsive to community needs (i.e., tactical) but also highly situated within institutional administration of the writing program (i.e., strategic). In my assessment of Parks's administrative approach, I believe he is able to achieve this balance by using the curriculum in ways that promote morphing. In other words, curricula, broadly speaking, are fairly stable and sustainable parts of institutional structures in higher education—courses will always be there in some capacity. However, individual courses themselves, bound by the academic calendar, are a fairly unsustainable structure in terms of a public pedagogy that remains responsive to public needs; the topic, students, and sometimes the professor change from term to term (Cushman, "Sustainable"). With Parks's next step courses, he seems to have harnessed the strategic components of the curriculum, knowing that there is a set of courses that will nearly always be offered in some capacity over the next several semesters, using that administrative planning in ways that will support a long-term project with a public partner. This method exploits the unsustainable nature of the course structure by seeing the change in topic and focus each semester as an advantage, a way to tackle a new piece of the larger project. Moreover, he, in some ways, subverts the traditional curricular structures that implicitly suggest that teachers passively wait for students to randomly register for courses, and instead invites students to continue on a curricular journey with a sustained project. I see Parks's next step sequencing as an ideal model for writing program administrators who want to engage in public pedagogies because it affords for a bit of planning ahead through the curriculum, while also remaining responsive by allowing the nature of projects to morph based around curricular needs and vice versa (allowing curricular needs to morph—through independent studies and special topics courses—to meet needs of public partners).

While course sequencing is a major component of Parks's approach, he uses a combination of methods, such as fellowships, independent studies, internships, and work with a community press, to keep students engaged in ongoing public pedagogies. Parks gave one example of a student who had been in three of his sequenced, next step courses; the student then graduated and was granted a fellowship to spend a year postgraduation to continue working with Parks on the project. Another example Parks cited was a student who took an independent study with him, and the work resulting from that independent study then grew into a new course Parks created; the student continued to work with Parks postgraduation also.

The roots of Parks's next step courses can also be seen in his scholarship on writing beyond the curriculum and in his years at Temple

University. In his publication *Gravyland*, Parks recounts and reflects on the evolution of Urban Rhythms, a community-based writing project that came out of his work with the Institute for the Study of Literature, Literacy, and Culture at Temple—the same collaborative organization Parks wrote about in his coauthored article with Eli Goldblatt. In *Gravyland*, Parks reveals how the Urban Rhythms project grew out of an Advanced Composition course he taught within the institute. He explains, similarly to Trubek's account, how the curriculum morphed to account for the public project: what began as a course focused on popular and politically motivated rap music morphed into the creation of an online journal publication, *Urban Rhythms*, that focused on "everyday culture in Philadelphia" (Parks, *Gravyland* 3–5). Of particular significance to my analysis of course sequencing and program administration is how Parks situates the course-based project within the broader goals of the institute, explaining that "no singular course could be expected to carry the full weight of institutional reform" (*Gravyland* 9). The way Parks employs next step courses likewise helps distribute the weight of reform within institutions of higher education and public pedagogies within writing programs. As an example of moving beyond the curriculum, the Urban Rhythms project demonstrated how writing programs "had moved beyond their traditional structure" to now exist "within a larger frame-work that also included public-school partnerships, community writing groups, literacy research projects, and service-learning courses" (*Gravyland* 10). In his past work at Temple and present work at Syracuse, Parks's projects serve as models for how writing programs might allow for curriculum to be driven (morphed and developed) by public pedagogies and projects, rather than the other way around.

While Parks notes that the kind of next step courses he sequences sometimes start outside of courses for the major, such as in first-year or professional writing, it seems that having an undergraduate major—like the one in Syracuse University's Writing Program—provides more opportunities for administrators to guide the development and morphing of extended course sequencing for projects that support public pedagogies. In their collection *What We Are*

Becoming: Developments in Undergraduate Writing Majors, editors Greg A. Giberson and Thomas A. Moriarty assert that the "growth of undergraduate majors in writing and rhetoric is unmistakable," and the authors specifically promote civic rhetoric as a potential focus for undergraduate degree programs "because such a degree will empower people in their public lives" (2, 216). As more programs develop undergraduate writing majors, composition specialists are finding a number of institutional advantages to having agency in how the work of writing on campus is framed, discussed, and valued. For example, Rebecca Moore Howard, a professor in Syracuse University's Writing Program, suggested in an article published in 2007 that "proposing the writing major provides an opportunity for curricular activism"; this moment, according to Howard, affords compositionists the chance to "circulate informed, nuanced, proactive visions of writing . . . that exceed the skill-based ideology of literacy instruction" (42). Indeed, an undergraduate writing major, especially one that is designed around public engagement, has the potential to transform the purpose of writing programs from "'serving' other academic programs to 'serving' a much more broadly defined public" (Rose and Weiser, *Going Public* 4). While not every institution or writing program administrator will have the support or resources to develop an undergraduate major, WPAs interested in public pedagogy might explore this option as a way to support course sequencing that productively sustains and responsively morphs public pedagogies within a program's curriculum.

In the cases of Parks at Syracuse and Trubek at Oberlin, both were able to sustain longer-term projects through some form of institutionalization that allowed for morphing, which, again, exploits the productive tensions between tactical and strategic administrative approaches to going public. For the CBWP at Oberlin College, institutionalization came from morphing into the Ninde Scholars Program; for community projects in the Writing Program at Syracuse University, institutionalization resulted from situating ongoing public outreach within curricular design that morphed the sequencing of next step courses. Both projects were able to employ strategic constructs, such as a program's writing center and/

or curriculum, in tactical ways that responded to the changing and ongoing needs of the public communities with which they partnered. This aligns with the kind of approach to institutionalization which Mathieu advocates, one that is mindful of institutional entanglements, and, in these cases, using them to an administrator's advantage.

PUBLIC EVENTS AND CURRICULA THROUGH FIRST-YEAR WRITING AND GRADUATE COURSES

The final example, from the University of Arizona Writing Program, demonstrates how threading curricula through interrelated projects and allowing the curriculum to morph can represent an effective approach to administering public pedagogy within composition programs. Whereas the administrative examples from Oberlin and Syracuse in this chapter highlight partnerships with public groups beyond the classroom and campus, this example shows how WPAs can create opportunities for students to go public with their writing while staying within the boundaries of campus (through a public but on-campus showcase of student writing). While some teachers I interviewed employ public pedagogies that require students to engage with places or persons beyond campus, other TAs used a combination of Writing Program initiatives to go public with their composition pedagogy: including using the program's custom-published textbook that emphasizes public argument and requiring student participation in the program's public writing showcase event; these assignments represent a public pedagogy in the way they invite students to engage with broader and sometimes unfamiliar publics beyond the classroom. Additionally, this administrative example from the University of Arizona shows how multiple components of a writing program can come together and overlap to support a public pedagogy within composition curricula.

In Spring 2011, I interviewed several graduate TAs in the University of Arizona Writing Program, as well as two of the WPAs: Anne-Marie Hall, who at the time was director, and Amy Kimme Hea, who at the time was the associate director.[8] The TAs and administrators discussed a range of ways in which the University of

Arizona's Writing Program is going public with its curricula and publications; how those public initiatives related to graduate curricula and TA training; and the strategies they used to assess the impact of going public. As Figure 5 graphically represents, the University of Arizona Writing Program employs a number of institutional structures, such as curriculum development, custom publication, public events, and assessment, to help initiate, support, and sustain their public pedagogies.

The initiatives within the University of Arizona Writing Program illustrate how overlapping faculty and students, as well as dovetailing of programs (e.g., the Writing Program and the graduate program in Rhetoric, Composition, and the Teaching of English [RCTE]), can result in a distributed model of more publicly focused pedagogy on a variety of fronts. In this case, the institutional entanglements were advantageous to the process of incorporating public pedagogies across curricula and programs. For example, Hall and Kimme Hea serve as both administrators in the Writing Program and faculty in the RCTE graduate program; similarly, a

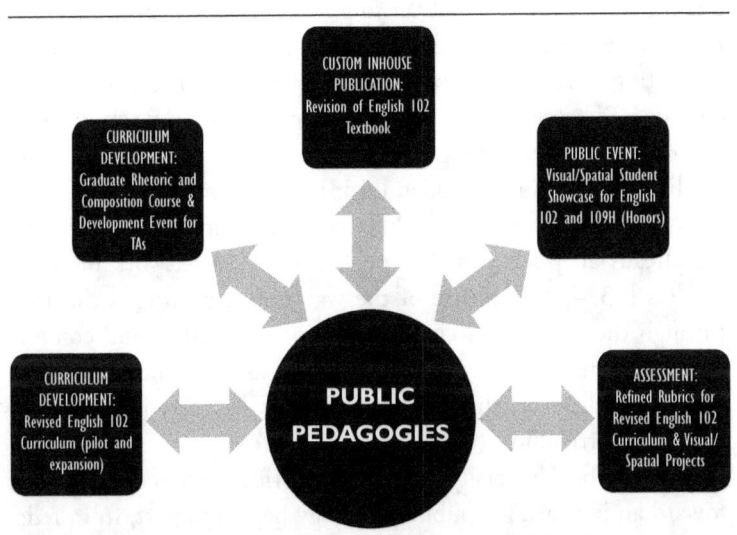

Figure 5. Interrelated public pedagogies in the University of Arizona's Writing Program.

number of TAs in the Writing Program also take graduate classes in RCTE. This overlap in roles resulted in graduate course projects that served the Writing Program, and Writing Program initiatives that bolstered graduate course curricula. The Writing Program has also created professional development opportunities for graduate students in the English department, including three editors for the custom publication used in first-year writing courses and three graduate assistant WPA positions. These graduate professional development positions resulted in a unified effort to make the Writing Program's curriculum more public and to support that public turn through the inhouse, custom textbook publication edited by the same TAs teaching the revised curriculum. Because of the multiple institutional hats that administrators and TAs wear, there was a synergy around going public with composition pedagogy that began to ripple through the writing and graduate programs.

Jessie L. Moore and Michael Strickland have argued for the benefits of administrators wearing multiple hats in order to inform and enhance program-specific public writing designs. Moore and Strickland discuss how their positions as co-coordinators of the undergraduate Professional Writing and Rhetoric concentration at Elon University overlapped in meaningful ways with their positions as Writing Across the Curriculum director and First-Year Writing coordinator, respectively, leading to internships, capstone projects, portfolios, and publishing opportunities that "take student work public" (Moore and Strickland 133). They conclude by offering WPAs strategies for going public, such as extending projects that are already in place and drawing on a shared network of stakeholders (137–38). Because of the way public writing is threaded through their program's curricula, Moore and Strickland contend that "students encounter public writing as a central element of PWR regardless of when or where in the design sequence—they enter the curriculum" (126).

Within the University of Arizona Writing Program, the turn toward an increasingly public pedagogy began, in part, from redesigning the English 102 curriculum. English 102 is the second of a two-course, first-year composition sequence required of the majority of incoming students. Though the Writing Program had been incorporating community outreach and service learning pedagogies in a small but growing number of sections of first-year and professional writing, the redesigned English 102 curriculum's emphases on rhetoric, research, and public argument helped grow and institutionalize a public focus.[9] In our interview, Hall explained how the public argument component of the revised curriculum, in particular, provided "opportunities for students to actually have a real audience and to write about something they really cared about"; this became especially true as the program started the First-Year Writing Showcase, which provided a public forum for presenting student arguments. Even though the revised English 102 curriculum became a fairly stable institutionalized structure required in all sections of English 102, the revisions began with a small pilot in only a few sections where teachers taught a sequence beginning with rhetorical analysis, then research into a controversy, and finally a public argument. As with other examples in this chapter, administrators allowed the curriculum to morph, expanding it to a requirement for all English 102 sections.

After revising the English 102 curriculum, Hall and other WPAs sought ways to sustain the public argument portion of the curriculum by creating a public venue for student projects to be showcased. This showcase of student writing began originally for students enrolled in honors writing courses (English 109H); however, the event continued morphing, expanding to an option for students in English 102 courses whose teachers chose to opt-in (Hall, Personal Interview). Because English 102 courses were now implementing the revised curriculum that culminated in a public argument, the public showcase event provided an opportunity for students to truly "go public" with their writing and projects, presenting arguments to peers, teachers, administrators, and community members in attendance. In the years since opening the showcase to English 102 students, the number of participants has grown significantly from four instructors and fifty-four students in the original honors-only showcase in 2007 to twenty-two instructors and 415 students in the more expanded showcase in 2009 (Hall, Kimme Hea, Kurtyka, and Holmes). This increased interest from instructors and students has further supported the public pedagogies within the revised curriculum. As the showcase expanded to be an option for a wider group of students and instructors, the Writing Program also put into place certain infrastructures to offer sustainability and support for this public event and curriculum: offering a presemester interest meeting, creating a website for the event, and providing instructor resources (Hall, Kimme Hea, Kurtyka, and Holmes).

Another way in which the First-Year Writing Showcase event morphed over time developed from productive institutional entanglements: the overlap of faculty and graduate students in the Writing Program and graduate RCTE program. What began as a public forum for student arguments morphed into a focus on showcasing students' visual and spatial arguments, and this focus on the visual and spatial dovetailed with the Spatial and Visual Rhetorics graduate course taught by Kimme Hea. In designing the graduate course, Kimme Hea "realized that our First-Year Writing Showcase, which had taken on the visual and spatial rhetorical emphasis, could be further enhanced with more direct inter-animation of theory and practice"; thus, she designed a final assignment that would offer English 102 instructors the "theoretical underpinnings to promote this work in the first-year writing classroom" (Kimme Hea, "Space, Event, Movement"). Kimme Hea invited graduate students in the seminar to create an event, SVR2 (Spatial and Visual Rhetorics 2), which offered interactive installations and mini-workshops to the English 102 and 109H instructors who were interested in having their students participate in the Writing Program's Visual and Spatial Showcase—the morphed version of the original First-Year Writing Showcase—in the following spring semester.[10] The SVR2 event offered graduate TAs peer-to-peer curricular support for teaching public arguments with visual and spatial components. For example, one SVR2 presentation provided rubrics, developed from key concepts in one of the graduate course readings, for assessing visual arguments (Crump and Verzosa); another SVR2 presentation outlined a sample assignment, spontaneous composing, to give students practice with visual and spatial approaches (Juarez). While not all writing programs will be within institutions that share a graduate program in rhetoric and composition, this example demonstrates the advantages of institutional entanglements and how program administrators can make strategic choices to support tactical public projects.

Two final pieces of the interrelated projects supporting the University of Arizona Writing Program's public pedagogies are the custom textbook and ongoing assessment of the revised curriculum. The custom textbook publication *Writing Public Lives* was edited and authored by lecturers and graduate TAs teaching the revised English 102 curriculum. Before the custom publication, many instructors found it challenging to teach public arguments with visual and spatial components. However, with chapters such as "Visual-Spatial Analysis," "Writing in Public," and "Creating Visual/Spatial Arguments for a Public Audience," instructors' public pedagogies were well supported by the newly developed textbook (Minnix and Nowotny-Young). In the same ways that Parks described New City Community Press in *Gravyland* as circulating arguments that redefine "who is an *intellectual*," custom textbook publications like the one in the University of Arizona's Writing Program can help redefine what is intellectual work in the composition classroom, helping expand this work to value broader publics in research, writing, and publication (130). Diana George and Paula Mathieu have also argued for the place of studying and replicating rhetorical practices of the dissident press in college writing courses; custom publications afford opportunities for individual writing programs to define worthy texts of study, whether that's *Hobo News*, in the case of George and Mathieu, or oral histories from Philadelphia's Chinatown, as one example from New City Community Press (George and Mathieu; Parks, *Gravyland*).

As the curriculum and first-year writing showcase kept morphing at the University of Arizona, assessment became an important consideration for the WPAs; according to Hall, "we're constantly evaluating." For example, after the shift to the Visual and Spatial Showcase, WPAs began noticing grade inflation; they hypothesized that "no one knew how to grade [the student projects], so [instructors] gave them extra credit" (Hall, Personal Interview). In response, Hall organized a group of graduate students to create rubrics to help instructors grade visual and spatial assignments; in fact, a number of the participating TAs had also been enrolled in the Spatial and Visual Rhetorics graduate course and participated in the SVR2 TA-development event. With the newly incorporated rubrics in place, students better understood the expectations of the public assignments and instructors had support for evaluating and assessing student learning from those projects. The University of Arizona's approach to assessment of its public pedagogy is an excellent example of what Bob Broad calls organic or homegrown assessment that is initiated by local, programmatic concerns. In the Introduction to *Organic Writing Assessment*, Broad rails against "generic, faceless, commercialized, off-the-shelf assessments," instead advocating for administrators to "grow their assessment cultures locally and organically" (4); indeed, assessments of public pedagogy at the University of Arizona grew organically out of local concerns about grade inflation and reflections on what would best support TAs and student learning. In the University of Arizona Writing Program, WPAs saw an opportunity to look closely at the curriculum and ask questions about how it might be implemented more effectively through a public turn, and, after making curricular revisions, the WPAs continued a cycle of reflective assessment, making adjustments (as with the rubric) to offer extended support for going public. In this example, assessment, reflection, and curriculum revision create an ongoing cycle, the "culture of changing" E. Shelley Reid has written about, that results in "more regularly and comprehensively" critiquing and revising the curriculum (12). The strength of the University of Arizona's public pedagogy comes from the multiple, interrelated ways in which public is threaded throughout the curriculum and programming. The combination of revised curricula with supporting textbooks, assessment measures, and public events works together to create an effective, institutionalized public pedagogy.

GOING PUBLIC WITH WRITING PROGRAM ADMINISTRATION

Going public with writing programs means opening the often closed-behind-institutional-walls work of writing program administration to more expansive publics; this public turn necessarily involves administrators looking outward for opportunities to work within local public spaces and to partner with local community members, instead of only looking inward, within one's institution. In the same ways that theories of public pedagogy invite teachers to broaden the scope of what we consider to be the educational field to include public spheres beyond the discipline, classroom, and campus, so too does public pedagogy invite WPAs to relocate administration, to reframe what has traditionally been defined as strategic, stable, institutionalized work in more tactical, localized ways. This chapter has argued for using curriculum design in tandem with morphing as an administrative strategy, which aligns with a tactical approach to support public pedagogies that are both situated within institutional structures but that also remain responsive to publics beyond the university. All three institution's examples suggest that administrators should not turn a blind eye to strategic approaches to going public—to do so would be to ignore the potential of projects to evolve and to serve both institutional and community interests.

4

Constructing Institutional Histories for Going Public

THE EXAMPLES FROM COMPOSITION TEACHERS AND administrators in Chapters 2 and 3 highlight the growing practice of employing a public pedagogy that positions student learning and experiences in public sites beyond the classroom or campus. While I have argued that public pedagogy involves critically attending to public places beyond the classroom or campus, understanding one's institutional context—the rich, contested, and varied histories of the colleges and universities from which our pedagogies are based—is an important task for grounding contemporary public work and illuminating the narratives that undergird our efforts to go public with composition pedagogy. As Elenore Long argues in *Community Literacy and the Rhetoric of Local Publics*, local publics and formal institutions have "a complex set of relationships . . . that shape and constrain" how people go public (7); this chapter broadens the analytical lens from writing courses and programs to consider the complex historical relationships between local publics and institutions of higher education, as well as how institutions frame their contemporary public work. As I maintained in Chapter 3, blurring the boundaries between binaries—academic/public, on-campus/off-campus, institution/community—can be a productive way to harness their tensions and productively disrupt exclusionary conceptions of what we mean by composition education, who has the authority to teach, and in what contexts students learn. Employing public pedagogy in composition studies means valuing public sites for student learning and writing, in turn allowing for public persons beyond solely the teacher to become arbiters of essential knowledge and for public places beyond the classroom to become the new chalkboard—a canvas for public learning, writing, and implementation of academic concepts. This chapter demonstrates the power of both constructing and rhetorically employing our institutions' histories to help us better understand the relationship between town and gown, as well as to use these histories strategically to support the implementation of public pedagogies in our writing courses and programs.

We can look to scholarship in community literacy and service learning for examples of an already strong tradition of carefully attending to the historical and contemporary relationships between town and gown. For instance, in Ellen Cushman's seminal essay "The Rhetorician as an Agent of Social Change," she analyzes how "the approach" at Rensselaer Polytechnic Institute, "a monument of granite stairs, pillars, and decorative lights," functions as a physical manifestation of the distanced relationship between the university and the surrounding city of Troy (10). Cushman's narrative of town-gown relations rang true as I began reading historical documents from Oberlin College, Syracuse University, and the University of Arizona; with each institution founded more than 100 years ago, the relations between institutions and their surrounding communities are deeply rooted and continually evolving. What became clear, and rhetorically interesting, as I shuttled between institutional histories and contemporary mission statements is that institutions and their leaders use histories to their advantage. Partial and constructed, these limited historical accounts function rhetorically to present each institution in a positive light, emphasizing stories that advance particular agendas while ignoring those that detract. Moreover, institutions construct historical values that spiral out into contemporary goals—such as diversity, social consciousness, and civic education—and that have the potential to map onto the goals of public pedagogy in composition studies. While ignoring unseemly parts of an institution's history raised some ethical concerns for me that I will address within this chapter, I ultimately began to see the rhetorical power of constructing institutional histories, and I came to see historical narrative as a valuable tool for supporting public pedagogies at an institutional level.

Of course, scholarship in composition studies and writing program administration already attests to the importance of preserving, archiving, and documenting teaching and administrative work of those who taught in and developed programs ahead of us. Researchers have argued for the significance of establishing and employing archives (Rose; S. Wells, "Claiming the Archive"), developing and interrogating histories of writing programs and their administration (L'Eplattenier; L'Eplattenier and Mastrangelo; Mirtz; Strickland), and telling stories of administrators from the past (L'Eplattenier and Mastrangelo). Programmatic histories are important, not only in how they serve to document the legacies of administration but also in their potential for bolstering current, often pressing, program needs. Knowing the histories of our writing programs, argues Barbara L'Eplattenier, is valuable in the way it "increases our ability to argue persuasively within institutional settings" and "creates legitimacy for contemporary work" (136). Historical narrative is a powerful rhetorical tool for supporting and framing work within composition studies, in part because of the way stories circulate and perpetuate values. Linda Adler-Kassner's *The Activist WPA*, for example, highlights the power stories have on public perceptions of student writers and the work of writing teachers. Drawing on framing theory, Adler-Kassner examines how frames help define stories in ways that "both reflect and perpetuate dominant cultural values" (12). She notes that while WPAs may not be able to change all of the erroneous stories about student writers that abound, "we can have some influence on how these discussions take place and how they are framed" (Adler-Kassner 163). The work of L'Eplattenier and Adler-Kassner suggests that composition specialists may find it advantageous to take an active role in framing historical narratives in order to gain some influence, argue effectively, and create legitimacy for the kinds of programmatic initiatives we value.

While the strong body of WPA scholarship effectively argues for historical and archival studies of writing programs and administrators, my research proposes that composition specialists may also find it valuable to broaden their scope to a study of *institutional histories*. As Doug Hesse cautions in "Understanding Larger Discourses in Higher Education," the insularity of a limited disciplinary perspective can be troublesome. Hesse urges WPAs to "analyze the broader contexts in which they and writing programs exist" (300). Similarly, Chris Anson and Robert L. Brown Jr. make the case for administrative research from the perspective of its "broader value and institutional legitimacy"; they argue that WPAs need to understand "ways of researching—reading—our own institutions, their practices, their politics, and the disciplinary relationships that affect our work" (141). These scholars call composition teachers and administrators to be mindful of how courses and programs exist within institutional contexts and within broader discourses in higher education.

Within this chapter, I aim to demonstrate how tracing the roots between institutions of higher education and their surrounding public communities can help composition specialists understand the legacies we tap in to when we go public with composition pedagogy. As a dominant trope that pervades official institutional discourse, historical narratives represent a language within the academy that carries weight—an economy of literacy that can be valuable to composition teachers and administrators seeking support for public pedagogies. Despite the growing prevalence of public engagement initiatives across institutions of higher education, the actual practices of going public with pedagogy continue to be challenged by department chairs, deans, and upper-level administrators who question the legitimacy of an approach that values public rather than traditional academic knowledge. As one strategy to help bolster institutional support, I contend that composition specialists should look to their institution's histories in order to construct narratives that carve a place for public pedagogy within the work of writing programs and courses.

To show the potential of such an approach, I analyze the contemporary mission statements of Oberlin College, Syracuse University, and the University of Arizona, examining how they function rhetorically and ideologically to construct a sense of belonging to an institution based on historically defined values; I then work backwards from contemporary mission statements to tease out historical threads that would corroborate an increasingly public focus in composition pedagogies. More specifically, I trace four threads within the histories of the three institutions in my study: (1) historical values of religion and morality at Oberlin and Syracuse, (2) historical precedents of coeducation and African American education at Oberlin and Syracuse, (3) Arizona's historical founding as a land-grant institution, and (4) historical ties to local Native populations at Oberlin and Arizona. I focus on these four threads because of their implications for public pedagogy—in particular, the implications for writing programs and courses that are interested in public pedagogy when their institutions translate contested histories into contemporary missions that connect with discourses of going public. I demonstrate how these threads have been rendered into contemporary institutional emphases in public service, education for the public good, social justice, diversity, public outreach, and community partnership—all values that intersect with public pedagogy in composition studies. The analysis in this chapter serves a dual purpose in the book: (1) to illustrate how one might employ history toward administrative ends and (2) to provide historical context for the institutions in my study as a way of showing the importance of understanding the relationship between towns and gowns. In each case, I demonstrate how to use an institution's history to construct a partial narrative that highlights the exigencies and traditions that would align with implementing a public pedagogy within composition courses and programs. Knowing that mission statements are often steeped with institutional lore and ethos, this chapter maintains that compositionists and WPAs can wield the power of historical narratives—constructing their own version of an institution's story—to support going public.

RHETORIC, IDEOLOGY, AND HISTORY IN INSTITUTIONAL MISSION STATEMENTS

As institutions each founded in the nineteenth century, one commonality among Oberlin College (founded in 1833), Syracuse University (founded in 1870), and the University of Arizona (founded in 1885) is the way in which university administrators draw from, frame, and reframe their institutional histories as they situate the mission and vision for their institutions today (see Appendixes A, B, and C). Institutional histories, as all histories, are invested—they have an institutionally defined interest in presenting a certain trajectory. Historian Geoffrey Blodgett identifies two common approaches to framing institutional histories: (1) "onward and upward"—the "long uphill progressive preparation for the present and future," and (2) the "Golden Age," which identifies "some point in the local past when things were better than they ever were before or have been since" (5–6). Both approaches draw on institutional history in rhetorical ways, constructing narratives that serve to persuasively support a claim, even when their packaging suggests an objective or unarguable series of factual events. Blodgett calls this "functional convenience"; in other words, "depending on what one is trying to prove," the same historical account can be told in different ways, to meet the needs of the narrator (5). In rhetorical terms, we might say that narratives can help rhetors more effectively communicate a message.

A significant component of how institutions use histories rhetorically is through the university or college mission statement. In her analysis of the impact of mission statements of a sample of US universities, Catherine Chaput demonstrates how the language in mission statements—often "having both religious and military connotations"—powerfully manifests itself in contexts worldwide (175). "Something as apparently trivial, inconsequential, or mundane as a mission statement," argues Chaput, "produces power-effects—rhetorically constructed enclosures within which material reality can be acceptably designed" (176). Chaput demonstrates the power of mission statements, and this power is derived in part because they are positioned as textual sites of institutional authority. Drawing on Bakhtin's definition of textual authority as "the word of our fathers," Nancy Myers argues that "text[s], as location[s] of authority, provide knowledge necessary to the stability and reproduction of the institution, discipline and society" (231). Particularly in the case of university mission statements, the legacy, traditions, and values represented function in a way that stabilizes and reproduces an image and ethos for the institution. Imbued with the textual authority of their institutional founding fathers, mission statements also function ideologically to interpellate and discipline. Chaput describes how a university's mission serves as a public statement of the institution's "ideological landscape" or "ideoscape," explaining its "self-proclaimed relationship to the broader historical materialist terrain" (182). The way mission statements communicate concepts, such as a student's role as a learned citizen of the world, is steeped with ideological discourse that, in Henry A. Giroux's view "must be investigated," especially because "the schools, the workplace, and the family" represent sites where "the production and investment of ideological discourses" are expressed and experienced (*Schooling* 7). Working ideologically, institutions of higher education use mission statements, among other strategies, to hail or interpellate subjects, recruiting them to serve a role within and perpetuate an articulated vision of the institution (Althusser).

One of the ways that institutional mission statements ideologically wield power is through the use of ideographs, which Michael McGee defines as "a high-order abstraction representing collective commitment to a particular but equivocal and ill-defined normative goal" (15). McGee is interested in how ideographs, such as "liberty," "equality," and "freedom," are used in political discourse to powerfully communicate messages. Ideographs, McGee contends, typically derive their meaning through historical association; in other words, we come to understand "equality" by connecting back to previous usages, what McGee identifies as a vertical structuring through time. The use of ideographs "guides behavior and belief," as "each member of the community is socialized, conditioned, to the vocabulary of ideographs as a prerequisite for 'belonging' to the society" (McGee 15). Oberlin College's mission statement uses ideographs such as "diversity" and "social engagement" (Appendix A); Syracuse uses "public good," "democracy," and "social innovation" (Appendix B); and the University of Arizona uses "innovation" and "community service" (Appendix C). These abstract ideals are most often defined through historical values and commitments, demonstrating how the ideographs come to be defined through vertical structuring. In this context, Syracuse's commitment to "social innovation," for instance, is defined by the region's "treasured history" of "abolitionism and the women's rights movement" (Appendix B). Moreover, the ideographs in institutional mission statements socialize students, faculty, staff, and alumni into the community's values—for example, understanding that Oberlin values diversity, and upholding that value for oneself, becomes an unstated prerequisite for "belonging" to that community (whether or not one chooses to accept the value).

Through the use of ideographs, a subject's role within the mission is limited and institutionally defined. Subjects who have responded to the institution's hail—i.e., have "bought in" to the vision of a college or university—perpetuate and protect that institution's expectations, traditions, and legacies. In other words, subjects help forward a "general surveillance" (Foucault) that disciplines other subjects to fall into a particular way of being within an institution—a set of values, ideals, life goals, and/or civic responsibilities. Repeatedly, through texts on the college's website and the university president's speeches, members of the Oberlin community, for example, are reminded of the institution's historical legacy and their part in continuing and strengthening those traditions. In the mission statement at Oberlin, the college is positioned as holding "a distinguished place among American colleges and universities" and being "known for its academic and musical excellence and its commitment to social engagement and diversity" (Appendix A); both of these phrases suggest that subjects—students, faculty, alumni—should adhere to the institution's historical commitments or risk damaging the college's legacy and reputation as "distinguished."

All three institutions in my study draw heavily on their histories to articulate their vision and values. The "Mission" page of Oberlin College's website, for instance, draws on its historical legacy to establish its ethos and to initiate members of its community (e.g., students, parents, faculty, staff), as well as members of broader publics (e.g., Oberlin residents, college boards, potential students), into its version of the institution's story and history: that "Oberlin was the first college to grant undergraduate degrees to women and, historically, was a leader in the education of African Americans" (Appendix A). Oberlin's positive framing of its institutional history through its mission statement elides the contested and contradictory nature of these histories, which I examine in more detail in a later section of this chapter.

Rhetorical texts such as college presidential speeches also serve to reinforce an institution's legacy, and administrative leaders commonly draw on institutional histories to frame contemporary work and values. For example, in each of his State of the College addresses since 2008, when he began his term as president, Martin Krislov has drawn on Oberlin's history and values to articulate a vision for what it means to be a contributing member of the Oberlin College community. In his first State of the College speech, he explains how common values—such as "the belief that [Obies, e.g., Oberlin students and alumni] can make the world a better place"—are "rooted in Oberlin's extraordinarily rich history" (Krislov). Krislov goes on to remind those who identify with the Oberlin Community that "we must honor our history," referencing the "moral character" of the college and upholding "Oberlin's blend of scholarly ambition and stubborn moral idealism." Through official texts, such as presidential speeches and the university's mission statement, the institution constructs a role for students, faculty, staff, and alumni: being a member of the Oberlin College community means knowing one's institutional history, taking pride in it, and using it as a guide for present and future acts.

By publicly stating, "this is who we are" and "this is what we value," mission statements define what it means to identify oneself as an Obie at Oberlin or a Wildcat at the University of Arizona. The power of the mission statement as a guiding vision for an institution is in how it convinces students to join the club—to self-identify as a contributing member to the vision—and a significant component of this entails upholding and protecting an institution's historical legacy. At the University of Arizona, the mission statement frames the university's work through the lens of innovation and discovery by extending the "fearless spirit" of the university's founders: "In 1885, establishing Arizona's first university in the middle of the Sonoran Desert was a bold move. But our founders were fearless, and we have never lost that spirit" (Appendix C). The rhetoric of this constructed institutional history hints at the cavalier tone of a university founded in the "Wild West"; the Top 10 list-style version of the University of Arizona's "About" page dramatically draws on that trope to highlight how the university was founded when Arizona was still a territory: "Our history runs deep. Before Arizona was a state, there was the University of Arizona" (Appendix C). Official university correspondence at Arizona also serves to reinforce the vision and mission that the institution has constructed for itself, at this particular moment. For example, three months into her position, President Ann Weaver Hart released a statement to the University of Arizona community in which she defined the university as a "hub for . . . innovation—a place of boundless possibilities," and she situated this institutional framing within the University of Arizona's history as a "research land-grant university." Making a rhetorical move common to university and college presidential speeches, Hart invites members of the University of Arizona community to both hold on to the traditional values of the institution and its founding, while re-envisioning them for contemporary and future application: "While grounded in the UA unique mission, emerging out of the 19th century and its statewide impact"—here, a reference to the institution's founding as a land grant that primarily served local agricultural efforts—"the challenges of the new century require the UA to engage in a thoughtful and rigorous imagining." Hart goes on to identify a "key theme" for the university as a "renewed focus on our land-grant mission." Hart's statements, combined with other components of the University of Arizona's history as represented in its "About" and "History" pages of the website, corroborate Chaput's claim that "public research universities . . . proudly advertise their land-grant heritage" (188), often using it rhetorically to garner support for local (as well as global) social and cultural activities.

Like Oberlin College and the University of Arizona, Syracuse University's vision statement rhetorically employs institutional history to construct a set of values and expectations for members of the Syracuse community. Not having a land-grant status on which to draw like the University of Arizona, Syracuse's vision statement draws on the broader implications of higher education as an enterprise that supports democracy: in other words, the "social charter" that purposes "higher education for the public good" (Kezar, Chambers, and Burkhardt xii). Referencing the work of the Kellogg Commission, Syracuse University constructs its role as reshaping the university's "historic agreement with the American people" by positioning itself as an "anchor institution in [their] community" (Appendix B).[1] Moreover, Syracuse's vision statement makes a move similar to President Hart at the University of Arizona by grounding contemporary choices in historical values. The statement references the "historical strength of the Central New York region and the City of Syracuse, as well as the University" and notes how the "treasured history of social innovation" in the region "played a key role in abolitionism and the women's rights movement" (Appendix B). Drawing on these institutionally defined historical strengths, Syracuse University today aspires to uphold the vision of the "University as Public Good," the theme of previous chancellor Nancy Cantor's inaugural year. While Cantor is no longer chancellor, her vision for Scholarship in Action is still pervasive in Syracuse's vision statement and other public initiatives throughout the university.[2] New chancellor Kent Syverud's inaugural speech demonstrated his commitment to preserve Syracuse's historical legacy, stating: "Each of us, including me, is called upon to do our part for this great place, and for its mission. Each of us, especially me, is a steward for the accumulated good works of the last 144 years." The message to students, faculty, staff, and alumni is clear: do not blunder the strong historical legacy of the institution. Syverud continues his inaugural speech by framing future aims of the university within "our unique history and with our values." Again, reminding subjects that to be a member of Syracuse University means to align with a certain set of values, based in the Christian faith tradition, to "know the truth and the truth shall make you free" (Syverud).

We should be mindful, of course, that the missions universities and colleges set out for themselves are not always what actually materializes in practice. Additionally, members within these institutional communities do not necessarily automatically accept the dominant ideologies that position them. While the aims of this chapter are not to analyze the extent to which these institutions instantiate the goals they set forth in their mission statements, nor the extent to which subjects accept or reject those goals, I believe it is valuable for members of institutions to be aware of how texts like mission statements and university speeches function ideologically and to understand the nature of that power. My study of contemporary mission statements and speeches suggests that administrative leaders commonly draw on institutional histories to both acknowledge history, while also carving a vision for the future that holds on to some essence, value, or commitment that was established and maintained through the years. Knowing and using this powerful rhetorical structure can be an asset to writing teachers and administrators—a way to not only read and research our institutions, as Anson and Brown suggest, but to also speak the language of power within institutional discourses.

TELLING STORIES, CONSTRUCTING HISTORIES

Even though writing teachers and administrators are not trained historians, nor experts in their institution's histories, what the previous analysis demonstrates is that one of our most valuable assets is our background in rhetoric. Composition specialists are most certainly rhetors mindful of audience and situation, storytellers who employ narratives to serve particular ends, and archivists who keep track of how pedagogies and programs have evolved over time. For example, Louise Wetherbee Phelps, in "Telling a Writing Program Its Own Story," makes a compelling case for the power of stories in helping shape and frame the histories of a writing program. Phelps reflects on the process of constructing and delivering a speech for the tenth anniversary of the founding of Syracuse University's Writing Program. Phelps focuses on the speech as a rhetorical task—one that was situated within a particular context of celebration, for the purposes of inspiration and historical documentation, and for a mixed audience of veterans and newcomers. In other words, she intimates that there were many historical narratives she *could* tell, but, based on the needs of the program and the rhetorical exigencies of the moment, Phelps constructed a certain kind of programmatic history—partial and fragmented—to meet the needs of "recollection and celebration" with an "inspiring and hopeful note" (169). Phelps analyzes her speech as rhetorical performance and intellectual work, but I also see her speech—its *kairos* and partiality—as representative of the kind of historical work that can be invaluable to compositionists wanting to go public with pedagogy.

Phelps's choice to tell a partial story reminds us that all historical work is partial, fragmented, and constructed. As Robert J. Connors argues, historians bring together their "perceptions of the present," "claims based on . . . the past," and "ongoing internal dialogue about cultural preconceptions and prejudices and the historian's own" (15). In other words, we bring to bear our current perceptions, or "predispositions" (North 76), on our interpretations of the past. While our preconceptions will necessarily result in a fragmented account, acknowledging that our stories are constructed and continuing to ask critical questions through the kind of internal dialoguing for which Connors advocates provides us with an opportunity to see partiality as advantageous—a chance to tell a version of a story to serve a rhetorical exigence.

Histories told by institutions often present one version of a story, but, as feminist scholars in rhetoric and composition have demonstrated, there is more historical work to be done to present a richer, more layered and polyvocal representation of our shared histories. Feminist rhetorical scholarship, though, is "now moving far beyond the rescue, recovery, and (re)inscription of a diversity of women participants" argue Jacqueline Jones Royster and Gesa E. Kirsch (31). Royster and Kirsch make the case that the new work of feminist rhetorical scholarship involves the "establishing of new watermarks of regard and worthiness in rhetorical studies more generally for the methodologies that we have been using and the types of insights that such methodologies have the capacity to yield" (31). In other words, feminist rhetorical practices are now being more widely applied, altering "the guiding assumptions and theoretical principles that underlie" our research methods (Royster and Kirsch 34). Indeed, I believe feminist historiography offers composition teachers and administrators a valuable methodology for approaching the construction of institutional histories for public pedagogies.

Feminist historiography provides opportunities for breaking out of the traditional frames institutions often use to tell their histories—the "onward and upward" or "golden age" narratives (Blodgett)—so that we may reread and reconstruct historical accounts in different ways. Drawing on postmodernist and resistant readings of history, Cheryl Glenn advocates for "look[ing] crookedly" at rhetorical histories as a means of seeing things differently (4). Postmodernism, Glenn emphasizes, forces us to "admit that we each have an angle" and that "all historical accounts, even the most seemingly objective historical records are stories . . . selected and arranged according to the selector's frame of reference" (5). Glenn argues that histories are never neutral and that postmodern historiographic practices "take for granted that histories *do* (or *should do*) something" (7). In this way, constructed histories "fulfill our needs at a particular time and place" (Glenn 7); or, stated differently, they have "functional convenience" (Blodgett). These rhetorical, *kairotic* components of constructed histories are exactly what make them advantageous to writing teachers and administrators, who most certainly have ongoing and multiple programmatic needs.

In her rereading of sophistic rhetoric, Susan Jarratt employs sophistic values as a means of articulating rhetorical, historiographic methods. Jarratt advocates for "breaking the chain" that attempts to "fit historical materials into a neat, continuous line from beginning to end" (19). This necessarily leads to a partial, fragmented, and overtly constructed historical account. Feminist scholars such as Donna Haraway contend that a partial perspective is a *privilege*—"not partiality for its own sake, but, rather, for the sake of the connections and unexpected openings situated knowledges make possible" (186–87). Jarratt similarly suggests that resisting the linear impulse offers opportunities for "critical distance" and "re-vision" and for the kinds of "unexpected openings," as Haraway phrases it, that partiality makes possible (19). Jarratt's conception of sophist historiography posits the rhetorical historian as a "storyteller [who] plays with the material like Frankenstein with body parts" (28). In other words, the opening up of history that re-vision affords leads to a regrouping and redefining of parts; to realignment, rearrangement, and revaluation for a purpose; and to a "consciously constructed story" (Jarratt 28). Approaching institutional history as a constructed story provides an opportunity for writing teachers and program administrators to have a stake in this valuable historical work without feeling like it is necessary (or even possible) to present a complete and comprehensive story.

While institutions may gloss over indecorous parts of their histories, compositionists can use feminist rhetorical practices to take a more ethical approach to constructing institutional histories. Kirsch and Royster emphasize how feminist rhetorical practices implicate ourselves as researchers; indeed, one of the values of a feminist framework, they contend, is "paying attention to the ethical self in the texts we study, the texts we produce, and the pedagogical frames we use to instruct and train our students" (18). In constructing institutional histories, this means acknowledging our positions as writing scholars and teachers who value public pedagogies and using our unique vantage points and locations within our institutions to critically imagine the intersections of public pedagogies with institutional history. Royster's conception of critical imagination is also productive here in the way "imagination functions as a critical skill in questioning a viewpoint, an experience, an event . . . " (19). Using critical imagination as an "inquiry tool," means using it as "a mechanism for seeing the noticed and the unnoticed" and "rethinking what is there and not there" (Royster and Kirsch 20). Royster emphasizes the necessity of acknowledging "the limits of knowledge and to be particularly careful about 'claims' to truth, by clarifying the contexts and conditions of our interpretations and by making sure that we do not overreach the bounds of either reason or possibility" (Royster qtd. in Royster and Kirsch 19). What Royster and Kirsch are advocating here is an ethical approach to critically imagining and constructing histories in a way that mindfully and explicitly acknowledges this work as partial, rhetorical, and from the vantage point of the storyteller. Compositionists also have the opportunity to account for and interrogate dominant, institutionally framed narratives. While I am advocating that writing teachers and administrators construct histories in order to draw on powerful discourses that resonate with institutional administrators, we should be mindful to not simply replicate problematic historical practices, and feminist historiography provides a framework for doing this work more ethically—by explicitly acknowledging partiality, power dynamics, and ideological authority. This historical work may also involve uncovering stories of minoritized populations and marginalized voices.

The positively framed historical legacies of Oberlin College, Syracuse University, and the University of Arizona function rhetorically as assets to college leaders who want to add gravitas to current institutional efforts. Writing program administrators and teachers can do the same to support and advocate for public pedagogies within their programs. We too can construct histories to serve the exigencies that arise in our programs, and our institutional histories may offer prime opportunities for doing so. In the following pages, I use the three institutions in my study to demonstrate how composition specialists might construct histories that show how current interests in public pedagogies have significant historical roots within institutions.

HISTORICAL VALUES OF RELIGION AND MORALITY TRANSLATED INTO CONTEMPORARY PUBLIC SERVICE AND EDUCATION FOR THE PUBLIC GOOD

Both Oberlin College and Syracuse University were founded as religious institutions, though neither institution maintains an official religious affiliation today. Based on my examination of how the historical roots of religion within these institutional histories have evolved over the years, these values are of significance to public pedagogy because they represent the foundations for contemporary goals of social justice, public service, and education for the public good. Charity, one of the three service learning paradigms Keith

Morton identifies, draws on students' sense of faith and religious calling. Morton defines charity as "spiritually based service . . . that bears witness to the worth of other persons" (128), and, based on survey data, he notes that "charity is a positive term for . . . students: a recognition of their obligation to help, and an expression of their recognition that our society affords them very few opportunities to make a contribution" (126). Thus, spirituality and a commitment to one's religious faith often have significant implications for students who may be interested in going public with their learning. Moreover, to understand how institutions rhetorically employ ideographs—like "social consciousness," in the case of Oberlin's mission statement, or "public good," in Syracuse's mission statement—we must work to uncover how those ideographs derive their meaning and what points of context within institutional histories serve to reinforce such conceptions.

Oberlin College was founded in 1833 by Presbyterian minister Reverend John Shipherd and missionary Philo Stewart. As Oberlin professor and historian Blodgett writes, "The college was very much a part of the utopian perfectionist enthusiasm that swept the country in the 1830s" (11). Shipherd, in a letter to his brother, wrote of his intention to form the colony "for the promotion of like, or superior, intelligence and Christian simplicity" (qtd. in Fletcher 87). Once Oberlin the colony was settled, the founders sought to build a school that could educate the youth of the community and spread the word of their faith. In fact, Oberlin's cofounder Shipherd required all potential recruits to the colony to sign the Oberlin Covenant, which articulated a vision for "missionary education to save a perishing world" (Blodgett 12). For the new Oberlin colonists, the school represented a chance to educate their children in the faith tradition in which they so firmly believed, and the college would also play an essential role in diffusing "sound morality and pure religion" by educating "ministers and pious school teachers" who would spread the colonists' faith (Fletcher 130–31). Thus, Oberlin College was created specifically to spread religious beliefs in what founders Shipherd and Stewart often referred to as the "Godless West" and to "conquer the Valley of the Mississippi for the Lord" (Fletcher 176, 92).

Almost forty years after Shipherd and Stewart began the colony and college of Oberlin, Syracuse University began as a charter—a contractual agreement—between church and city in 1870. The founders of Syracuse University relied heavily on contributions from donors in the United Methodist Church (UMC), and many Church members also served as trustees on the school's board. However, unlike the founding of Oberlin College, Syracuse University was not established exclusively for the spread of Christian ideals. From its start, Syracuse did not advocate one particular kind of religion, despite its overwhelming monetary and leadership support from the UMC. According to some scholars, the UMC historically supported institutions of higher education for their educational value, "rather than for the purposes of religious indoctrination" (Elliot et al. qtd. in Rincon 40). On the other hand, historians note that Syracuse's Methodist origins and Christian mission resulted in an education that was intended to be a "hand-maid of God" (Galpin 254). This commitment to the Christian faith became manifest in Syracuse University's aim to develop not only the minds of its students but also their moral character (Smalley 7). For example, faculty initiated an "Annual Day of Prayer" to "quicken the moral tone of every student," and chapel was a "fixed feature" from the earliest days of the University (Galpin 255, 259). Speeches by Syracuse University chancellors in the early years also emphasized the significance of moral character. For example, Chancellor James Roscoe Day, in an address to students in 1920, declared: "You will not all be President. You will not all be rich. You will not all be famous. But every one of you . . . may reach the greatest estate ever seen on this earth—a true character" (Smalley 173). The university's religious affiliation undoubtedly fostered this commitment to teaching morality and good character.

Even though Oberlin and Syracuse were founded by religious groups, both institutions eventually shifted toward academic agendas as they became more competitive and selective. Oberlin College became increasingly secularized, and what had previously been presented as the school's moral values shifted into extracurricular social or political programs. The late 1840s represented a transition away from the "rhetoric of the evangelical years" that was rooted in a value of morality toward an interest in the more secular "electoral politics" (Ginzberg 75). And, this less evangelical tone continued with the presidency of James H. Fairchild in 1866 (Barnard 4). Whereas previous Oberlin president Rev. Charles Finney preached lively revivals at First Church and Tappan Square—a public green space area between Oberlin the town and Oberlin the college— Fairchild had "neither the talent nor the desire" to do so (Barnard 5). However, Fairchild remained committed to the college's Christian ideals, remarking in his inaugural address that Oberlin students should be "deeply engaged in the great moral concerns" of their time (Barnard 6). By the time Fairchild's presidency drew to a close at the end of the nineteenth century, though, Oberlin was beginning to relax its requirements for religious worship, and the "daily chapel and class prayer meetings were increasingly defended on a social rather than a religious basis" (Barnard 104).

Similarly, at the start of the nineteenth century, Syracuse University became increasingly secularized, changing its charter in 1920 to be "nonsectarian" ("Chancellor James").[3] Within the university's chronology represented on their website, Syracuse articulates this historical shift as a "loosening" of its ties with the Methodist Church. Much like Oberlin College, the school began shifting what had previously been religious-based, moral education to service for the public good. As Richard L. Phillips and Donald G. Wright note in their history of Syracuse University's Hendricks Chapel, "in our current society . . . the roles once performed by 'religion' have been incorporated into schools and government agencies" (80). They illustrate how this "secularization" of society is reflected in the increasingly secularized history of the university's beloved Hendricks Chapel. In the 1960s, Dean John H. McCombe took a flexible approach to the religious mission and activities of the chapel, taking a "broad understanding of the purpose of religion in society" (Phillips and Wright 214). Syracuse University's historical commitment to religious tolerance and its increasing secularization are reflected in the initiatives of Hendricks Chapel today. For example, the chapel is the foundation of many campus-community initiatives through its Office of Engagement Programs, which "fosters a commitment to service in order to promote a more caring, just and democratic society" and operates within a "social justice context" ("Hendricks"). These initiatives indicate a shift in the contemporary purpose of Hendricks Chapel away from an explicit religious mission toward more secular community outreach, social justice, and public engagement programs.

Rather than the evangelical ideals of salvation and personal morality, the twentieth century at Oberlin College brought about an interest in social service—a new faith that combined "reverence for the worth of the individual with social redemption" (Barnard 115). During the first half of the 1900s, students learned the importance of service through faith-based organizations such as the YMCA and YWCA, a "model of social justice rooted in white evangelical Christian social activism" (Baumann 8). This progressive model of social justice bore many similarities to the religious evangelical movement, "reflect[ing] many of the same social, religious, and academic assumptions that shaped education at Oberlin" (Barnard 126). While Oberlin's religious affiliation and mission have evolved over its 180 years—indeed, the college no longer has an official religious affiliation—the institution's historical commitment to Christian ideals can still be traced in its contemporary commitments to social justice.

In tracing the religious and moral roots of these institutions, composition specialists can begin to understand the complex relationships between their institutions and the surrounding local publics. They also equip themselves with narratives that speak a language of power—institutional history—to upper-level administrators. Take, for example, a composition instructor who has designed an assignment where students go public by partnering with a local nonprofit to compose documents that help forward the mission of a youth runaway prevention organization. The instructor, who may need to defend her public pedagogy to WPAs or deans, can show how this kind of public engagement aligns with the institution's historical tradition of charitable public outreach rooted in the Christian religious and moral goals of helping others. In other words, writing teachers and administrators looking for a rationale and supporting arguments for going public with composition pedagogy can use these historical narratives to make the case for why going public is deeply ingrained in the institution's values. Of course, while not every institution has a history of religious affiliation or commitment to moral education, many institutions do; moreover, the following sections highlight other threads that may intersect with different kinds of institutional histories.

HISTORICAL PRECEDENTS OF COEDUCATION AND AFRICAN AMERICAN EDUCATION TRANSLATED INTO CONTEMPORARY VALUES OF SOCIAL JUSTICE AND DIVERSITY

Another shared distinguishing feature in the histories of Oberlin College and Syracuse University is that both institutions were among the first—in the case of Oberlin, *the* first—institutions to admit and grant degrees to women alongside men. Oberlin also touts its legacy as a "leader in the education of African Americans" (Appendix A), and Syracuse notes that its region "played a key role in abolitionism" (Appendix B). Both of these points within institutional histories have been translated into contemporary values of diversity, social justice, and social engagement, even though the conditions under which they came into being are more contested than the institutions typically acknowledge.

Oberlin College was the first school to grant degrees to both men and women (Ginzberg), and, upon reviewing various historical accounts, this decision seems to be closely linked with the original moral mission of the college. While the historical legacy of coeducation is significant to Oberlin College's values of inclusivity and social justice today, many scholars have argued that this choice was not rooted in the college's commitment to equality for women, nor for social justice reasons. Blodgett notes how, remarkably, "little discussion or debate was devoted to the subject [of coeducation] at the outset" (12). This casual inclusion of women was intended more as a means of furthering the religious goals of the institution than of seeing women as equal in their rights. As Blodgett argues, educating women meant more Christian teachers and missionaries, as well as more mothers who would train their children in the faith (13). In fact, few women graduates of Oberlin College went on to participate in the suffragist movements (Blodgett 13). Thus, even though the College today frames coeducation through a social justice lens, various historical accounts call this historical construction into question.

Furthermore, in the eyes of Oberlin College's founders, having women on campus afforded opportunities for greater moral influence (Lasser). Carol Lasser emphasizes that the founders' logic was "less concerned with the progress of women toward equality" (3). Lori D. Ginzberg also argues that "Christian virtues were, increasingly, defined as inherently—and aggressively—female virtues," and the "evangelical and domestic world-view of [Oberlin College's] founders and students demanded . . . that men live up to the standards of women" (68–69). However, rather than faulting the early founders for not placing women on par with men, Ginzberg maintains that Oberlin's leaders, "by exalting 'female' qualities and virtues and working to incorporate them into male students," were actually questioning what was inherent in the "gender identities of women and men [that] could be modified by education and exposure to the other sex" (68). Judging their coeducation experiment a success in 1836, leaders of the college attributed the college's avoidance of riots at all-male colleges to the "very presence of women" (Ginzberg 70). In many ways, Oberlin's decision to allow coeducation is inextricably linked to the religious and moral mission of the college. Indeed, Ginzberg believes that interest in Oberlin College as a "coeducational and interracial college," two of its claims to fame, "has obscured its significance as a religious community, that is, an experiment in Christian virtue which grew directly out of the spirit of the Second Great Awakening" (69). Ginzberg's claim further emphasizes the significant role of religion in Oberlin's history, which I highlighted in the previous section.

In the decades after the founding of Oberlin College, their model of coeducation spread to several religious colleges, including Bates, Swarthmore, and Syracuse. Though these colleges were of "different denominations, . . . all shared the same Christian values about the relationships of men and women" (Solomon 84). Both Oberlin College's and Syracuse University's coeducation are contested histories, even though they are often positioned within contemporary institutional documents as uncontested decisions toward social justice and equality. For example, not all students and trustees were in support of coeducation at Syracuse University. In an article in the campus newspaper, male students argued that "women's inability to learn was an established fact" (qtd. in Gorney 9). Despite resistance from some parties, first chairman of the board Reverend Peck and first chancellor Reverend Haven agreed that admissions should be open "to all qualified persons, regardless of sex" (Gorney 9). In fact, among the seven young women who enrolled in the first class was Chancellor Haven's daughter (Gorney 9).

Yet another contested history, often elided in contemporary representations, is the admittance of African American students at Oberlin College. In official institutional documents, Oberlin often pairs coeducation and African American education as indicators of the community's "commitment to social engagement and diversity" (Appendix A). However, much like coeducation, these histories are not seamless "onward and upward" trajectories. Oberlin's tradition of African American education came about as part of a bargaining deal rather than for an explicit social or political mission, as it is often portrayed in official university histories. In 1835, two years after the founding of the college, Shipherd saw an opportunity to enhance the college by enticing antislavery leaders and their abolitionist rebel student groups. Blodgett's historical analysis suggests that this move was calculated based on the college's particular needs in 1835; this was a time when Oberlin "was still very hungry for students and money, had no president and few notable teachers, and seemed on the brink of collapse" (15). Oberlin capitalized on a rebellion at Lane Seminary in Cincinnati during which a group of students, professors, and trustees threatened to leave because their abolitionist activities were being squelched by the majority of the seminary's board of trustees (Blodgett 15). Asa Mahan (a prominent antislavery voice and Lane Seminary trustee) and John Morgan (a Lane Seminary professor) were both discontented with

Lane's lack of support for abolitionist initiatives, and they were ready to leave for Oberlin College along with their rebel student followers (Blodgett).

However, Oberlin needed money to bring in these professors, so Shipherd made a trip to New York City to make his case to antislavery merchant philanthropists. Shipherd convinced brothers Arthur and Lewis Tappan to finance the hiring of Mahan and Morgan. The Tappan brothers also wanted their friend Rev. Charles Finney, "the nation's foremost revival minister," to be hired to "head up the college theological department in which the Lane rebels were expected to enroll" (Blodgett 15). Notably, the hiring of Mahan, Morgan, and Finney was wrapped up in the "biggest and most crucial package deals in Oberlin's history," because none of the leaders would come to Oberlin, nor would the Tappans provide the money they promised, unless Oberlin agreed to "a policy of open admissions irrespective of color" (Blodgett 14–15).

The issue of admitting African American students was heavily debated within the college and the surrounding town. The board of trustees and the student body were divided on the issue, and the people of Oberlin were "worried about what it might do to the village" (Blodgett 15–16). In the end, abolitionist and trustee Rev. John Keep cast the deciding vote that allowed for the admission of African American students ("About Oberlin"). The history of division surrounding the issue of African American admissions at Oberlin, though, continued throughout the nineteenth and twentieth centuries. Tracing the issue through archived, historical college documents, Baumann argues that the college's original commitment to admit black Americans thrived under the presidencies of Mahan and Finney; however, in the late nineteenth century and first half of the twentieth century, Oberlin retreated from this commitment (5). While African American students were still permitted to enroll, Oberlin College did not make efforts to recruit them, and curricular programming did little to support these student populations. In the 1960s, driven mostly by the protests of Oberlin students themselves, the administration and board of trustees redefined and reshaped admissions policies, and minoritized programming and course offerings in order to recruit more minoritized students and faculty to what had become an increasingly white and privileged Oberlin community (Baumann 5, 12). As the twentieth century drew to a close and Oberlin sought to remain true to its traditions in the twenty-first century, the college "reaffirmed its principles and practices of racial equality in the context of multiculturalism, which broadened the notion of equality to include all people of color" (Baumann 5). We see this represented within contemporary institutional documents today, such as the mission statement's claim that "recognizing diversity broadens perspectives, Oberlin is dedicated to recruiting a culturally, economically, geographically, and racially diverse group of students" (Appendix A).

While the admittance of African Americans at Syracuse does not figure prominently within their institutionally framed historical accounts, the mission statement highlights the "treasured history of social innovation" in the "Central New York region" that led to the region playing a "key role in abolitionism" (Appendix B). Drawing on the history of abolitionism within the region allows for further support of claims that universities "must connect more tangibly with their communities, and . . . Syracuse University, in particular, is remarkably well positioned to do so" (Appendix B).

The constructed histories of coeducation and African American education at Oberlin College and Syracuse University reveal how institutions can smooth over contested histories by positioning certain features within contemporary goals of social justice, equality, and diversity. As with institutional roots in religious and moral education, the tracing of coeducation and African American education at these institutions provides an example of how composition specialists can find ways to connect contemporary efforts to go public with the social justice and diversity missions often rooted in an institution's history and values. For example, a WPA who wanted to revise the course objectives of first-year composition to involve students going public to study social issues and use public writing for social change could defend this choice to a dean or provost by situating the program's public goals within the institution's tradition of social justice. However, WPAs also have the opportunity to highlight the complexities of our institutional histories as a means of demonstrating the ongoing needs of addressing social inequalities. In other words, while we may use partial histories of social justice to defend public pedagogy to upper-level administrators, we can also continue to document silenced, unseemly, or complicated parts of institutional histories to further support why we need to go public with pedagogy in the first place: going public with composition pedagogy helps break down some of the barriers between public/academic and community/institution that have resulted in strained relations between town and gown.

HISTORICAL FOUNDING AS A LAND-GRANT INSTITUTION TRANSLATED INTO CONTEMPORARY PUBLIC OUTREACH

The University of Arizona was established through a land grant in 1885 in Tucson, Arizona. Unlike Syracuse University and Oberlin College, the University of Arizona does not have historical ties to religion nor is the school private. Bearing some similarity to Oberlin College's founding in a new colony in what at the time (1830s) was considered "the West," the University of Arizona was established in a place that was newly settled by Americans but in the middle of the desert—what would eventually be the southwestern United States.[4] In fact, the University of Arizona was founded only twenty-two years after Arizona first became an American territory and twenty-seven years *before* Arizona officially joined the United States—a historical fact that the institution currently uses to position its "deep roots" and "fearless spirit" (National Association 35).[5] However, the University of Arizona's history deviates in significant ways from the two other schools in this study, and a noteworthy point of departure is in the relationship between the town and university at its founding. Whereas Oberlin College was an important part of its founders' original utopian vision for the community, and Syracuse University was a welcome collaboration between the Methodist Church and business owners in the community, the University of Arizona began with public rejection from the Tucson community. As with coeducation and African American education at Oberlin and Syracuse, the land-grant legacy of the University of Arizona is a contested history.

"It was 1885 and the mood was mean," begins the story on the University of Arizona's website ("UA History"). Cities in the territory of Arizona needed new sources of revenue funded by taxes, such as buildings and institutions, which would produce future income (Ball). The territory's legislature debated where to establish the state capital, a new insane asylum, a teachers' college, and its first university. The capital and insane asylum were considered valuable assets, whereas "no one really wanted" the latter two, especially since there were no high schools in the territory at the time (Ball 2). To the great disappointment of Tucson residents, Prescott retained the capital and Phoenix was granted $100,000 to establish the asylum; Tempe was given the teacher's college (Ball).[6] And, as "an unwelcome consolation prize," Tucson was given $25,000 to establish the state's first university ("UA History"). Pima County legislative representative C. C. Stephens "was bitterly rebuked by his Tucson constituents" when they learned of his inability to persuade the legislature to establish either the capital or the asylum in their community (Ball 2). Expecting a hearty welcome with his news of the university, Stephens was instead greeted by angry citizens who showered him with "ripe eggs, rotting vegetables, and, some say, a dead cat" (Martin 24).

To make matters worse, the legislature required that forty acres of land be granted by people in the community in order for the town to receive the $25,000 to start the university; this requirement was in accordance with the Morrill Act of 1862, which established land-grant universities across the country.[7] No one in Tucson was willing to contribute land for the university, and, if it had not been for the leadership of Jacob S. Mansfeld, who was "deeply interested in the city's development, believing steadfastly in the concept of the University," the University of Arizona would likely not exist today (Ball 2). Mansfeld, a new member of the Board of Regents, was able to convince three Tucson businessmen to donate the required forty acres of land, and thus began the founding of the University of Arizona ("UA History").

With a mission to teach "agriculture and the mechanic arts in order to promote the liberal and practical education of the industrial classes," land-grant universities were intended to be for the service of the people, particularly farmers ("The First Morrill Act"). Prior to the Morrill Act of 1862, higher education was "preserved for, and helped preserve, the aristocracy of society" (McDowell 4). As University of Arizona president Richard A. Harvill explained in a 1953 speech, "[t]he Country's early private colleges, like their European prototypes, served a small group. They prepared those who wanted to be lawyers, doctors, ministers, or teachers, and those who wished to enjoy more abundantly a life of leisure" (10–11). Thus, the introduction of land-grant universities opened many opportunities for young people from less wealthy backgrounds and from families in industries, such as farming and agriculture, that were not typically associated with higher education. Yet, this legislation, which was intended for "the maintenance of political democracy" (Morrill qtd. in McDowell 4) continued to exclude many local minoritized populations, which is unfortunate especially given the University of Arizona's location within a high concentration of Native American populations.

Despite the turmoil surrounding the university's early beginnings in 1885, the groundbreaking ceremony in 1887 was attended by a "crowd of about 600 Tucsonians" (Ball 5). And, when classes first began in 1891, the University of Arizona's website claims that Tucson citizens were no longer angry; they celebrated their town's accomplishment ("UA History"). In the years to come, the university offered many cultural and economic benefits to the surrounding community—from public events, to the sense of pride for the university's stadium, to the employment of local men for government-funded public projects from the Public Works Administration during the Depression (Sonnichsen 232, 245). Nonetheless, it is impossible to overlook the impact of such a contested beginning—that the University of Arizona was "unwelcome, undervalued, and resented in Tucson" from the start (Sonnichsen 136).

In the University of Arizona's mission statement today, they position themselves as "partners with the community," stating "whether we're teaming up with local schools to improve K–12 education, or working with rural communities to improve the health of residents, we're helping society meet its grand challenges" (Appendix C). The university's mission statement also contends that students have opportunities to "apply the knowledge they learn in the classroom in the real-world" through internships and community service (Appendix C). The land-grant mission of the University of Arizona is also echoed through references to the "economic influence" of the university that "helps infuse billions into the state economy every year" (Appendix C)—a message that harkens back to the implied reciprocal relationship between town and gown, despite the rocky start to that relationship.

An institution's land-grant status presents a prime opportunity for writing program administrators and teachers to connect public pedagogies in composition with the core mission of a university. If an upper-level administrator, for instance, questioned a composition instructor's public pedagogy that involved students visiting a local park to research and write about the flora and fauna for a local newsletter, the instructor could situate this public pedagogy within the institution's land-grant mission, citing the importance of students learning about and giving back to the public land and community that granted the existence of their university in the first place. Because the historical founding represents a relationship between town and gown through the granting of local lands, this historical thread—common to a number of US institutions—can be rhetorically used to help support an increasingly public pedagogy in writing courses and programs.

HISTORICAL TIES TO LOCAL NATIVE POPULATIONS TRANSLATED INTO CONTEMPORARY VALUES OF COMMUNITY PARTNERSHIP

A final historical thread that I would like to draw on involves the connections between institutions and local Native American populations, in the cases of Syracuse University and the University of Arizona. Syracuse's institutional history includes the use of American Indian symbols and images in the school's former mascot: the Saltine Warrior named Chief Bill Orange. While Syracuse celebrates its historical ties to abolitionism and women's rights, the complicated histories surrounding this Native American character are often deemphasized, though not entirely ignored, within official historical accounts on the university's website ("Syracuse University History"). Donald M. Fisher argues that when Syracuse was founded in the late 1800s, it established "mythical ties with the Onondaga people of the Iroquois Confederacy," who had been in the Syracuse region since the early 1500s (26). During this time, competitiveness in university recruiting and intercollegiate athletics "led the university to create an identity rooted in local Native antiquity" (Fisher 26). Syracuse University's Chief Bill Orange and the Saltine Warrior both drew on the image of a primitive noble savage (Fisher 41). Fisher illustrates how Syracuse's "ill-defined historical link between Natives and the university" led students to believe (incorrectly) that the university had inherited lands from the Natives (27). Moreover, Syracuse's American Indian mascot helped "reinforce notions of race and class superiority" by positioning students within "the doctrine of the inevitability of progress, of Indian savagery giving way to collegian civilization" (Fisher 30).

In 1978, members of a Syracuse University Native American student group led protests against the use of the Saltine Warrior mascot, and local Onondagan chief and Syracuse alumnus, Oren Lyons, agreed that the mascot was "derogatory" ("Syracuse University History"). Despite criticism from many alumni and community members, the university discontinued its use of the American Indian mascot in 1978. Fisher contends that the extreme backlash to this decision reveals "white disinterest in the views of Indians, anxiety over the loss of white control of imagery, and fear of the undermining doctrine of racial hierarchy" (37). The new mascot ultimately evolved through the 1980s and 1990s into Otto the Orange (the citrus fruit). As recently as the mid-1990s, the Syracuse community reinitiated debate about the use of the Native mascot, with many advocating for the university to revert back to the racist and derogatory imagery of its past. This aspect of Syracuse University's history demonstrates the continued complications the institution has in its relationship with the surrounding community and Native populations.

While the University of Arizona does not have ties to a racist mascot, the institution similarly has had complicated relations with surrounding Native American groups. The state of Arizona is home to more than 250,000 Native Americans among twenty-one federally recognized tribes ("Inter Tribal Council of Arizona"). The university's campus is in close proximity to a number of reservations, including the New and Old Pascua Yaqui Reservation, the San Xavier Reservation, and the Tohono O'Odham Reservation ("Native American Student Affairs"). However, racist attitudes in the late nineteenth century reveal the tensions between white legislators and Native peoples. For example, Arizona's Governor Safford advocated for the raising of taxes to support education in the 1860s, but the people of Arizona argued that they could not afford additional taxes because Apache raids kept them in "poverty and distress" (Harvill 11). To this, Governor Safford retorted: "Unless we educate the rising generation we shall raise a population no more capable of self government than the Apaches themselves" (qtd. in Harvill 11–12).[8] Safford's racist comments portray Native populations as savages, unable to govern themselves, and his comments are a vivid reminder of how exclusionary education for the "public good" was conceived of at the time.[9]

While the University of Arizona has a number of programs specifically aimed at supporting Native American populations,[10] the university mission statement does not explicitly reference ties with Native populations in the surrounding community. These connections are implied through statements about partnering with the community and helping "rural communities to improve the health of residents" (Appendix C). While Arizona has a number of rural communities, the surrounding Native American reservations are typically rural and are often in need of health services; thus, this reference in the mission statement implies rather than explicitly identifies public support and partnership with local Native American groups. Syracuse University's mission statement more explicitly acknowledges historical ties to Native populations, while still omitting some of the difficulties surrounding the mascot Chief Bill Orange. Syracuse's mission, noting the "historical strength" of the region, states that the revolutionary ideas of the women's rights movement "found inspiration in the indigenous culture of the Haudenosaunee [also known as the Iroquois] people, whose matriarchal society thrived in the region before the arrival of Europeans and whose form of government inspired our nation's founders" (Appendix B). Interestingly, whereas Oberlin College highlights its historical legacy of African American education and translates this into a contemporary value of diversity in its student population, neither the University of Arizona nor Syracuse University mission statements mention diversity, which might have easily been drawn from their historic relationship with local Native populations.

CONCLUSION

In *Community Literacy and the Rhetoric of Public Engagement*, Linda Flower makes the claim "people who stand within circles of privilege (like myself and many readers of this book) may also be standing in need of empowerment" (216). Flower goes on to explore the ways scholars, teachers, students, and citizens might begin to affirm a contested agency, and how we can use our "institutional authority to scaffold an intercultural dialogue" (224). Constructing institutional histories is yet one more rhetorical tool we can use to empower our efforts to serve public communities; doing so further authorizes our sense of agency and our abilities to persuade upper-level administrators of how public pedagogies in composition studies connect with the legacies and traditions of our institutions. Compositionists also have the opportunity to acknowledge the contested and partial nature of our constructed institutional histories, to confront ideographs that abstractly tout values without attending to material conditions we see within communities (Coogan).

While this chapter is intended to demonstrate the kind of partial and constructed histories compositionists might construct to support public pedagogies at their own institutions, this work is not without its flaws and limitations. For instance, many of the historical and archival sources I consulted are published by or were commissioned by the institutions themselves or were authored by historians employed by the institution. I want to acknowledge that giving voice to these kinds of histories silences other perspectives—historical accounts from students, community members, women, minoritized populations, and others, and we most certainly need more polyvocal historical accounts and counter-stories that work to preserve and highlight these important histories. As Connors reminds us, histories must be "examined, again and again, not merely accepted. That is . . . why we need multiple histories" (34). The constructed histories within this chapter are meant to serve as one starting point (not *the only* starting point) for analyzing more broadly how historical institutional values are reinterpreted and reinscribed in current missions and projects.

If you are teaching or administering writing at an institution other than one of the three within my study, you may be wondering how the constructed histories within this chapter may be useful to you. For one, I hope that readers will see value in the method presented here—the significance of constructing institutional histories that trace the historical roots of tropes that connect with our efforts to incorporate public pedagogies today. Indeed, the categories I have begun to identify are common to a number of institutions. In other words, while not every institution will have the same histories as Oberlin College, Syracuse University, or the University of Arizona, many institutions will have at least one feature in common with these institutions, whether a public mission for a state or land-grant institution or a commitment to social justice because of an institution's location and history.

Institutions with shorter and perhaps less storied histories often still draw on those histories in significant ways that carry rhetorical power. For example, my current institution, Georgia State University, was originally founded as an "evening school of commerce" in 1913 (Becker). In President Mark P. Becker's 2013 State of the University speech, he constructs the university as an adaptable institution that has changed to "meet the needs of Georgia and the metro Atlanta region"; he notes the change from an all-white, all-male student body to one of the most diverse universities in America today; from the development of an evening school of commerce into a comprehensive research university; from a purely commuter campus to one with more than 4,100 beds in our residential inventory. (Becker) Making a similar rhetorical move to previously analyzed university president speeches, Becker maintains that "through all the change . . . an essential feature of Georgia State remains constant. . . Georgia State is a destination of choice for hardworking students who aspire to improve themselves" (Becker). At Georgia State, I have come to understand that I can align and defend (for yearly reviews, promotion, and tenure) my public pedagogy work with my institution's historical values of diversity and urban renewal—two threads that President Becker highlights in his 2013 speech. In sum, part of the economy of discourse within institutions involves references to an institution's past. Speaking the language of university deans and presidents means connecting our arguments for public pedagogies to the histories of our institutions. We can also use our constructed histories to educate others about the complexities of our institutional histories; in this way, our constructed histories become yet another form of public pedagogy, a way to document and educate the kinds of stories we need and want to tell. Finally, investigating and constructing partial histories becomes valuable in helping us understand the complicated relationships between local publics and formal institutions as places.

CODA

Since the time of this writing, Syracuse University administrators and students have been in an ongoing debate about the future of the university's mission. On June 24, 2014, Chancellor Syverud announced his plans for "Fast Forward Syracuse," a program that entails developing and implementing a new strategic plan and campus master plan, as well as a revision of the university's vision and mission statements ("Fast Forward"); these changes seem to be partially related to the change in chancellorship. Syracuse's past vision statement—the one analyzed in this chapter—was filled with references to previous chancellor Nancy Cantor's vision for the university as an "anchor institution" that engages in "scholarship-in-action"; thus, with a change in leadership, these initiatives and goals are undergoing a process of change. While Syracuse invited feedback and comments on the proposed new statement, a group of students calling themselves THE General Body organized a movement called "Rewind Syracuse" to protest some of the proposed changes (Mulhere). THE General Body wrote "a 43-page outline of demands and grievances, which states that the administration has made repeated changes to university services without enough student input and that the university is not a safe space for students from marginalized groups" (Mulhere). Through a series of rallies, sit-ins, and protests, the group garnered the attention of upper-level administrators who agreed to meet with members of THE General Body to discuss their grievances in late 2014 (Mattingly). However, despite the protests of THE General Body, the steering committee has approved a revised mission and vision statement, effective April 2016, which omits words and phrases such as "public good," "committed citizens," "democratic institutions," and "public intellectuals" ("Fast Forward Vision and Mission Statements").

The debate, protests, and revisions call attention to the fact that institutions are constantly in flux, changing their mission and vision to suit their current needs and interests. I see this as all the more reason for composition teachers and administrators to become adept at translating our interests and work with public pedagogies into terms that resonate with university leaders, and aligning this work with constructed institutional histories seems to be a rhetorically savvy move.

5

Transformative Learning, Affect, and Reciprocal Care in Public Pedagogy

AS THE EXAMPLES THROUGHOUT THE PREVIOUS chapters demonstrate, taking a public approach to composition pedagogy can lead to deeply meaningful, even transformative, learning experiences for students. However, when we open our pedagogies to more expansive publics, any safety that a classroom could provide may be entirely absent. Partnering with publics beyond the classroom and/or campus can be risky, disorienting, and emotionally demanding for students and teachers. Part of the work of asking students to go public, according to Nancy Welch, is helping students explicitly differentiate terms like *public*, *private*, *personal*, and *social* to help students see them as contested (42). One of Welch's goals is to help students see that the "experiences and genres we've been taught to regard as personal and private are very much bound up in what is social and public" (46). When we ask students to go public with their experiences in our composition courses, what may be seen as their personal learning or private, affective reactions become public in a way that can be disorienting. Moreover, students' affective responses may be dismissed as private and insignificant to their learning. However, the riskiness of public pedagogy and the potential for an affective response can be rewarding, and many advocates of community-based learning value such an approach precisely because of the growth and profound learning students may experience. Going public with pedagogy may expose students to diverse populations and prompt them to confront pressing problems in their community; in these scenarios, the traditional classroom becomes a reflective space for students to work through the dissonance that may accompany these experiences. My recent work with public pedagogies has prompted me to question the affective components of this style of teaching and learning and whether, as a teacher who strives to approach students as whole learners, I am fully prepared to embrace the emotions that may arise for students in my courses. Overwhelmingly, the teachers I interviewed for my study noted their commitment to going public because of its positive impact on student engagement and learning. However, paired with the praise were comments that indicated teachers' awareness of the potential risks and emotional demands of incorporating public projects that involve students venturing beyond the classroom and/or situating student writing within increasingly public contexts.

The narratives teachers shared about going public with composition pedagogy raised questions for me about how we should respond to affective reactions. As much as I value the way going public can be productively disruptive or unsettling, I also question a pedagogy that purposefully exposes students to emotionally demanding scenarios without providing the kind of support to help them make sense of their experiences and move toward learning. In spring 2014, debates about the values and risks of purposefully exposing college students to challenging and emotionally demanding course content arose in response to moves on several campuses to institute "trigger warnings" on syllabi (Medina). Commonly used on feminist blogs, though also used in other feminist and nonfeminist spaces, trigger warnings are meant to caution readers/viewers about graphic or explicit content—e.g., rape, abuse, torture—that may be upsetting and which may trigger a flashback for someone who has experienced trauma. While proponents argue that using trigger warnings in higher education would protect students, many faculty opponents counter that supporting such alerts "suggest[s] a fragility of mind that higher learning is meant to challenge, not embrace" (Medina); in other words, many teachers believe that an important part of learning in college means discussing and experiencing texts and issues that may be out of students' comfort zones. While the trigger warning debates did not explicitly interrogate the role of public pedagogy as a potential trigger, asking students to go public in composition courses opens up more opportunities in which they may encounter scenarios or interactions that could be upsetting. Indeed, such moments of discomfort can be transformative for students' learning, echoing what opponents of trigger warnings have contended. However, as proponents of trigger warnings continue to question, how much discomfort is too much?

In an effort to find an approach to public pedagogy in composition studies that addressed some of my concerns, I turned to feminist scholarship, which I believe provides a frame through which we can problematize disorientation and theorize a reciprocal approach to care. In the following pages, I highlight some of the emotional risks that may arise for students, public partners, and teachers when we situate our pedagogies in public sites beyond the university. I suggest how theories of transformative learning might help teachers and community partners productively theorize affective dimensions of learning that may arise with public pedagogies in composition courses. Using an example from one of the teachers in my study, I analyze a moment of emotional distress a student experienced resulting from the service learning component of her business writing course. Reflecting on the role of affect for students, teachers, and community partners in this public pedagogy, I maintain that the example should cause composition specialists to pause and contemplate our responsibilities to each other in public projects. I conclude by suggesting a reciprocal model of care that draws on the strengths of a feminist standpoint while discarding the traditional, gender-specific positioning of care and nurturance as women's work. By employing transparency and decentering authority, we open opportunities to acknowledge and validate the emotions that students, teachers, and community members may experience through a transformative, community-based education. I situate transparency and decentering authority within the lens of a well-known tenet of scholarship in service learning and community literacy: reciprocity; I call for teachers of public pedagogies in composition studies to see the power of all participants to both give and receive care in transformative education.

RISKS AND REWARDS OF GOING PUBLIC

Teachers who choose to employ public pedagogies do so for a number of reasons, ranging from improving one's local community to helping instill in students a sense of civic responsibility to putting course content into action. However, the foundation of the choice—whether or not to include a public component in one's course—is primarily pedagogical; we choose to engage students in the public work of composition because we believe it is valuable for their learning. Situating student experience, learning, and writing in public sites beyond the classroom provides a meaningful context through which to explore social issues while facilitating student learning. The rewards of higher levels of engagement, transfer of knowledge, and potential transformation are certainly attractive, but do they outweigh the risks of situating one's pedagogy in the often messy unknowns of publics beyond the classroom?

In the interviews I conducted for my study, writing teachers repeatedly noted that students became more engaged when the course design involved community-based and/or public writing projects. For example, Jan Cooper, who co-taught the field-based writing course at Oberlin College discussed in Chapter 2, noted that getting students out into the local community to conduct ecological labs in the river watershed and interview local farmers resulted in "a level of immediacy that engaged [students] more thoroughly" (Cooper). Similarly, Crystal Fodrey, who taught composition courses at the University of Arizona that were also discussed in Chapter 2, asked students to analyze spaces that "exhibit inequalities of race, class, gender, sexuality, ability, etc.," and she found that prompting students to leave the classroom and enter local community spaces "woke [students] up" in ways that made them "more engaged" (Fodrey). High levels of engagement have an impact on how successfully students learn concepts. "Students must engage to learn," note Peter Felten and H-Dirksen L. Bauman, "and high quality institutions support frequent, deep engaged activities by students to promote learning" (367). In other words, higher levels of engagement can have a positive impact on students' learning.

Higher levels of student engagement can lead to the possibility of long-term transfer of core concepts from the course. Research on knowledge transfer notes that a learner may have a "life transforming experience" in which she or he "becom[es] someone . . . new" (Tuomi-Gröhn and Engeström 27). When the transfer of knowledge is transformative, learners experience "changes in identity as well as knowledge and skill" (28). A transformative education that alters students' worldview aligns with many of the social justice goals of community-based projects, such as challenging dominant ideologies, deconstructing hierarchies, and critiquing biases. The long-term benefit for students is a new frame of reference for understanding the world, and the benefit for teachers, community members, and society is moving one step closer toward an informed citizenry who asks critical questions and works to eradicate injustice.

When we partner with publics beyond the classroom, however, students are exposed to different kinds of risks that can be disorienting, even if they are ultimately productive for their learning. Public pedagogies pose a unique set of risks, in part because teachers have little control over what students may experience in the publics beyond the classroom and how those experiences may clash with students' personal worldviews. The risks associated with public pedagogies are part of what makes them attractive to many teachers, including myself, because such contexts prompt students to address issues that may not have come up within the relative safety of the traditional four-walled classroom. Some research on knowledge transfer also suggests that risk taking can enhance learning and transfer; however, as David Guile and Michael Young note, "learners need to be supported" through processes of collaboration, discussion, and risk taking (74). How can teachers create a productive tension between risk and safety, and, at what point does risk-taking complicate the goals of learning and transfer in one's public pedagogy? Without risk, students may not have the opportunity to address tough issues or face dilemmas that would prompt a transformation in their worldview. However, without some degree of safety, support, and care, students may shut down—unable to deal with the overwhelming dissonances, let alone move toward any meaningful learning. As teachers trained in our disciplines, not in therapy, how can we acknowledge and give credence to students' valid emotions while still moving toward more meaningful learning? To begin answering these questions, I review scholarship on theories of transformative learning and education, as well as the role of affect and emotion in public pedagogies.

TRANSFORMATION AND AFFECT

Transformative learning, as a theory coming out of education and curriculum studies, can be a valuable tool for composition teachers interested in public pedagogy to understand the potential disorientation and emotional responses that may accompany transformation within public learning contexts. In his theory of transformative learning developed in the early 1990s, Jack Mezirow describes a kind of conversion that can happen when adults wrestle with new information. Through what Mezirow calls "perspective transformation experiences," learners shift their assumptions to cope with and make sense of newly learned information. He defines transformative learning as "the process by which we transform our taken-for-granted frames of reference (meaning perspectives, habits of mind, mind-sets) to make them more inclusive, discriminating, open, emotionally capable of change, and reflective so that they may generate beliefs and opinions that will prove more true or justified to guide action" (Mezirow, *Learning as Transformation* 8). Transformation involves becoming self-reflective and critically aware of our assumptions and how they "constrain the way we perceive, understand and feel about our world"; as a result of this critical self-awareness, we open possibilities for a new perspective—one that may be more "inclusive, discriminating and integrative" (Mezirow, *Transformative Dimensions* 168). Mezirow describes ten phases that learners may go through when experiencing transformation, beginning with (1) a disorienting dilemma and (2) self-examination with feelings of fear, anger, guilt, or shame (Mezirow, *Learning as Transformation*).[1] For this chapter, I focus on these first two phases—rather than all ten—because they represent the root or spark of transformative learning, but also because they are the most explicitly emotional, drawing attention to the affective dimensions of teaching and learning. Other education researchers and cognitive psychologists have theorized the disorientation that may accompany new knowledge, but these theories are much less attentive to the emotional components of transformation. For example, Leon Festinger theorizes "cognitive dissonance" as the condition during which one's existing set of beliefs, knowledge, or opinions are questioned and which leads to an activity meant to reduce the dissonance (3–4). Similarly, Jean Piaget theorized learning as an ongoing cycle of equilibration, with disequilibrium leading to equilibrium (7). Cognitive dissonance and disequilibrium are useful concepts, but because both lack attention to the role of affect, they connote a hyper-rational, masculinized approach to learning that serves to replicate divisions between cognition and emotion. In fact, the study of emotions in pedagogy has traditionally been undertheorized because of the unnecessary divides between cognition and affect, mind and body. Moreover, affect continues to be dismissed as "something dangerous, personal, irrelevant, and counter-productive" (DeGenaro 195). In his analysis of Lynn Worsham's seminal article, "Going Postal: Pedagogic Violence and the Schooling of Emotion," William DeGenaro highlights that even critical pedagogies, according to Worsham, "lack a useful understanding of affect and tend to reinforce a reason/mind-emotion/body binary" (195). While Mezirow's theory of transformative learning is certainly not a panacea for these deep-seated binaries, it perhaps offers teachers a more nuanced, integrated approach to theorizing student learning because it implicates emotional considerations in the processes of making meaning.

A number of transformative learning theorists have identified the important role of emotions—such as loss, grief, and frustration—in the process of transformation. Sue M. Scott likens the process of transformation to letting something go: "an old way of seeing or doing is changed to a new way of seeing or doing. Something that is familiar must be denied" (41); such a loss can be upsetting and disorienting. Similarly, Sue L. T. McGregor found overlap between theories of transformative learning and stages of grief. McGregor analyzes student freewrites from an intensive, seven-day summer institute on consumerism and peace. Like Scott, McGregor ultimately realizes that what her students were experiencing was a sense of loss, what she identifies as "grief before growth" (51). The grief in students' writing represented feelings of being overwhelmed and powerless, as well as frustrated by their new perspectives. McGregor used the institute as a reflective, supportive space to help students move through their emotions with the goal of helping them arrive at a position of empowerment and agency.

Grief and other emotions can present barriers to learning, but they can also be necessary steps toward transformation. Barbara Schneider argues that we need to more fully explore affective barriers to learning; she looks at affect in terms of students' racist dispositions when confronting multicultural texts. Schneider employs Cornel West's conception of discernment, which "requires an examination of consciousness, a search for insight, [and] a self-reflexivity . . . [in] affective as well as cognitive processes" (927). Schneider argues that teachers can use discernment in the classroom as a method of "schooling the emotions" to help students avoid habitually racist ways of reading and discussing difference (927). Through discernment students can gain empathy, taking on what West identifies as an "other-centered rather than self-centered" attitude—a change that mirrors the way Mezirow describes a transformed perspective or worldview (qtd. in Schneider 928). To initiate these changes in students' dispositions, teachers must shift their attention from the "rational or mechanical . . . to the affective and attitudinal" (Schneider 928). Schneider's argument for the use of discernment to change students' attitudes and dispositions is quite similar to the use of critical self-reflection in order to transform one's perspective. Part of the significance of Schneider's contribution is how she directs our attention to the role of affect in this process; in short, attending to students' emotions is a necessary component for the deep learning that results in transformation.

In "The Affective Dimensions of Service Learning," DeGenaro claims that affect and the role of emotions in the teaching of writing have garnered "much critical attention from compositionists writ large but little attention in the service learning literature" (192). Nonetheless, emotional responses continue to emerge in community literacy work. For example, Ellen Cushman and Erik Green note that an unexpected result of their work with the Cherokee Nation was the "very emotional response that we had with the material"; during the process of sharing research papers, they recall that one student "broke into tears" (187). Like DeGenaro, though, I agree that compositionists interested in going public with pedagogy would benefit from a "more careful consideration of the affective affinities of both students and teachers," as well as public partners (192). Though DeGenaro does not employ transformative learning theory explicitly, many of his ideas align with how Mezirow has theorized perspective transformation; for example, DeGenaro contends that, as a result of service learning, "students and teachers both have the potential to have their respective world views changed" (197). DeGenaro describes affect in service learning as "initial felt senses"; his work highlights how an encounter with a homeless person at a food bank, for instance, results first and foremost in a sensation:

> Before [students] begin to rationalize, analyze, critique, form a response, take action, or even just describe the experience, (all of which are cognitive activities we ask service learning students to do as part of their writing assignments), a sensation occurs, contributing to a potential to feel, act, think, and formulate verbal responses. (197)

Like Mezirow's first phases of transformation—a disorienting dilemma and self-examination with a range of potential feelings—students in service learning courses may very well be disoriented the first time they encounter a homeless person, and they would certainly have initial felt senses resulting from that interaction. DeGenaro acknowledges the important role of affect in service learning experiences, especially because those experiences have the potential for being emotionally demanding and potentially transformative.

Theories of transformation often distinguish between transformative learning and transformative education (Karpiak; Mezirow; McGregor). The former might be prompted by a life event, such as the loss of one's job or the death of a family member, whereas the latter involves a "planned for and facilitated" educational journey (McGregor 55). Transformative learning may happen as the result of transformative education, though not necessarily, and transformative learning can happen outside of educational contexts. However, movements toward self-reflection and transformation can be "significantly influenced by educational interventions" (Mezirow, *Transformative Dimensions* 161). I see choosing to implement public pedagogies in one's composition course as a kind of educational intervention because these approaches likely result in a higher probability of students confronting unexpected problems that may result in disorientation. Public pedagogy overlaps with transformative education in significant ways—but this overlap makes me somewhat uneasy. Do I want to purposefully construct learning scenarios that expose students to risks that may be upsetting, even if I believe an emotional response could result in a deeply meaningful, perhaps transformative, learning experience?

In reviewing scholarship on transformative learning, I found very limited coverage of ethics when implementing a purposefully designed transformative education. In the case of McGregor, she critically self-reflects on her own motivations for employing a transformative education that initiates grief before growth: "'What do you get out of this for yourself, by exposing people to a planned loss and hopeful recovery or shift? Are you looking for power, for control?' I am working on that one, with no answer just yet" (McGregor 68). While the transformation McGregor's students experienced was unintentional on her part—she only came to understand their transformation through analysis of freewrites after the class was over—she concludes that she now sees the importance of an educational experience "intentionally designed as a collection of disorienting moments serving to instill a loss leading to shifts in world views" (51). Even still, her reflections suggest an inner turmoil about transformative education.

The writing teachers I interviewed for my study expressed their own concerns about how to balance the risks of going public—many of which overlap with components of transformative education—even though they found those pedagogies valuable for student learning. For example, Faith Kurtyka, a graduate teaching assistant at the University of Arizona at the time of our interview, reflected on the risks of students going into the community and her responsibilities to them as the teacher who initiated a public pedagogy: "anything can happen, and I worry about what can happen. . . . I feel as a teacher, you're responsible for the things that happen in the classroom, and if bad things happen, that becomes your problem." Kurtyka also noted that she gravitates toward certain kinds of partnerships because of what she feels comfortable with as a teacher: "I guess I really only did one type of service learning [a partnership with a local school], but that's because of my ethical issues of what do I want students to get involved in or what do I feel like I can manage as a teacher—what do I feel like I can ask them to do that's not too problematic." Kurtyka's comments prompt us to consider how students are implicated by the educational choices we make, such as whether or not to incorporate public pedagogies and in what ways, as well as the responsibilities we have to support them through the learning scenarios we develop.

Another writing teacher I interviewed expressed concerns for students' emotional responses to community-based learning as a result of her own transformative learning experiences. University of Arizona graduate teaching assistant Rachael Wendler said she is committed to critical pedagogies, but she also has reservations about the emotionally demanding aspects of such approaches:

> I really believe in critical pedagogy, and . . . I want students to understand structural inequality. But, when I think back to my own experience, . . . I came to understand those issues . . . in an intensive summer-long [community] program where I had a lot of support. It can be very emotionally demanding to deal with issues of privilege and power, both for students who are new to thinking about these concepts and for those who experience structural inequality in their everyday lives.

Wendler's remark highlights the emotions that may arise when we ask students to critically reflect on and engage with issues of privilege, power, and inequity within increasingly public spheres. While many teachers would argue that a degree of discomfort may be productive for student learning, Wendler's reflection reminds us to put ourselves in the shoes of our students and to be mindful of how to provide support through emotional moments in order to lead toward productive learning. In the next section, I analyze an example of a disorienting dilemma from a service learning course taught by one of the teachers in my study. I use this example to provide a snapshot of the first two phases of Mezirow's theory and to explore the emotional reactions—from the perspective of students, teachers, and public partners—that may accompany disorientation.

EMOTIONAL RESPONSES IN PUBLIC PEDAGOGIES

In my interview with Rebecca Richards, who at the time was a graduate teaching assistant at the University of Arizona, she told me about her experiences teaching a business writing course that incorporated a service learning partnership.[2] Richards described how her course design exposed students to increasingly public audiences and experiences. The first assignment was a memo of introduction that students posted to Desire2Learn (a course management system). Students read and responded to each other's memos in ways that Richards described as a kind of "public forum" with "hybrid cyber-interaction" that Richards did not mediate; the public forum created through the online discussion space, though, was closed to a more expansive public beyond the students' peers and teacher. As the semester progressed, students began to engage with more expansive public groups through service learning partnerships that Richards initiated: "I . . . form alliances with non-profit organizations in the community and interview them and establish stakeholder relationships with them across semesters, across years. And then the students . . . come in to that relationship and I eventually back out." Students in Richards's business writing course collaborated with the owners of local nonprofit organizations to assess organizational writing needs, write a proposal, and work in groups to produce communication "deliverables" that could be used by the organizations.

An additional public component of Richards's course involved students posting reflections about their service learning experiences to online blogs.[3] She described the blogging assignment as students creating "micro-communities that are more public." This assignment required that the students blog about their service learning project and "invite people in the classroom to join their blog group, read their blog, and comment on it." Richards gave students the option of making their blogs public or private, using it as an opportunity to teach audience awareness and differences in writing style and purpose when writing in digital, public contexts. Deciding whether or not to make one's blog public or private—a decision that could change throughout the semester—was something that Richards prompted students to consider carefully. She noted the benefits of "having an online space that can be opened up or closed down" with the possibility of keeping the blog private if the student, for instance, was "having a difficult experience that semester." When talking about writing for blogs that students choose to make public, Richards specifically asked students to think about "what kinds of information you should share and what kinds of information you should not share, especially because [students were] blogging about their service learning project, which [involved] a real person in the community." Having students think about whether and when to go public or stay private with the service learning blog, noted Richards, was a "good critical thought process for [students] to work out with their collaborators and me" (Richards, Personal Interview).

Despite Richards's recommendation that students carefully consider audience when choosing whether to make their blogs public, she explained that her students were "always surprised when people just show[ed] up on their [public] blog." Richards saw these moments as opportunities to help students reflect on public and professional writing contexts: they were "writing in this different kind of public space," but she used it as a reflective moment inquiring of students: "you've chosen [to make your blog public], and so how does that change your writing?" (Richards, Personal Interview). For one of Richards's students, though, the surprise of a truly more public readership for her blog led to what I argue was a disorienting experience for the student, teacher, and public partner.[4]

When I asked about problems with students going public, Richards described an issue that arose with the public component of the blogging assignment. As the students' experiences, interactions, and writing became increasingly public through service learning and blogging assignments, the risk of miscommunication, abrupt reactions, and emotional responses also increased. The moment of disorientation for the student, as narrated by Richards, happened during a class session:

> One of my students met with her service learning client and blogged about the experience—which, it was a positive experience—but from it she got the impression that her client . . . [seemed] very demanding, hard to please. She wrote in her blog that person's name and put, "My client . . . seems like she might be hard to please, so we'll have to work extra hard to make her happy." Well, sure enough, that organization has one of the trackers for looking up on the Web any instance of its organizational name and any of its key stakeholders in that conversation, so [the student's] blog popped up the next day on her client's program. [The client] emailed the student and said, "please do not talk about me in public: if I have given you any reason to think that I am hard to please or difficult, I hope you know I'm committed to this." . . . It happened in class that [the student] received the email. . . . [The student] blurted out with tears in her eyes "my client's stalking me." (Richards, Personal Interview)

I would like to consider this moment of disorientation from a variety of standpoints (e.g., the student's, her peers' in the classroom, the teacher's, and the client's) in the hopes that we may begin to understand the complexity of stakes, responses, and emotions at play here. First, I analyze the student's reaction as a moment of disorientation that has the potential to spark a transformative learning experience.

The student's reaction, as narrated by Richards, represents two key components of the transformative learning process Mezirow theorized: she experienced a disorienting dilemma with an accompanying emotional response. Receiving the email was clearly disorienting to the student; she may have thought she was being a perceptive observer, using a critical fieldworker's eye to assess her client and the rhetorical context of the service learning partnership. Indeed, Richards noted that in some ways the student's comment was a fairly "innocuous thing." Richards believed the student "meant no harm by it; she didn't mean this person is impossible to work with, or I don't like this person, or I'm not happy with the project. She just literally was reporting her impressions." For the student who likely thought she was doing a good job of completing her assignment, receiving the emailed reprimand from her client would have been jarring; this would be especially true for a student who Richards described as "a really good student who was conscientious [and] kind."

The student's disorientation was followed by her emotional reaction, what Richards portrayed as the student having "tears in her eyes." Richards interpreted the situation as "painful" for the student (Richards, Personal Interview); this kind of language maps onto the ways in which Mezirow describes perspective transformation as a potentially painful process (Mezirow, *Transformative Dimensions* 168). Additionally, the student's emotional response aligns with the feelings of "fear, anger, guilt, or shame" that Mezirow theorizes in the second phase of transformative learning. We might conjecture, based on her tearful reaction, that the student may have been feeling angry at the client for sending her an "aggressive email" (Richards, Personal Interview); fearful regarding the future of her service learning partnership, as well as her grade and potential for success in the business writing course; and likely bewildered that the writing on her blog was in fact truly public. The outburst, "my client's stalking me," supports the idea that what was perhaps most disorienting for the student was the public nature of her blog writing, but the word choice of *stalking* also suggests that the student felt betrayed and perhaps threatened. Something about the method through which the client discovered the public writing on the student's blog—the online tracker—may have felt surreptitious to the student, further complicating the situation, mixing in additional layers of emotional response.

If the standpoint is flipped in this scenario, though, we might consider the range of reactions the client felt when she discovered the student's public blog. I want to acknowledge that I have very limited data in regard to the public partner in this scenario, but I believe it is productive to consider her possible reactions as well.[5] Based on Richards's explanation of the situation, it seems that the community partner's response demonstrated concern for her public image and the public image of the nonprofit organization. It may have been hurtful, even disorienting, for the community partner to read that the student perceived her as being "very demanding, hard to please," especially if she thought that the meeting with the student had gone well and that she was being cordial. Her comments suggest that she was interested in correcting what she saw as the student's misperception of her personality: "if I have given you any reason to think that I am hard to please or difficult, I hope you know that I'm committed to this." Richards described the email as "very aggressive" and noted that, "even though I stepped in at that moment and spoke with the client, told her they're students, they're learning," she was not sure the community partner "ever really got past that," further indicating that the students' words were likely upsetting. Even if the client's email came across as harsh, the overall purpose of it seems to have been to extend an olive branch to the student, to communicate that she wanted to move forward with the partnership, that she was committed to it. Another way to read this community partner's email is as a lesson to the student about the nature of public writing and professional partnerships—exactly what Richards had been trying to get across to her students in the business writing course (Richards, Personal Interview).

Whether the client purposefully intended it or not, the email came to represent a lesson within Richards's business writing course, in part because of the student's public outburst during class time and because of the way Richards chose to address the situation in the moment. From the perspective of the other students in the class, they were drawn into this student's moment of emotional distress. According to Richards, the student's reaction "created an interesting moment for the class," and she took time to have students work through a response to what had happened: "we unpacked that." Richards's choice to address the student's issue through whole-class discussion transitioned the scenario into a teachable moment, not only for the disoriented student but also for her classmates. Richards could have brushed the student's comment aside, not taking it seriously and thus not validating the student's emotional reaction; she also could have asked the student to see her after class or during office hours to address the issue more privately and/or to give them both more time to process a response. However, Richards's on-the-spot response acknowledged the student's emotional reaction, primed the class for a moment of self-reflection, and, thus, facilitated the scenario as meaningful in terms of learning for the entire class. In our interview, Richards began telling the story as an example of a pitfall, but she ultimately reflected on how the experience was positive for student learning: "I think [the experience] was productive in the end, a good learning lesson for everybody about digital footprints and how [students] go about representing themselves and others in their writing and how that circulates beyond the public that [they] intended it for" (Richards, Personal Interview). Even as Richards expertly handled the moment, validating the students' affective response and helping her and her peers see this as a moment of learning, we might imagine that this was also a challenging moment from her perspective as a teacher.

From Richards's perspective, the student's outburst was somewhat disorienting for her as well. In our interview, Richards reflected that "it took a few minutes for [her] to figure out what had happened; [she questioned], how did this happen?" In recounting the scene, Richards said she was "horrified" for the student, suggesting both her empathy for the student's emotional response but perhaps also her own emotional reaction to the unfolding events (Richards, Personal Interview). Richards also noted that the student's outburst, combined with the follow-up class discussion, "sort of derailed class for the day," causing her to rearrange her pedagogical plans. Richards's experiences in some ways represent disorienting dilemmas that may be all too familiar to composition specialists who employ public pedagogies. The messiness of engaging with public groups outside of the classroom means that we, as teachers, often have little control over the kind of responses students receive or the kinds of experiences they have in public contexts. Indeed, I see this as a productive tension in public pedagogies: the possibility for moments of learning that are unexpected, just like the preceding scenario. What interests me as a teacher who values public approaches to teaching composition is how we might be able to both anticipate and support affective responses for students, ourselves as teachers, and public partners.

The moment of disorientation from Richards's course provides a point from which those of us interested in public pedagogies can reflect on how affect and transformation impact teaching and learning in our classrooms. Without further evidence from the student herself, we cannot know whether she was transformed and whether her perspective changed as a result of this experience.[6] We also do not know how the community partner was ultimately influenced by the experience. However, I view this snapshot of the student's experience as important for examining experiences that may spark transformation—experiences that as teachers we might exploit, prompt, avoid, or use as teachable moments. Richards's off-the-cuff decision to use the outburst to facilitate a meaningful learning experience provides an excellent model for teachers who may be faced with and/or experiencing disorienting dilemmas. Her response also suggests that in moments of disorientation, teachers have responsibilities to students.

In the final section, I consider how we might employ a reciprocal notion of care in public pedagogy projects with transformative goals, while avoiding the reinscription of problematic gender-roles. Theories of transformative learning and feminist pedagogy prompt us to break down the divisions constructed by dominant discourses that work to subordinate affect to intellect and women's work to men's work, thwarting efforts to develop a pedagogy of care that would more successfully guide students through processes of transformation. This traditional discourse also replicates gender dualities that read feminist pedagogies of nurturance as women's work (Worsham). One approach for composition specialists who also value feminist pedagogies would be to work to change the discourses of dominant pedagogy by reconstructing conceptions of nurturance and care that are not gender-specific. I suggest that some of the concerns raised in regards to transformative learning and education might be addressed by employing tenets of feminist pedagogy, such as decentralizing classroom authority, aiming to empower students as agents in control of their own transformative learning, and transparently challenging them to transform within a context of care.

DECENTERING AUTHORITY, TRANSPARENCY, AND RECIPROCAL CARE

Feminism calls us to be mindful of our positions of power in the classroom and our efforts to subvert those traditionally defined roles. For example, Rebecca Ropers-Huilman, reflecting on teaching her first graduate seminar, explains how she "felt trapped by the constraints of a pedagogy that attempts to enact power in efforts to empower, and care in efforts to ensure comfort, ease, and positive outcomes in learning" (131). The circularity of these feelings reflects many of the dilemmas within transformative education: how can we empower students without exerting power ourselves, and how can we care for students in ways that are not self-serving? Thinking back to McGregor's self-critical line of questioning regarding transformative learning—"[w]hat do you get out of this for yourself? . . . [a]re you looking for power, for control?" (68)—we should be prepared to carefully consider our pedagogical choices and what motivations guide those decisions. Moreover, as Ropers-Huilman notes, not all students are interested in the care we may offer. Similarly, Worsham has critiqued the traditional, patriarchal role of the teacher "as the sign of power and the agent of empowerment, as the one who has the power to know students better than they know themselves and to transform their relation to the world" (1020). In transformative education, teachers may be particularly prone to this risk—believing we have the power to transform students' understanding of the world. We, once again, want to empower students, while wanting to avoid exerting power to empower, while also knowing that we can never fully eliminate the power that accompanies our position of authority as the teacher.

I believe we can forge a new path to avoid this circularity by approaching transformative education in public pedagogies through reciprocal care that is based on (1) a continual shifting of teacher and learner roles and (2) transparency. Community literacy practitioners familiar with reciprocity know that the give-and-take in public partnerships "need[s] to be openly and consciously negotiated by everyone participating" (Cushman, "The Rhetorician" 16). Though not always discussed using the same terminology, reciprocity is a shared value in the feminist classroom. As Ropers-Huilman concludes in her feminist analysis of teaching graduate students: "regardless of the seemingly clear lines between teachers and students in classroom contexts, all educational participants have the ability to enact the power to care" (131). When we consider care in transformative education, especially in public pedagogies, I believe reciprocity should be a central value because of its self-critical focus on power relations among students, teachers, and public partners. Without an attention to reciprocity for all participants, we risk abusing our position of authority in the classroom to exert power and control over students or community members—whether that control is through disorientation, transformative education, and/or care. By taking a reciprocal approach, teachers can offer to care for students and community partners, but perhaps more important, we can be open to accepting the care that students and community partners may offer to us.

Acknowledging that all participants have the potential for power and the potential to give and receive care can help us move toward decentering authority and shifting teacher and learner roles. Both feminist classrooms and public pedagogies attempt to shift the loci of power and authority, positioning students and community partners as teachers and teachers as learners, blurring traditionally defined roles. The opening up and shifting of teacher and learner positions is unlikely to happen in a classroom where the teacher does not present herself as ready to learn and, at times, vulnerable. As hooks emphasizes in *Teaching to Transgress*, "engaged pedagogy does not seek simply to empower students. Any classroom that employs a holistic model of learning will also be a place where teachers grow, and are empowered by the process" (21). Integral to this holistic model of empowerment is that teachers are open to being "vulnerable while encouraging students to take risks" (hooks 21). Presenting oneself as a learner who may be just as vulnerable as a student and community partner may seem too risky to some teachers; but, if we support a model of reciprocal care, we can hope that our students and public partners will offer the support we need in moments of disorientation or distress.

To be attentive to the dynamics of power and reciprocity, I believe we must also strive to be transparent with students and the publics with which we partner. In her self-reflections, McGregor questions the extent to which teachers should prepare students for the grief that may accompany transformation; she questions whether telling students they will go through fairly predictable stages of "grief toward growth" would have a negative impact on their transformation. Feminist pedagogies value transparency in the classroom, and my position is that the most ethical approach to transformative education is to be open and honest with students, sharing our misgivings and enthusiasm for the processes we may experience with them. A transparent approach to public pedagogy might involve telling students from the start that we do not know exactly what will transpire over the course of the semester or how they might respond. In fact, I have started including the following disclaimer on my syllabi to that effect:

> I can assure you that there will be many unknowns. I will not be able to tell you exactly how your experiences and assignments will unfold because they will develop through your interactions with our community partners. The unknowns of the process can be disconcerting for some students, but, as long as you keep an open line of communication with me and your community partner, we will be able to work through

things so that you can succeed in the course assignments. (Holmes, English 3120)

This disclaimer on my syllabus functions as a kind of trigger warning for students, even though I am not able to identify what the triggers may be. In fact, in their critique of mandated trigger warnings, seven humanities professors identify the number one flaw with a proposed mandate as the fact that "faculty cannot predict in advance what will be triggering for students" (Freeman et al.). While I agree with many concerns faculty have raised in regards to censoring course content, requiring trigger warnings on syllabi, and protecting untenured and non-tenure-track faculty, I also believe that we have responsibilities to be transparent and care for students when we employ pedagogies that may be risky and disorienting. However, we also must be willing to "share our struggles with students as we negotiate relationships supported and disrupted by power and caring practices" (Ropers-Huilman 133). When we share our struggles, students have a better sense of how we as teacher-learners experience disorienting dilemmas and move toward transformation.

Though I am still honing what it means to enact a reciprocal model of care in courses where I incorporate public pedagogies, I can offer a brief example from a recent graduate course I taught at Georgia State University called Public Rhetorics for Social Change. One component of the course involved a collaborative "public project" that I did not define for students, in part as an attempt to decenter my authority and in part to provide a context for students to experience the messy and challenging process of finding a meaningful public with which to engage. I tried to be transparent with students at the start of the semester, noting on the syllabus that I did not know what this project would ultimately look like but that we would work together to define how they would contribute and be assessed. After months of discussions about possible prison literacy initiatives or direct service to nonprofit organizations, the class decided they/we wanted to lead a series of group discussions (modeled on Linda Flower's intercultural communication strategies) about the experiences of international students with writing on campus. While the proposed public pedagogy project would have involved graduate students remaining on campus, some graduate students saw it as an opportunity to investigate and engage with what was for many of them an unfamiliar public: students who are nonnative speakers of English at our university; on the other hand, I had several nonnative speakers of English enrolled in the graduate seminar who saw it as an opportunity to serve as a liaison between two groups with which they identified (graduate student peers and nonnative English speakers). Moreover, aligning with a public approach to pedagogy, the class members critically attended to the university as a place in their selection of this issue: as one of the most diverse campuses in the country and with a large and growing international population, Georgia State University represented a prime place for students to interrogate literacy issues for nonnative English speakers, perhaps identifying ways in which these students might be better supported.

Once the group decided on this project, I sent a collaboratively drafted query on behalf of the class to a faculty member in another department who we considered a stakeholder and who we hoped might be an ally for us. Unfortunately, our good intentions were either unwanted or ill received as the faculty member replied with what I interpreted as a somewhat defensive and aggressive email listing the programs already in place to help nonnative speakers transition into college writing. The email response was upsetting and disorienting to me, in part because the faculty member rhetorically positioned herself as expert and our class (and by extension me) as novices—noting a number of publications she and her colleagues had published on nonnative speakers—but also because I felt our intentions had been misunderstood. We were hoping to collaborate and partner with an unfamiliar public on campus, but the response we received suggested we were stepping on toes, questioning the effectiveness of programs already in place, and/or overstepping our bounds.

During the next class, I tried to be transparent in explaining why I would suggest we move in a different direction for the project. This level of transparency, as I reflect back, made me vulnerable to my students: I noted my concerns about "rocking the boat" by moving forward with the project because I was a newcomer to the campus community, a pretenure faculty member, and not an expert in scholarship on Teaching English as a Second Language. I also conveyed my disappointment and frustration that I felt hemmed in by these institutional constructs, and I emphasized that my vote was only one vote, that I would help the class move forward with whatever project we came to agree upon. Ultimately, the class moved in a different direction, choosing a supportive inhouse partner within the Lower Division Studies program.

Part of what was frustrating for me in this shift was that the on-campus group, Lower Division Studies—who administers first-year composition—with which the class ended up partnering was an on-campus group with which most of the students, as TAs, were familiar; thus, students did not go public in the ways I had originally intended or hoped for. However, the graduate students and I made this decision after careful consideration of the constraints noted earlier and of our one-semester commitment to a project, ultimately deciding to draw on our already-existing knowledge of the campus community and the first-year writing curriculum in order to contribute a one-time project, rather than initiate an unsustainable project with a community partner off campus (see Chapter 3 for a more fully developed discussion of sustainability and unsustainability in public pedagogies). The project that resulted from the graduate students' work was a collaboratively written chapter, titled "Civic Engagement and Community-Based Writing," for the custom published first-year writing textbook and a corresponding online resource guide for writing instructors interested in incorporating civic engagement, service learning, and/or community-based writing into their courses. Students' writing projects became public in terms of publication within the textbook and on the program's website, even though their experiences remained within traditional academic spaces and with familiar groups. In many ways, this project bears similarity to the way the University of Arizona brought together a range of overlapping programs, curricula, and initiatives to support the administration of public pedagogies (see Chapter 3).

What I see as significant in terms of affect and reciprocal care in this example is the process our class went through of reacting to the disorienting email from the faculty member in another department and then negotiating a revised project. I attempted to care for students by shepherding a project that they would be invested in and promoting reflection on why we received such a negative reaction to our originally proposed project. The graduate students in the course offered their care for me both in terms of how they carefully considered the complex demands on me as their instructor (tenure-track, newcomer, not expert in second language writing instruction) and how they negotiated with each other and me to decide on a project that would meet our needs in the course and fulfill their interests. Not all students were satisfied with the amended "public" project, and even I look back with hesitance at even calling the project public, but I think it models the messiness that often arises when attempting to go public with pedagogy—it's not always easy or clear-cut. The difficulty of going public, as Welch has argued, is rewarding, even if our "attempts to make voices heard are foiled" (92). Moreover, I believe this example models the role of the personal in the public, of affect in teaching and learning, and of the potential for a model of reciprocal care when we employ a public pedagogy.

As I think back to the interviews I conducted with writing teachers, I realize how their narratives prompted me to transform my approach by being mindful of the affective components of public pedagogies and by shifting to a more transparent and decentered role in the classroom. And, as I begin another semester of courses with the hope of going public with my pedagogy, I have already begun considering how I might prompt students to critically self-reflect in ways that may lead to transformative learning. However, I also approach these transformative goals mindful of the unknowns of the real world contact zone and the emotional responses that may emerge for students. A reciprocal and feminist approach to a transformative public pedagogy reminds us that we are all learners who need to be challenged and supported. When we position ourselves as learners, teachers, and caretakers, inviting students and public partners to do the same, the traditional gender-basis of those roles becomes further removed, and we begin to see the potential for a truly transformative experience.

Part of the power of public pedagogy in composition studies is the possibility of transforming student learners by having them engage with local publics and critically attend to our surrounding communities: in doing so, community people and places become valuable arbiters of knowledge; public pedagogies, when approached from a position of transparency and reciprocity, also have the potential to positively impact and change local publics, too. As Manuela Guilherme contends in the introduction to her interview with Giroux, his scholarship on public pedagogy and schooling "draws our attention to the transformative potential of the academy and school within a wider society," while also "critically unveiling the political and economic forces that threaten academic school independence and creativity" (Giroux, "Is There a Role" 182). Public pedagogy as a liberatory and transformative approach to composition education demonstrates the value of higher education bolstered by public, everyday experiences and writing. Despite the neoliberal threats that may challenge our experiences in publics beyond the traditional university classroom (as well as within our university space), opening our pedagogies to more expansive publics provides an opportunity for forging a different path, to publicly model what it means to be an engaged citizen, to both learn from and educate our local publics.

Conclusion

In an increasingly privatized society, the public turn in composition studies is more important than ever. Composition teachers and administrators have the opportunity to lead efforts in going public with pedagogy in ways that respect and ethically engage with the public knowledge our students can gain from persons and locations beyond the academy. As Nancy Welch argues in *Living Room*, scholars in our field need to actively "stand against constructions of expertise that have already dramatically narrowed the place of who is authorized to argue about pressing public questions" (144). Taking a public approach to pedagogy broadens the scope of local, public issues to be addressed in our composition courses, while also supporting students and everyday citizens confronting important community issues. As Welch notes, even though we face growing pressures to "create a program, or product, with market appeal," we are valuing public knowledge over privatized expertise when we view the work of writing and rhetoric as a "mass practical art," instead of a "specialized or bureaucratic *techne*" (144).

Throughout *Public Pedagogy in Composition Studies*, one of my goals has been to draw on the wealth of knowledge already existing in scholarship on public writing, service learning, and geographies of writing, as well as the innovative practices of administrators and composition teachers I interviewed, to document the ways in which our discipline is shifting toward public sites for student writing and learning. In doing so, I intended to build on these foundations to offer new approaches to writing pedagogy and program administration, while highlighting the role of institutional histories and the risks and rewards of going public. However, the findings of the study are limited primarily to perspectives of teachers and administrators, and our field would benefit from more research that includes the voices of public partners and students, as well as direct analysis of student writing, in order to better understand issues of engagement and reciprocity, learning and transfer. Additionally, the schools in my study represent only a small sampling of the diverse types of institutions and communities in which composition specialists teach and live. While I sought to represent some of that diversity, there are more stories to be told and more public pedagogies to be documented.

Recently, I've begun exploring how relocation in public pedagogy may be impacted by digital, particularly mobile, composing technologies. Mobile composition is a growing area of research within composition studies, and recent and forthcoming collections such as Amy C. Kimme Hea's *Going Wireless* and Claire Lutkewitte's *Mobile Technologies and the Writing Classroom* show that compositionists are considering the ways mobile devices affect composition teaching and learning. Within *Going Wireless*, for instance, Olin Bjork and John Pedro Schwartz suggest a "paradigm for mobile composition"—what they call "writing in the wild"— that would involve students visiting "places of rhetorical activity," such as "city parks, waiting rooms, shopping malls," in order to "research, write, and (ideally) publish on location" (224). Public pedagogies invite students to engage with nonschool publics, physically and materially, in ways that are similar to the assignments Bjork and Schwartz suggest; mobile technologies advantageously afford opportunities for students to bridge separate physical locations through mobile writing and publishing. The linking of academic and nonacademic literate practices was also one of Stacey Pigg's findings from her study of mobile composition habits. She notes: "while instructors often observe students bringing the extracurriculum into classrooms (e.g., texting or using social networking sites), students also located academic literacy practices in nonclassroom locations" (Pigg 269). Pigg's study emphasizes the role of "public social places," such as coffee shops and on-campus social learning areas, as essential places for students to "dwell and locate writing" when working from a mobile device (250–51).

The schema I suggest at the end of Chapter 2 (see Figure 1) depicts a continuum with opposing poles of physical and local places on one side, with digital and global spaces on the other; however, mobile publishing via laptops, tablets, and smartphones troubles these divisions in constructive ways. The proliferation of geo-locative social media technologies (Fagerjord; Løvlie; Schmidt), such as dropping a pin on a Google map, adding a location to a Facebook post, checking-in on Foursquare, or scanning a QR code, provide opportunities for students to physically engage with local public spaces while also composing in digital public spaces. Here, I see opportunities for connecting the material to the digital (and vice versa) in ways that may meaningfully address some of the concerns I have with public pedagogy projects that exist entirely within a digital realm (see Holmes, "Virtual Volunteerism"). I am not sure that there is yet a digital substitute for the kind of physical interaction with local public places and people that I expect of students in my courses that incorporate public pedagogy. However, a place-based approach to mobile composing offers the potential to ground student experience and writing in material places, carving out and reclaiming local public space (see Holmes, "Write on Location"). Blurring the perceived boundaries between digitality and materiality may also help students connect mobile composition to the everyday local, public places through which they move. As Pigg argues, we cannot "assume that all students will acquire strategies for effectively locating mobile composing habits on their own" (269). Public pedagogies can begin to help students locate their writing and learning, and a place-based approach to mobile composition can support students in connecting their digital and material writing spheres.

Public pedagogy helps bridge our institutions of higher education with their surrounding communities to engage students within their local publics and to address important public issues through writing. Even as institutions tout their values in social justice, diversity, and community engagement, as analyzed in Chapter 4, the reality is that the goals espoused in lofty mission statements do not always translate to visible and meaningful public projects within the community. In "The Scholarship of Engagement," Ernest L. Boyer, writing twenty years ago, remained hopeful for the future of America's colleges and universities as institutions that help advance "intellectual and civic progress in this country"; to do so, though, Boyer argued that "the academy must become a more vigorous partner in the search for answers to our most pressing social, civic, economic, and moral problems" (11). Broadening the scope of our scholarship and partnering with public communities, as Boyer contended, will help "academic cultures communicate more continuously and creatively" (20). However, I believe broadening the scope of our pedagogies also holds an important key to demonstrating for students—future members of our local publics—that the world is our classroom, that we can bring our academic perspectives to bear on everyday, public issues and that these public issues have import in our study and discussions within academic spaces. Designing and implementing public pedagogies in our composition courses and programs provides us with an opportunity to reeducate publics beyond the academy about the relevance and importance of institutions of higher education today, not as cordoned-off ivory towers but as engaged campuses.

APPENDIX A

Oberlin College Mission Statement

Oberlin College, an independent coeducational institution, holds a distinguished place among American colleges and universities. Oberlin was the first college to grant undergraduate degrees to women and, historically, was a leader in the education of African Americans. The Oberlin community is known for its academic and musical excellence and its commitment to social engagement and diversity.

The college uniquely combines an outstanding professional school of music with a leading undergraduate college of arts and sciences. The Oberlin Conservatory of Music provides flexible programs to prepare students as professional musicians and teachers of music. Deeply committed to academic excellence, the College of Arts and Sciences offers a rich and balanced curriculum in the humanities, social sciences, and natural sciences. Within that framework the college expects that students will work closely with the faculty to design an educational program appropriate to their own particular interests, needs, and long-term goals.

Oberlin seeks a disparate and promising student body. Recognizing that diversity broadens perspectives, Oberlin is dedicated to recruiting a culturally, economically, geographically, and racially diverse group of students. Interaction with others of widely different backgrounds and experiences fosters the effective, concerned participation in the larger society so characteristic of Oberlin graduates. Oberlin seeks students who are talented, highly motivated, personally mature, and tolerant of divergent views. The conservatory in particular seeks talented musicians with considerable potential for further growth and development. Performance is central to all of the curricula including music education, history, theory, composition, and technology.

For its students, the aims of Oberlin College and the Oberlin Conservatory of Music are to:

- Graduate liberal arts and conservatory students who have learned to think with intellectual rigor, creativity, and independence
- Provide the highest level of conservatory education to exceptionally talented young musicians
- Offer superb liberal education across the arts and sciences, in the humanities, natural and social sciences, and the arts
- Open the world to its students and develop in them the skills and knowledge they will need to engage with and navigate in highly diverse communities and in a global society
- Nurture students' creativity by providing rich curricular and cocurricular opportunities for studying and making art and music
- Help students clarify and integrate their intellectual strengths and interests, social commitments, and vocational aspirations
- Enable students to integrate and apply their knowledge
- Nurture students' social consciousness and environmental awareness
- Provide outstanding preparation for success at the highest level of graduate and professional education and in careers
- Graduate individuals who are humane, thoughtful, and influential actors in the world who will provide leadership in their communities and professions and in the arts, politics, education, international relations, public service, science, business, and communications.

From "A Strategic Plan for Oberlin College"
Adopted by Board of Trustees and General Faculty, March 5, 2005

Retrieved 29 Dec. 2014 from http://new.oberlin.edu/about/mission.dot.

APPENDIX B

Syracuse University Vision Statement

Our Vision

Syracuse University is driven by its vision, Scholarship in Action—a commitment to forging bold, imaginative, reciprocal, and sustained engagements with our many constituent communities, local as well as global. SU is a public good, an anchor institution positioned to play an integral role in today's knowledge-based, global society by leveraging a precious commodity—intellectual capital—with partners from all sectors of the economy: public, private, and non-profit. Each partner brings its strengths to the table, where collectively we address the most pressing problems facing our community. In doing so, we invariably find that the challenges we face locally resonate globally.

We understand that this represents an expansive definition of the role of a university, but as the Kellogg Commission has observed, it is incumbent upon universities today "to reshape our historic agreement with the American people so that it fits the times that are emerging instead of the times that have passed." Today, in a world in which knowledge is paramount, we believe that we best fulfill our role as an anchor institution in our community when:

- We educate fully informed and committed citizens;
- We provide access to opportunity;
- We strengthen democratic institutions;
- We create innovation that matters, and we share knowledge generously;
- We inform and engage public opinion and debate; and
- We cultivate and sustain public intellectuals.

Serving the public good in these ways pervades our daily decision making and connects us not just with our immediate community, but with communities throughout the world. These outward-looking engagements both optimize education and yield new forms of scholarship and new scholarly arrangements, propelling us forward as an academic institution. They allow us not only to create innovations that matter, but to test our notions of who is a scholar and what scholarship is.

Roots of the Vision

Scholarship in Action captures a vital, historical strength of the Central New York region and the City of Syracuse, as well as the University. Our region has a treasured history of social innovation, having played a key role in abolitionism and the women's rights movement. Even those ideas—revolutionary in their own times—found inspiration locally in the indigenous culture of the Haudenosaunee people, whose matriarchal society thrived in the region before the arrival of Europeans and whose form of government inspired our nation's founders.

The process of adopting Scholarship in Action as our vision was organic as well. Chancellor Nancy Cantor dedicated her inaugural year to the theme "University as Public Good: Exploring the Soul of Syracuse." All of SU's stakeholders were invited to share their reflections on our strengths and aspirations for our future—from students, faculty and staff members to alumni to friends of the University to members of the local, regional, and global communities. The many activities of that reflective year revealed profound thoughts and feelings, from which two very clear messages were distilled: (1) universities today must connect more tangibly with their communities and (2) Syracuse University, in particular, is remarkably well positioned to do so. Scholarship in Action is a faithful translation of these messages, a bona fide expression of the identity to which the Syracuse University community aspires.

Retrieved 29 Dec. 2014 from http://www.syr.edu/about/vision.html.

APPENDIX C

University of Arizona Mission

The University of Arizona (UA) is a place without limits—where teaching, research, service and innovation merge to improve lives in Arizona and beyond. We aren't afraid to ask big questions, and find even better answers.

We're innovators and discoverers.
In 1885, establishing Arizona's first university in the middle of the Sonoran Desert was a bold move. But our founders were fearless, and we have never lost that spirit. To this day, we're revolutionizing the fields of space sciences, optics, biosciences, medicine, arts and humanities, business, technology transfer and many others. Since it was founded, the UA has grown to cover more than 380 acres in central Tucson, a rich breeding ground for discovery. Where else in the world can you find an astronomical observatory mirror lab under a football stadium? An entire ecosystem under a glass dome? Visit our campus, just once, and you'll quickly understand why the UA is a university unlike any other.

Here, "Bear Down" is more than just a motto.
Before UA student body president and revered football quarterback John "Button" Salmon died in 1926, his last words to his teammates were "Tell them . . . tell the team to bear down." Whether it's academics, athletics or research, we've adopted the stance that when the going gets tough, the tough #BearDown.

Our curiosity knows no bounds.
As a leading-edge public research university, we're inspired to explore humanity's most fundamental questions—about science, medicine, the arts and business. Our faculty includes members of esteemed national academies, Pulitzer Prize winners, White House Champions of Change and cel-

ebrated thought leaders in numerous disciplines. We are leading projects that will change how we see the world, such as the OSIRIS-REx mission, which will scoop samples from a near-Earth asteroid in 2020.

We're partners with the community.
Whether we're teaming up with local schools to improve K-12 education, or working with rural communities to improve the health of residents, we're helping society meet its grand challenges.

The UA's Tech Parks are where dynamic innovators and business leaders work side by side to test and develop new technologies. The UA Medical Center, part of the UA Health Network, is a 479-bed hospital that has been ranked among the nation's best hospitals by *U.S. News & World Report* for more than a decade. Together, the UA, UA Tech Parks and the UA Health Network generate billions of dollars of economic activity in Arizona each year—$8.3 billion in 2011 alone.

Our graduates are workforce-ready.
At the UA, 100 percent of our undergraduates will have the opportunity to apply the knowledge they learn in the classroom in the real-world, through internships, community service, on-campus jobs and research opportunities. Our mission is to graduate students who are sought after by the best employers and postgraduate programs, and who are ready to embark on engaging, fulfilling careers.

Equipped with skills, knowledge, experience and the entrepreneurial spirit they gain at the UA, our students become highly skilled members of society who lead with determination, innovate without limits and create companies that generate more jobs, benefitting our state, our nation and the world, in boundless ways. Our alumni include astronauts and actors; Grammy, Tony, Emmy and Oscar winners; media stars; Olympic athletes; Fortune 500 CEOs; public servants; Nobel scientists; inventors and best-selling authors.

We're thinkers and doers.
From the heart of the Southwest to the edges of the universe, there are no limits to how far we can reach. We'll never stop pushing to make sense of the world and to find ways to make it better. At the University of Arizona, we have the power to make a difference.

Bigger Questions. Better Answers. Bear Down.

Top 10 Facts about the University of Arizona

#10 Our history runs deep.
Before Arizona was a state, there was the University of Arizona.

#9 A premier, public research university.
As one of the world's premier public research universities, the University of Arizona conducts more than $625 million of research annually, a key measure of productivity. The National Science Foundation ranks the UA 19th among public universities and 29th overall in research expenditures.

#8 Arizona's only M.D. granting medical school.
The UA Health Networks helps treat more than 100,000 patients each year, and the UA Medical Center houses the only Level I trauma center in Southern Arizona.

#7 Creativity flourishes here.
Iconic photographer Ansel Adams helped found the UA's Center for Creative Photography, the largest institution in the world devoted to documenting the history of modern North American photography.

#6 We transform ideas into reality.
Researchers at the UA's BIO5 Institute develop and commercialize new technologies, diagnostics and health care treatments, and have helped form 20 spinoff companies in the past eight years.

#5 The best and the brightest internationally.
The UA is one of the nation's top producers of Fulbright Scholars.

#4 Our economic influence is felt statewide.
The UA directly and indirectly impacts more than 30,000 jobs, and helps infuse billions into the state economy every year.

#3 Uncharted territory is our playground.
The UA is leading a first-of-its-kind mission to send a spacecraft to a near-Earth asteroid in 2020. The spacecraft will scoop samples to bring back to Earth, helping us understand the origins of the Solar System.

#2 One hundred percent.

That's how many UA undergraduates can complete their degrees with real-world experience on their transcript.

#1 The first and only.

The UA offers the nation's only Bachelor of Arts in Law degree.

Retrieved 29 Dec. 2014 from http://www.arizona.edu/about.

NOTES

1. Public Pedagogy in Composition Studies

1. Of course, pedagogies that incorporate cultural critique and civic writing can also invite students to venture beyond the classroom; my point is to highlight moving beyond the classroom as a key feature of public pedagogy.
2. The Syracuse University Writing Program recently obtained approval and officially changed its name to the Department of Writing Studies, Rhetoric, and Composition.
3. In the spring of 2011, I interviewed teachers and administrators via Skype at Oberlin College, during a three-day site visit at Syracuse University, and in-person over the course of two months at the University of Arizona, where I was a PhD student completing my dissertation research.
4. This study had Institutional Review Board approvals or exemptions at Oberlin College, Syracuse University, the University of Arizona, and Georgia State University. During the time of data collection, I was a graduate student at the University of Arizona, and all participants, including faculty, administrators, and graduate students from all three schools in the study gave me permission to identify them by name and institution. I collected these permissions when I invited participants to sign the IRB-approved informed consent form, which gave participants the option of me using their full name or a self-selected pseudonym in the study. None of the participants selected a pseudonym and all signed and checked the box for me to use their full name in the research and future publications. I contacted via email the participants who I quote from significantly and whose pedagogies I analyze in detail; I invited them to review their specific chapters to make sure I am representing them and their pedagogies accurately and to confirm their choice to be named (and to confirm their selected name and preferred gender pronoun).

Some study participants responded to my emails and several read their chapters, providing follow-up details and/or clarifying information, whereas other participants did not respond to follow-up requests. I want to be transparent with readers about the consent processes and my choice to respect the participants' wishes to be named.

5. Enrollment numbers are representative of combined graduate, undergraduate, and professional (e.g., law, pharmacy) student populations and are for 2014-2015 at the University of Arizona and 2015-2016 for Syracuse University and Oberlin College ("Fact Book"; "SU Facts"; "Enrollment").

2. Relocating the Composition Classroom: Going Public with Pedagogy

1. Long's five pedagogies correspond to prominent literacies that students use to take public action; she labels the literacies using the same categories as the pedagogies: interpretative, institutional, tactical, inquiry-driven, and performative (155).
2. I was not able to interview the other co-teacher, Mary Garvin, for this study. Thus, my analysis of the pedagogy for this course is based on my interview with Jan Cooper, as well as teaching materials from the course that Cooper shared with me.
3. Because I interviewed Luce in March, his commentary about the course was while it was still in progress. Following our face-to-face interview, I accessed publicly available documents related to Luce's course through Syracuse's website; these documents included his syllabus, as well as some writing prompts and assignment sheets.
4. On the assignment sheet, Luce described the "honesty box" journal entry as a series of statements that make explicit students' assumptions about "your [service learning] site, your participation, your research, and the course."
5. In fact, in *Understanding by Design*, Grant Wiggins and Jay McTighe advocate for using "backwards design" to more purposefully craft learning experiences. This approach to pedagogical planning involves starting with the course learning goals, objectives, and standards first, and then deriving the curriculum from the evidence of student performance (see Holmes, "Advancing"; Wiggins and McTighe).

3. Productive Tensions: Administering Public Pedagogies

1. Much of the scholarship on service learning and community engagement within composition studies has focused on classroom

practices and, in general, much less has been published on writing programs and administration. In her bibliographic essay "Writing Program Administration and Community Engagement," Jaclyn M. Wells identifies and reviews three perspectives that have emerged historically: WPA scholarship that addresses community engagement, community engagement scholarship in composition that addresses administration, and community engagement scholarship outside composition that addresses administration. "Even though administrative concerns reverberate throughout composition's community engagement literature," Wells concludes, "little of that literature directly connects community engagement with writing program administration" (237).

2. Campus Compact represents one of the most centralized forces behind institutionalizing community engagement programs within higher education. The organization was formed in 1985 by the presidents of Brown, Georgetown, and Stanford Universities to combat the media's negative portrayals of college students as "materialistic and self-absorbed, more interested in making money than in helping their neighbors." "The founding presidents," according to Campus Compact's telling of its organization's history, "believed this public image was false" based on their observations of students' community engagement work; therefore, they created Campus Compact to help colleges and universities construct "support structures" that would further encourage those engagement efforts ("Who We Are").

3. Many of these programs are literally top-down in that they were created by leaders of institutions. Campus Compact is an organization initiated and enacted by university presidents, and the authors of *Becoming an Engaged Campus* who advocate for the alignment process are three top-level administrators (associate provost for outreach, president, and vice president for academic affairs/provost) at Northern Kentucky University.

4. Campus Compact is a "national coalition of more than 1,100 college and university presidents," and the organization boasts that more than 98 percent of those schools have "one or more community partnerships" and more than 90 percent include "service or civic engagement in their mission statements" ("Who We Are").

5. I met with staff in the campus service learning center to discuss the kinds of writing projects I would like for students in my course to work on and the staff member suggested six organizations that might be a good fit. I believe the center's staff did their best to

match up my needs and interests with those of the partnering organizations; however, because there was an intermediary negotiating the terms, I feel that the lines of communication were crossed and I never built firm partnerships with the leaders of the organizations.

6. When Cushman left her position and partnerships at CU Denver, she narrates how she built capacity to help sustain the program and the service learning curriculum by introducing other professors to "key organizational representatives," by delivering teaching materials to "the instructor next in line to teach the course," and by training other faculty members to do the digital composition work she started. As Cushman explains, "the program design included a kind of capacity building knowledge, social connections, and resources that stay within the project even when stakeholders change" ("Sustainable" 61).

7. When Trubek started the CBWP that would eventually become the Ninde Scholars Program, she was able to pay the tutors through their association with the Writing Associates Program, thus the Department of Rhetoric and Composition provided the financial support for the tutors (Arbogast). As the program evolved, the population of tutors expanded to include students who had been trained as writing associates as well as those who had not. However, the three or four Ninde Scholars tutors who have taken the RHET 401: Teaching and Tutoring Writing Across the Curriculum course continue to be funded from the Department of Rhetoric and Composition (Arbogast). In fact, the pay scale for other tutors is still "tagged to the writing associates' pay scale; if that goes up, we go up [for all tutors]" (Arbogast).

8. Hall has since retired from the University of Arizona. In 2012 Kimme Hea took over as the director of the Writing Program at the University of Arizona and served until 2015. Kimme Hea is now associate dean for instruction in the College of Social and Behavioral Sciences. Kimme Hea served as the chair and Hall served as one of the readers on my dissertation committee; both reviewed earlier draft versions of pieces that have made their way into *Public Pedagogy in Composition Studies*.

9. For a more detailed account of earlier outreach efforts in the University of Arizona Writing Program, see Anne-Marie Hall's "Expanding the Community: A Comprehensive Look at Outreach and Articulation."

10. The SVR2 event was a second iteration of the first SVR event. The first SVR event was not pedagogically focused; however, this event

also "morphed" to meet the needs of the UA Writing Program, as well as the graduate course curriculum.

4. Constructing Institutional Histories for Going Public

1. Syracuse University defines itself as an "anchor institution" in the city of Syracuse that pursues "extensive partnerships with the public, private, and non-profit sectors" to "create meaningful opportunities for students and faculty to learn and discover, while tackling pressing issues in our city that resonate in our nation and world" ("SU as Anchor Institution").
2. Nancy Cantor was chancellor of Syracuse University from 2004 to 2013. Kent Syverud took over the chancellorship in 2014 ("Chancellor").
3. Even today, Syracuse University maintains some ties with the United Methodist Church (UMC), including its membership in the International Association of Methodist Schools, Colleges, and Universities and the membership of three members on SU's board of trustees to represent the UMC as stated in the university bylaws ("International"; "Syracuse University Bylaws").
4. Of course, a number of Indian populations settled in Arizona for centuries before Americans.
5. Abraham Lincoln signed the Congressional Act that created the Territory of Arizona in 1863 (Ball 2). Arizona became the forty-eighth state—and last contiguous state—to be admitted to the United States in 1912 ("Arizona History").
6. The teachers' college in Tempe, Tempe Normal School, eventually became Arizona State College and then Arizona State University (Ball 2).
7. The 1862 Act established an agriculture college in each state and territory. The second Morrill Act in 1890 established an additional seventeen institutions, primarily in the Southeast and primarily for African American students (*Colleges of Agriculture* 1).
8. When the American Civil War broke out, leading to the departure of Arizona federal garrisons, the territory of Arizona was in bitter conflict with Apache Indians for nearly twenty-five years until the surrender of Geronimo in the 1880s (Harvill 8).
9. The state of Arizona's history illustrates its ongoing complications with the democratic participation of minoritized populations. Native American populations were barred by law from voting in Arizona until 1948 (King and Springwood 192). More recently, Arizona has passed laws that are increasingly oppressive to Mexican Ameri-

can populations, including voter ID and proof-of-citizenship laws, as well as laws that permit law enforcement officers to stop and inquire about an individual's immigration status.

10. Some of the Native programs for students at the University of Arizona are sponsored by the Office for Native American Student Affairs, including social justice speakers and film series and Native American heritage month events. Additionally, the university's College of Medicine houses the Native American Research and Training Center, which conducts research and training projects intended to improve the quality of life for Native Americans and specifically targets local Native American populations.

5. Transformative Learning, Affect, and Reciprocal Care in Public Pedagogy

1. The complete list of the ten phases of Mezirow's original theory of transformative learning are as follows: (1) a disorienting dilemma, (2) self-examination with feelings of fear, anger, guilt, or shame, (3) a critical assessment of assumptions, (4) recognition that one's discontent and the process of transformation are shared, (5) exploration of options for new roles, relationships, and actions, (6) planning a course of action, (7) acquiring knowledge and skills for implementing one's plans, (8) provisional trying of new roles, (9) building competence and self-confidence in new roles and relationships, and (10) a reintegration into one's life on the basis of conditions dictated by one's new perspective (Mezirow, *Learning as Transformation*).

2. Because I offer an in-depth analysis of an example from Richards's interview, I want readers to know that Richards read several drafts of this manuscript, offering feedback and confirmation on how I represent her and analyze her pedagogy.

3. Reflection has been theorized as an important component of learning for professionals (Schön), for students in the writing classroom (Yancey), and for students engaging in service learning (Ash, Atkinson, and Clayton). Critical self-reflection is also a significant component of transformative learning theory (Mezirow).

4. In a recently published article on cyberfeminist pedagogy in *Feminist Teacher*, Richards discusses a different dilemma that arose in her business writing course with a service learning component (see Richards, "I Could Have Told You").

5. I want to underscore that the lack of community partner perspectives is a significant issue within community literacy and service

learning scholarship—an issue that has been noted and has begun to be addressed by Marie Sandy and Barbara A. Holland's research on community partner perspectives, as well as Randy Stoecker and Elizabeth A. Tryon's edited collection *The Unheard Voices: Community Organizations and Service Learning*.

6. Moreover, collecting the kind of evidence that would document and track a student's transformation is particularly challenging because the process could take years; the student may experience an emotional trigger that she continues to reflect on and unpack for months or years to come (Mezirow). Despite these challenges, this is an area ripe for future research—tracking whether and how students transform after service learning experiences.

WORKS CITED

"About Oberlin: Overview." *About Oberlin*. Oberlin College. 2011. Web. 22 July 2011. <http://new.oberlin.edu/about/>.

Ackerman, John M. "Rhetorical Engagement in the Cultural Economies of Cities." *The Public Work of Rhetoric: Citizen-Scholars and Civic Engagement*. Ed. John M. Ackerman and David J. Coogan. Columbia: U South Carolina P, 2010. 76–97. Print.

Ackerman, John M., and David J. Coogan, eds. *The Public Work of Rhetoric: Citizen-Scholars and Civic Engagement*. Columbia: U South Carolina P, 2010. Print.

Adler-Kassner, Linda. *The Activist WPA: Changing Stories about Writing and Writers*. Logan: Utah State U P, 2008. Print.

Alexander, Robin J. "Border Crossings: Towards a Comparative Pedagogy." *Comparative Education* 37.4 (2001): 507–23. *JSTOR*. Web. 21 Mar. 2012.

Althusser, Louis. "Ideology and Ideological State Apparatuses: Notes Towards an Investigation." *Lenin and Philosophy and Other Essays*. Trans. Ben Brewster. New York: Monthly Review Press, 2001. 85–126. Print.

Anson, Chris M., and Robert L. Brown, Jr. "Subject to Interpretation: Researching the Textual Representation of Writing Programs and Its Effects on the Politics of Administration." *The Writing Program Administrator as Researcher: Inquiry in Action and Reflection*. Ed. Shirley K Rose and Irwin Weiser. Portsmouth: Heinemann/Boynton-Cook, 1999. 141–52. Print.

Arbogast, Bo. Personal Interview via Skype. 3 May 2011.

"Arizona History." *Arizona Spotlight: All about the State of Arizona*. Office of the Arizona Governor Doug Ducey. Web. 21 July 2016. < http://azgovernor.gov/governor/arizona-history>.

Ash, Sarah L., Maxine P. Atkinson, and Patti H. Clayton. "Integrating Reflection and Assessment to Capture and Improve Student Learning." *Michigan Journal of Community Service Learning* 11.2 (2005): 49–60. *Academic OneFile*. Web. 4 Sept. 2011.

Ball, Phyllis. *A Photographic History of the University of Arizona 1885–1985*. 2nd printing, with corrections. Tucson: U of Arizona Foundation, 1987. Print.

Barnard, John. *From Evangelicalism to Progressivism at Oberlin College, 1866–1917*. Columbus: The Ohio State U P, 1969. Print.

Baumann, Roland M. *Constructing Black Education at Oberlin College: A Documentary History*. Athens: Ohio U P, 2010. Print.

Becker, Mark P. "State of the University 2013." *Office of the President*. Georgia State University. 2 Oct. 2013. Web. 30 Dec. 2014. <http://president.gsu.edu/2013/10/02/state-of-the-university-2013/>.

Beere, Carole A., James C. Votruba, and Gail W. Wells. *Becoming an Engaged Campus: A Practical Guide for Institutionalizing Public Engagement*. San Francisco: Jossey-Bass, 2011. Print.

Bergmann, Linda S. "The Writing Center as Site for Engagement." *Going Public: What Writing Programs Learn from Engagement*. Ed. Shirley K Rose and Irwin Weiser. Logan: Utah State U P, 2010. 160–76. Print.

Berlin, James A. "Social-Epistemic Rhetoric, Ideology, and English Studies." *Rhetorics, Poetics, and Cultures: Refiguring College English Studies*. Urbana: NCTE, 1996. 77–94. Print.

Bjork, Olin, and John Pedro Schwartz. "Writing in the Wild: A Paradigm for Mobile Composition." *Going Wireless: A Critical Exploration of Wireless and Mobile Technologies for Composition Teachers and Researchers*. Ed. Amy C. Kimme Hea. Cresskill: Hampton Press, 2009. 223–38. Print.

Blodgett, Geoffrey. *Oberlin History: Essays and Impressions*. Kent: Kent State U P, 2006. Print.

Bousquet, Marc. *How the University Works: Higher Education and the Low-Wage Nation*. New York: NYU P, 2008. Print.

Boyer, Ernest L. "The Scholarship of Engagement." *The Journal of Public Service and Outreach* 1.1 (1996): 11–20. Print.

Broad, Bob. "Organic Matters: In Praise of Locally Grown Writing Assessment." *Organic Writing Assessment: Dynamic Criteria Mapping Action*. Ed. Bob Broad et al. Logan: Utah State U P, 2009. 1–13.

Cella, Laurie JC. "Introduction: Taking Stock of Our Past and Assessing the Future of Community Writing Work." *Unsustainable: Re-Imagining Community Literacy, Public Writing, Service-Learning, and the University*. Ed. Jessica Restaino and Laurie JC Cella. Lanham: Lexington Books, 2013. 1–16. Print.

"Chancellor." Syracuse University. Web. 30 Dec. 2014. <http://chancellor.syr.edu/chancellors/>.

"Chancellor James Roscoe Day Papers." *Syracuse University Archives.* Web. 25 July 2016. <http://archives.syr.edu/collections/chancellors/sua_day_jr.htm>.

Chaput, Catherine. *Inside the Teaching Machine: Rhetoric and the Globalization of the U.S. Public Research University.* Tuscaloosa: U of Alabama P, 2008. Print.

"Classes Canceled: Monday, March 4." Office of Communications, Oberlin College. *The Source.* 4 Mar. 2013. Web. 17 June 2013. <https://oncampus.oberlin.edu/source/articles/2013/03/04/classes-canceled-monday-march-4-2013>.

Claycomb, Ryan, and Rachel Riedner. "Cultural Studies, Rhetorical Studies, and Composition: Towards an Anti-Disciplinary Nexus." *Enculturation* 5.2 (2004). Web. <http://www.enculturation.net/5_2/claycomb-riedner.html>.

Colby, Anne, Thomas Elrich, Elizabeth Beaumont, and Jason Stephens. *Educating Citizens: Preparing America's Undergraduates for Lives of Moral and Civic Responsibility.* San Francisco: Jossey-Bass, 2003. Print.

Colby, Anne, Elizabeth Beaumont, Thomas Elrich, and Josh Corngold. *Educating for Democracy: Preparing Undergraduates for Responsible Political Engagement.* San Francisco: Jossey-Bass, 2007. Print.

Colleges of Agriculture at the Land Grant Universities: A Profile. Committee on the Future of the Colleges of Agriculture in the Land Grant University System. Washington: National Academy Press, 1995. Print.

"Community-Based Writing Program." *Department of Rhetoric and Composition.* Oberlin College. 11 Nov. 2011. Web. 2011. < http://new.oberlin.edu/arts-and-sciences/departments/rhetoric/writing-associates-program/community-based-writing-program.dot>.

Connors, Robert J. "Dreams and Play: Historical Method and Methodology." *Methods and Methodology in Composition Research.* Ed. Gesa Kirsch and Patricia A. Sullivan. Carbondale: Southern Illinois U P, 1992. 15–36. Print.

Coogan, David. "Service Learning and Social Change: The Case for Materialist Rhetoric." *College Composition and Communication* 57.4 (2006): 667–93. *JSTOR.* Web. 21 Mar. 2012.

Cooper, Jan. Personal Interview via Skype. 27 Apr. 2011.

Cooper, Jan, and Mary Garvin. "FYSP 116-01: Field-Based Writing Course Syllabus." Fall 2008. Shared via email correspondence.

Crump, Adrienne, and Elise Verzosa. "Visualizing Writing Space: A Reflection." *Kairos: A Journal of Rhetoric, Technology, and Pedagogy* 16.3 (2012). Web. 30 Dec. 2014. <http://kairos.technorhetoric.net/16.3/praxis/hea-et-al/crump-verzosa/index.html>.

"Current and Recent Course Offerings." *Writing Program.* Syracuse University. Spring 2012. Web. 28 Mar. 2012. <http://wrt.syr.edu/course offerings/index.html>.
Cushman, Ellen. "The Rhetorician as an Agent of Social Change." *College Composition and Communication* 47.1 (1996): 7–28. *JSTOR.* Web. 22 Jan. 2010.
———. "Sustainable Service Learning Programs." *College Composition and Communication* 54.1 (2002): 40–65.
Cushman, Ellen, and Chalon Emmons. "Contact Zones Made Real." *School's Out: Bridging Out-of-School Literacies with Classroom Practice.* Ed. Glynda Hull and Katherine Schultz. New York: Teachers College Press, 2002. 203–32. Print.
Cushman, Ellen, and Erik Green. "Knowledge Work with the Cherokee Nation: The Pedagogy of Engaging Publics in a Praxis of New Media." *The Public Work of Rhetoric: Citizen-Scholars and Civic Engagement.* Ed. John M. Ackerman and David J. Coogan. Columbia: U of South Carolina P, 2010. 175–92. Print.
DeGenaro, William. "The Affective Dimensions of Service Learning." *Reflections: Writing, Service-Learning, and Community Literacy* 9.3 (Summer 2010): 192–220. Print.
Dewey, John. *Democracy and Education: An Introduction to the Philosophy of Education.* New York: Macmillan, 1916. Print.
Di Leo, Jeffrey R., Walter R. Jacobs, and Amy Lee. "The Sites of Pedagogy." *Symploke* 10.1-2 (2002): 7–12. *Project Muse.* Web. 23 Jan. 2010.
Dobrin, Sidney I., and Christian R. Weisser. *Natural Discourse: Toward Ecocomposition.* Albany: SUNY P, 2002. Print.
Donehower, Kim, Charlotte Hogg, and Eileen E. Schell. "Constructing Rural Literacies: Moving Beyond the Rhetorics of Lack, Lag, and the Rosy Past." *Rural Literacies.* Ed. Kim Donehower, Charlotte Hogg, and Eileen E. Schell. Carbondale: Southern Illinois U P, 2007. 1–36. Print.
"Enrollment." *Oberlin College Office of Institutional Research.* Oberlin College. 2015. Web. 18 June 2016. <http://oberlin.edu/instres/irhome/>.
"Fact Book 2014-2015." *Fact Book.* University of Arizona. 2014. Web. 18 June 2016. <http://factbook.arizona.edu/2014-15/at_a_glance>.
Fagerjord, Anders. "Between Place and Interface: Designing Situated Sound for the iPhone." *Computers and Composition* 28.3 (2011): 255–63.
"Fast Forward Syracuse." *Chancellor.* Syracuse University. 31 Dec. 2015. Web. 31 Dec. 2015. <http://chancellor.syr.edu/messages/m/fast-forward-syracuse.html>.

"Fast Forward Vision and Mission Statements." *Syracuse University*. April 2015. Web. 10 Aug. 2016. <http://fastforward.syr.edu/strategic-plan/vision-and-mission-statements/>.

Feigenbaum, Paul. "Tactics and Strategies of Relationship-Based Practice: Reassessing the Institutionalization of Community Literacy." *Community Literacy Journal* 5.2 (Spring 2011): 47–66. Web. 20 Feb. 2012.

Felten, Peter, and H-Dirksen L. Bauman. "Reframing Diversity and Student Engagement: Lessons from Deaf-Gain." *The Student Engagement Handbook: Practices in Higher Education*. Ed. Elisabeth Dunne and Derfel Owen. Bingley: Emerald Group Publishing, 2013. 367–79. Print.

Festinger, Leon. *A Theory of Cognitive Dissonance*. Stanford: Stanford U P, 1957. Print.

"The First Morrill Act (1862): Donating Public Lands for Colleges of Agriculture and Mechanic Arts." *Colleges of Agriculture at the Land Grant Universities: A Profile*. Committee on the Future of the Colleges of Agriculture in the Land Grant University System. Washington: National Academy Press, 1995. Print.

Fisher, Donald M. "Chief Bill Orange and the Saltine Warrior: A Cultural History of Indian Symbols and Imagery at Syracuse University." *Team Spirits: The Native American Mascots Controversy*. Ed. C. Richard King and Charles Fruehling Springwood. Lincoln: U of Nebraska P, 2001. 25–45. Print.

Fletcher, Robert Samuel. *A History of Oberlin College from Its Foundation through the Civil War*. Vol. 1. Oberlin: Oberlin College, 1943. Print.

Flower, Linda. *Community Literacy and the Rhetoric of Public Engagement*. Carbondale: Southern Illinois U P, 2008. Print.

Fodrey, Crystal. Personal Interview. 28 Apr. 2011.

Foucault, Michel. "Panopticism." *Discipline & Punish: The Birth of the Prison*. Trans. Alan Sheridan. 1975. New York: Vintage Books, 1995. 195–230. Print.

Fraser, Nancy. "Rethinking the Public Sphere: A Contribution to the Critique of Actually Existing Democracy." *Social Text* 25/26 (1990): 56–80.

Freeman, Elizabeth, et al. "Trigger Warnings Are Flawed." *Inside Higher Ed*. 29 May 2014. Web. 20 June 2014.

Galpin, W. Freeman. *Syracuse University: The Pioneer Days*. Vol. 1. Syracuse: Syracuse U P, 1952. Print.

Garvin, Mary C., and Jan Cooper, eds. *Living in the Vermilion River Watershed*. Chardon: POV Communications, 2008. Web. 8 Aug. 2013. <http://www.wrlandconservancy.org/vermillion/pdf/book.pdf>.

Gee, James Paul. *Good Video Games and Good Learning: Collected Essays on Video Games, Learning, and Literacy.* New York: Peter Lang, 2007. Print.

George, Diana, and Paula Mathieu. "A Place for the Dissident Press in a Rhetorical Education: 'Sending Up a Signal Flare in the Darkness'." *The Public Work of Rhetoric: Citizen-Scholars and Civic Engagement.* Ed. John M. Ackerman and David J. Coogan. Columbia: U South Carolina P, 2010. 247–66. Print.

Giberson, Greg A., and Thomas A. Moriarty, eds. *What We Are Becoming: Developments in Undergraduate Writing Majors.* Logan: Utah State U P, 2010. Print.

Ginzberg, Lori D. "The 'Joint Education of the Sexes': Oberlin's Original Vision." *Educating Men and Women Together: Coeducation in a Changing World.* Ed. Carol Lasser. Urbana: U of Illinois P, 1987. 67–80. Print.

Giroux, Henry A. "Cultural Studies, Public Pedagogy, and the Responsibility of Intellectuals." *Communication and Critical/Cultural Studies* 1.1 (2004): 59–79. *Communication & Mass Media Complete.* Web. 4 June 2010.

———. "Cultural Studies in Dark Times: Public Pedagogy and the Challenge of Neoliberalism." *Fast Capitalism* 1.2 (2005). www.fastcapitalism.com. Web. 4 Apr. 2011.

———. "Is There a Role for Critical Pedagogy in Language/Cultural Studies? An Interview with Henry A. Giroux." By Manuela Guilherme. 2006. *The Giroux Reader.* Ed. Christopher G. Robbins. Boulder: Paradigm, 2006. 181–95. Print.

———. "Mouse Power: Public Pedagogy, Cultural Studies, and the Challenge of Disney." 1999. *The Giroux Reader.* Ed. Christopher G. Robbins. Boulder: Paradigm, 2006. 219–30. Print.

———. "Neoliberalism as Public Pedagogy." *Handbook of Public Pedagogy: Education and Learning beyond Schooling.* Ed. Jennifer A. Sandlin, Brian D. Schultz, and Jake Burdick. New York: Routledge, 2010. 486–99. Print.

———. "Public Pedagogy and Rodent Politics: Cultural Studies and the Challenge of Disney." *Arizona Journal of Hispanic Cultural Studies* 2.1 (1998): 253–66. Print.

———. *Schooling and the Struggle for Public Life: Democracy's Promise and Education's Challenge.* 2nd ed. Boulder: Paradigm Publishers, 2005. Print.

Glenn, Cheryl. *Rhetoric Retold: Regendering the Tradition from Antiquity through the Renaissance.* Carbondale: Southern Illinois U P, 1997. Print.

"Goal 1." *Strategic Plan.* Georgia State University. 27 May 2013. <http://strategic.gsu.edu/preamble/goal-1/>.

Goggin, Peter, ed. *Rhetorics, Literacies, and Narratives of Sustainability.* New York: Routledge, 2009. Print.

Goldblatt, Eli. *Because We Live Here: Sponsoring Literacy beyond the College Curriculum.* Cresskill: Hampton, 2007. Print.

Gorney, Jeffrey. *Syracuse University: An Architectural Guide.* Syracuse: Syracuse U P, 2006. Print.

Grabill, Jeffrey T. *Writing Community Change: Designing Technologies for Citizen Action.* Cresskill: Hampton Press, 2007. Print.

Grabill, Jeffrey T., and Lynée Lewis Gaillet. "Writing Program Design in the Metropolitan University: Toward Constructing Community Partnerships." *Writing Program Administration* 25.3 (2002): 61–78. Print.

Guile, David, and Michael Young. "Transfer and Transition in Vocational Education." *Between School and Work: New Perspectives on Transfer and Boundary-Crossing.* Ed. Terttu Tuomi-Gröhn and Yrjö Engeström. Amsterdam: Pergamon, 2003. 63–84. Print.

Hall, Anne-Marie. "Expanding the Community: A Comprehensive Look at Outreach and Articulation." *The Writing Program Administrator's Resource: A Guide to Reflective Institutional Practice.* Ed. Stuart C. Brown and Theresa Enos. Mahwah: Lawrence Erlbaum, 2002. 315–30. Print.

———. Personal Interview. 18 Apr. 2011.

Hall, Anne-Marie, Amy C. Kimme Hea, Faith Kurtyka, and Ashley J. Holmes. "Ecologies of Writing Programs: A Heuristic for Building Sustainability." Writing Development in Higher Education (WDHE) Conference. London, England. June 2010.

Haraway, Donna "Situated Knowledges: The Science Question and the Privilege of Partial Perspective." *Technology and the Politics of Knowledge.* Ed. Andrew Feenberg and Alastair Hannay. Indianapolis: Indiana U P, 1995. 175–94. Print.

Hart, Ann Weaver. "Fall Semester Beginnings." *Executive Office of the President.* University of Arizona. 19 Sept. 2012. Web. 29 Dec. 2014. <http://president.arizona.edu/memos_letters/fall-semester-beginnings>.

Hartzog, Carol P. *Composition and the Academy: A Study of Writing Program Administration.* New York: MLA of America, 1986. Print.

Harvill, Richard A. "Arizona: Its University's Contributions to the Southwest." Newcomen Address. 25 Feb. 1953. Princeton U P: Newcomen Publications, 1953. Print.

Heilker, Paul. "Rhetoric Made Real: Civic Discourse and Writing Beyond the Curriculum." *Writing the Community: Concepts and Models for Service-Learning in Composition*. Ed. Linda Adler-Kassner, Robert Crooks, and Ann Watters. Washington: AAHE and NCTE, 1997. 71–78. Print.

"Hendricks Chapel: Home." Hendricks Chapel. *Syracuse University*. Web. 18 July 2011. <http://hendricks.syr.edu/>.

Hesse, Douglas. "Understanding Larger Discourses in Higher Education: Practical Advice for WPAs." *Allyn & Bacon Sourcebook for Writing Program Administrators*. Ed. Irene Ward and William Carpenter. Boston: Longman, 2002. 299–314. Print.

Holland, Barbara A. "Institutional Differences in Pursuing the Public Good." *Higher Education for the Public Good: Emerging Voices from a National Movement*. Ed. Adrianna J. Kezar, Tony C. Chambers, and John C. Burkhardt. San Francisco: Jossey-Bass, 2005. 235–59. Print.

Holmes, Ashley J. "Advancing Campus-Community Partnerships: Standpoint Theory and Course Re-Design." *Reflections: A Journal of Writing, Service-Learning, and Community Literacy* 8.3 (2009): 76–98. Print.

———. English 3120: Electronic Writing & Publishing. Syllabus. 2013. Web. 23 May 2014. <http://3120fall2013.wordpress.com/about/service-learning/>.

———. "Street Art as Public Pedagogy & Community Literacy: What Walls Can Teach Us." *Ubiquity: The Journal of Literature, Literacy, and the Arts*. 1.1 (Winter 2014). Web. 19 June 2016. <http://ed-ubiquity.gsu.edu/wordpress/holmes-1-1/>

———. "Virtual Volunteerism: Review of *LibriVox* and *VolunteerMatch*." *Community Literacy Journal* 6.1 (Fall 2011).

———. "Write on Location: A Place-Based Approach to Mobile Composition." *Mobile Technologies and the Writing Classroom: Resources for Teachers*. Ed. Claire Lutkewitte. Urbana: NCTE, 2016. 179–93. Print.

hooks, bell. *Teaching to Transgress: Education as the Practice of Freedom*. New York: Routledge, 2000. Print.

Howard, Rebecca Moore. "Curricular Activism: The Writing Major as Counterdiscourse." *Composition Studies* 35.1 (2007): 41–52. EBSCOhost. Web. 1 Dec. 2010.

Illich, Ivan. "Phenomenology of School." *Deschooling Society*. New York: Harper and Row, 1971. 25–33. Print.

Inter Tribal Council of Arizona. Web. 21 July 2016. <http://itcaonline.com/>.

Jarratt, Susan. *Rereading the Sophists: Classical Rhetoric Refigured*. Carbondale: Southern Illinois U P, 1998. Print.

Juarez, Marissa M. "A Visual-Spatial Approach to Spontaneous Composing in First-Year Composition." *Kairos: A Journal of Rhetoric, Technol-

ogy, and Pedagogy 16.3 (2012). Web. 30 Dec. 2014. <http://kairos .technorhetoric.net/16.3/praxis/hea-et-al/juarez/index.html>.

Karpiak, Irene E. "Evolutionary Theory and the 'New Sciences': Rekindling Our Imagination for Transformation." *Studies in Continuing Education* 22.1 (2000): 29–44. *EBSCOhost Academic Search Complete*. Web. 9 June 2013.

Keller, Christopher J., and Christian R. Weisser, eds. *The Locations of Composition*. Albany: SUNY P, 2007. Print.

Kezar, Adrianna J., Tony C. Chambers, and John C. Burkhardt. *Higher Education for the Public Good: Emerging Voices from a National Movement*. San Francisco: Jossey-Bass, 2005. Print.

Kimme Hea, Amy C., ed. *Going Wireless: A Critical Exploration of Wireless and Mobile Technologies for Composition Teachers and Researchers*. Cresskill: Hampton Press, 2009. Print.

———. Personal Interview. 4 May 2011.

Kimme Hea, Amy C., et al. "Space, Event, Movement: Reflections on a Spatial and Visual Rhetorics Graduate Course." *Kairos: A Journal of Rhetoric, Technology, and Pedagogy* 16.3 (2012). Web. 30 Dec. 2014. <http://kairos.technorhetoric.net/16.3/praxis/hea-et-al/index.html>.

King, C. Richard, and Charles Fruehling Springwood, eds. *Team Spirits: The Native American Mascots Controversy*. Lincoln: U of Nebraska P, 2001. Print.

Krislov, Marvin. "2008 State-of-the-College Address." Oberlin College & Conservatory. 2008. Web. 29 Dec. 2014. <http://new.oberlin.edu/ events-activities/commencement/speech-2008presidentialaddress .dot>.

Kurtyka, Faith. Personal Interview. 27 Apr. 2011.

Lasser, Carol, ed. *Educating Men and Women Together: Coeducation in a Changing World*. Urbana: U of Illinois P, 1987. Print.

L'Eplattenier, Barbara. "Finding Ourselves in the Past: An Argument for Historical Work on WPAs." *The Writing Program Administrator as Researcher: Inquiry in Action & Reflection*. Ed. Shirley K Rose and Irwin Weiser. Portsmouth: Boynton/Cook, 1999. 131–39. Print.

L'Eplattenier, Barbara, and Lisa Mastrangelo, eds. *Historical Studies of Writing Program Administration: Individuals, Communities, and the Formation of a Discipline*. West Lafayette: Parlor Press, 2004. Print.

Long, Elenore. *Community Literacy and the Rhetoric of Local Publics*. West Lafayette: Parlor Press, 2008. Print.

Løvlie, Anders Sundnes. "Annotative Locative Media and G-P-S: Granularity, Participation, and Serendipity." *Computers and Composition* 28.3 (2011): 246–54.

Luce, A. V. Personal Interview. 8 Mar. 2011.

Lutkewitte, Claire, ed. *Mobile Technologies and the Writing Classroom: Resources for Teachers*. Urbana: NCTE, 2016.

Martin, Douglas D. *The Lamp in the Desert: The Story of the University of Arizona*. Tucson: U of Arizona P, 1960. Print.

Mathieu, Paula. "After Tactics, What Comes Next?" *Unsustainable: Re-Imagining Community Literacy, Public Writing, Service-Learning, and the University*. Ed. Jessica Restaino and Laurie JC Cella. Lanham: Lexington Books, 2013. 17–32. Print.

———. *Tactics of Hope: The Public Turn in English Composition*. Portsmouth: Heinemann, 2005. Print.

Mattingly, Justin. "Student Protestors Meet with Senior Administrators Sunday Night, Continue Negotiations." *Daily Orange*. 10 Nov. 2014. Web. 30 Dec. 2014. <http://www.dailyorange.com/2014/11/student-protesters-meet-with-senior-administrators-sunday-night-continue-negotiations/>.

Mauk, Johnathon. "Location, Location, Location: The Real (E)states of Being, Writing, and Thinking in Composition." *College English* 65.4 (2003): 368–88. *JSTOR*. Web. 27 Nov. 2009.

McAllister, Ken S. *Game Work: Language, Power, and Computer Game Culture*. Tuscaloosa: U of Alabama P, 2006. Print.

McClennen, Sophia A. *America According to Colbert: Satire as Public Pedagogy*. New York: Palgrave Macmillan, 2011. Print.

McDowell, George R. *Land-Grant Universities and Extension into the 21st Century: Renegotiating or Abandoning a Social Contract*. Ames: Iowa State U P, 2011. Print.

McGee, Michael Calvin. "The 'Ideograph': A Link Between Rhetoric and Ideology." *Landmark Essays on Contemporary Rhetoric*. Ed. Thomas B. Farrell. Mahwah: Lawrence Erlbaum, 1998. 85–102. Print.

McGregor, Sue L. T. "Transformative Education: Grief and Growth." *Narrating Transformative Learning in Education*. Ed. Morgan Gardner and Ursula Kelly. New York: Palgrave Macmillan, 2008. 51–74. Print.

Medina, Jennifer. "Warning: The Literary Canon Could Make Students Squirm." *New York Times*. 17 May 2014. Web. 1 June 2014.

Mezirow, Jack. *Learning as Transformation: Critical Perspectives on a Theory in Progress*. San Francisco: Jossey-Bass, 2000. Print.

———. *Transformative Dimensions of Adult Learning*. San Francisco: Jossey-Bass, 1991. Print.

Minnix, Christopher, and Carol Nowotny-Young, eds. *Writing Public Lives: From Personal Interests to Public Rhetoric*. Plymouth: Hayden-McNeil, 2010.

Mirtz, Ruth M. "WPAs as Historians: Discovering a First-Year Writing Program by Researching Its Past." *The Writing Program Administrator as Researcher: Inquiry in Action & Reflection.* Ed. Shirley K Rose and Irwin Weiser. Portsmouth: Boynton/Cook, 1999. 119–30. Print.

Moore, Jessie L., and Michael Strickland. "Wearing Multiple Hats: How Campus WPA Roles Can Inform Program-Specific Writing Designs." *Going Public: What Writing Programs Learn from Engagement.* Ed. Shirley K Rose and Irwin Weiser. Logan: Utah State U P, 2010. 122–39. Print.

Mortensen, Peter. "Going Public." *College Composition and Communication* 50.2 (1998): 182–205. *JSTOR.* Web. 23 Jan. 2010.

Morton, Keith. "The Irony of Service: Charity, Project, and Social Change in Service-Learning." *Writing and Community Engagement: A Critical Sourcebook.* Ed. Thomas Deans, Barbara Roswell, and Adrian J. Wurr. Boston: Bedford St. Martin's, 2010. 117–37. Print.

Mulhere, Kaitlin. "Fast Forward or Rewind?" *Inside Higher Ed.* 5 Nov. 2014. Web. 30 Dec. 2014. <https://www.insidehighered.com/news/2014/11/05/syracuse-students-sit-demand-changes>.

Myers, Nancy. "Relocating Knowledge: The Textual Authority of *Classical Rhetoric for the Modern Student.*" *The Locations of Composition.* Ed. Christopher J. Keller and Christian R. Weisser. New York: SUNY P, 2007. 229–50. Print.

National Association of State Universities and Land-Grant Colleges. *Serving the World: The People and Ideas of America's State and Land-Grant Universities.* Washington: National Association of State Universities and Land-Grant Colleges, 1987. Print.

"Native American Student Affairs." *University of Arizona.* Web. 20 Aug. 2011. <http://nasa.arizona.edu/>.

"Ninde Scholars Program." Oberlin College. 23 Nov. 2011. Web. 2011. <https://new.oberlin.edu/office/bonner-center/bcsl-programs/ninde-scholar/ninde-scholar.dot/>.

North, Stephen M. *The Making of Knowledge in Composition: Portrait of an Emerging Field.* Upper Montclair: Boynton/Cook, 1987. Print.

O'Malley, Michael P., Jennifer A. Sandlin, and Jake Burdick. "Public Pedagogy." *Encyclopedia of Curriculum Studies.* Ed. Craig Kridel. Thousand Oaks: SAGE, 2010. 697–701. *SAGE Reference Online.* Web. 7 Mar. 2012.

Owens, Derek. *Composition and Sustainability: Teaching for a Threatened Generation.* Urbana: NCTE, 2001. Print.

Parks, Steve. *Gravyland: Writing Beyond the Curriculum in the City of Brotherly Love.* Syracuse: Syracuse U P, 2010. Print.

———. Personal Interview. 7 Mar. 2011.
Parks, Steve, and Eli Goldblatt. "Writing Beyond the Curriculum: Fostering New Collaborations in Literacy." *College English* 62.5 (2000): 584–606. *JSTOR*. Web. 29 Mar. 2010.
Pérez-Peña, Richard, and Trip Gabriel. "Racist Incidents Stun Campus and Halt Classes at Oberlin." *New York Times*. 4 Mar. 2013. Web. 17 June 2013.
Phelps, Louise Wetherbee. "Telling a Writing Program Its Own Story: A Tenth-Anniversary Speech." *The Writing Program Administrator as Researcher: Inquiry in Action & Reflection*. Ed. Shirley K Rose and Irwin Weiser. Portsmouth: Boynton/Cook, 1999. 168–84. Print.
Phillips, Richard L., and Donald G. Wright. *Hendricks Chapel: Seventy-Five Years of Service to Syracuse University*. Syracuse: Syracuse U P, 2005. Print.
Piaget, Jean. *Six Psychological Studies*. Trans. Anita Tenzer. Ed. David Elkind. New York: Random House, 1967. Print.
Pigg, Stacey. "Emplacing Mobile Composing Habits: A Study of Academic Writing in Networked Social Spaces." *College Composition and Communication* 66.2 (Dec. 2014): 250–75.
Pisani, Elizabeth. *The Wisdom of Whores: Bureaucrats, Brothels, and the Business of AIDS*. London: Granta Books, 2008. Print.
Portman-Daley, Joannah. "Subtle Democracy: Public Pedagogy and Social Media." *Currents in Electronic Literacy*. Aug. 2013. Web. <http://currents.cwrl.utexas.edu/2013/subtle-democracy-public-pedagogy-and-social-media>.
Reid, Alex. "Social Media, Public Pedagogy, and the End of Private Learning." *Handbook of Public Pedagogy: Education and Learning Beyond Schooling*. Ed. Jennifer A. Sandlin, Brian D. Schultz, and Jake Burdick. New York: Routledge, 2010. 194–200. Print.
Reid, E. Shelley. "A Changing for the Better: Curriculum Revision as Reflective Practice in Teaching and Administration." *WPA* 26.3 (2003): 10–27. Web. 6 Feb. 2010.
Restaino, Jessica. "Conclusion: Rejecting Binaries and Rethinking Relationships." *Unsustainable: Re-Imagining Community Literacy, Public Writing, Service-Learning, and the University*. Ed. Jessica Restaino and Laurie JC Cella. Lanham: Lexington Books, 2013. 253–62. Print.
Restaino, Jessica, and Laurie JC Cella. *Unsustainable: Re-imagining Community Literacy, Public Writing, Service-Learning, and the University*. Lanham: Lexington Books, 2013. Print.
Reynolds, Nedra. *Geographies of Writing: Inhabiting Places and Encountering Difference*. Carbondale: Southern Illinois U P, 2004. Print.

Richards, Rebecca. "'I Could Have Told You *That* Wouldn't Work': A Cyberfeminist Pedagogy in Action." *Feminist Teacher* 22.1 (2011): 5–22. *JSTOR*. Web. 14 June 2013.

———. Personal Interview. 20 Apr. 2011.

Riedner, Rachel, and Kevin Mahoney. *Democracies to Come: Rhetorical Action, Neoliberalism, and Communities of Resistance*. Lanham: Lexington Books, 2008. Print.

Rincon, Frank Legleu. *Factors Related to the Founding and Development of Special Purpose Private Institutions of Higher Education*. Diss. U of Arizona, 1982. *ProQuest*. Web. 13 July 2011.

Ritter, Kelly. "Extra-Institutional Agency and the Public Value of the WPA." *WPA* 29.3 (2006): 45–64. <http://www.wpacouncil.org/archives/29n3/29-3-ritter.pdf>. Web. 6 Feb. 2010.

Ropers-Huilman, Rebecca. "Scholarship on the Other Side: Power and Caring in Feminist Education." *NWSA Journal* 11.1 (1999): 118–35. *JSTOR*. Web. 14 Feb. 2013.

Rose, Shirley K. "Preserving Our Histories of Institutional Change: Enabling Research in the Writing Program Archives." *The Writing Program Administrator as Researcher: Inquiry in Action & Reflection*. Ed. Shirley K Rose and Irwin Weiser. Portsmouth: Boynton/Cook, 1999. 107–18. Print.

Rose, Shirley K, and Irwin Weiser, eds. *Going Public: What Writing Programs Learn from Engagement*. Logan: Utah State U P, 2010. Print.

Royster, Jacqueline Jones, and Gesa E. Kirsch, eds. *Feminist Rhetorical Practices: New Directions in Rhetoric, Composition, and Literacy Studies*. Carbondale: Southern Illinois University Press, 2012. Print.

Ryder, Phyllis. *Rhetorics for Community Action: Public Writing and Writing Publics*. Lanham: Lexington Books, 2011. Print.

Sandlin, Jennifer A., Michael P. O'Malley, and Jake Burdick. "Mapping the Complexity of Public Pedagogy Scholarship: 1894–2010." *Review of Educational Research* 81.3 (2011): 338–75. Print.

Sandlin, Jennifer A., Brian D. Schultz, and Jake Burdick, eds. *Handbook of Public Pedagogy: Education and Learning Beyond Schooling*. New York: Routledge, 2010. Print.

Sandy, Marie, and Barbara A. Holland. "Different Worlds and Common Ground: Community Partner Perspectives on Campus-Community Partnerships." *Michigan Journal of Community Service Learning* 13.1 (Fall 2006): 30–43. Print.

Savage, Glenn C. "Problematizing 'Public Pedagogy' in Educational Research." *Handbook of Public Pedagogy: Education and Learning beyond*

Schooling. Ed. Jennifer A. Sandlin, Brian D. Schultz, and Jake Burdick. New York: Routledge, 2010. 103–15. Print.

Schmidt, Christopher. "The New Media Writer as Cartographer." *Computers and Composition* 28.4 (2011): 303–14.

Schneider, Barbara. "Uncommon Ground: Narcissistic Reading and Material Racism." *The Norton Book of Composition Studies.* Ed. Susan Miller. New York: Norton, 2009. 919–32. Print.

Schön, Donald. *The Reflective Practitioner: How Professionals Think in Action.* New York: Basic Books, 1984. Print.

Schubert, William H. "Outside Curricula and Public Pedagogy." *Handbook of Public Pedagogy: Education and Learning Beyond Schooling.* Ed. Jennifer A. Sandlin, Brian D. Schultz, and Jake Burdick. New York: Routledge, 2010. 10–19. Print.

Scott, Sue M. "The Grieving Soul in the Transformation Process." *New Directions for Adult and Continuing Education* 74 (1997): 41–50. EBSCOhost Academic Search Complete. Web. 10 June 2013.

Smalley, Frank, ed. *The Golden Jubilee of Syracuse University 1870–1920.* Geneva: W. F. Humphrey, 1920. Print.

Solomon, Barbara Miller. "The Oberlin Model and Its Impact on Other Colleges." *Educating Men and Women Together: Coeducation in a Changing World.* Ed. Carol Lasser. Urbana: U of Illinois P, 1987. Print.

Sonnichsen, C. L. *Tucson: The Life and Times of an American City.* Norman: U of Oklahoma P, 1982. Print.

Stoecker, Randy, and Elizabeth A. Tryon, eds. *The Unheard Voices: Community Organizations and Service Learning.* Philadelphia: Temple U P, 2009. Print.

Strickland, Donna. *The Managerial Unconscious in the History of Composition Studies.* Carbondale: Southern Illinois U P, 2011. Print.

"SU as Anchor Institution." Syracuse University. Web. 30 Dec. 2014. <http://www.syr.edu/suanchorinstitution/>.

"SU Facts 2015-2016." Syracuse University. 2015. Web. 18 Feb. 2016. <http://www.syr.edu/about/facts.html>.

"Syllabus WRT205 M081: Critical Research and Inquiry." A.V. Luce. Spring 2011. Web. 8 Aug. 2013.

"Syracuse University Bylaws." *Syracuse University Policies.* Syracuse University. 14 May 2011. Web. 28 Mar. 2012. < http://supolicies.syr.edu/ethics/bylaws.htm>.

"Syracuse University History." *Syracuse University Archives.* Syracuse University. 2010. Web. 10 July 2011. < http://archives.syr.edu/history>.

Syverud, Kent. "Chancellor Inauguration." Syracuse University. 2014.

Web. 29 Dec. 2014. <http://inauguration.syr.edu/remarks/transcripts/chancellor_syverud.html>.

Trubek, Anne. Personal Interview via Skype. 25 Apr. 2011.

Tuomi-Gröhn, Terttu, and Yrjö Engeström. "Conceptualizing Transfer: From Standard Notions to Developmental Perspectives." *Between School and Work: New Perspectives on Transfer and Boundary-Crossing.* Ed. Terttu Tuomi-Gröhn and Yrjö Engeström. Amsterdam: Pergamon, 2003. 19–38. Print.

"UA History & Traditions." University of Arizona. 2011. Web. 30 July 2011. < http://www.arizona.edu/about/ua-history-traditions>.

"Unit 1 Assignment Sheet: Rhetorical Analysis." Crystal Fodrey. English 102. Spring 2012. Shared via email correspondence.

"Unit 2 Assignment Sheet: Research Essay." Crystal Fodrey. English 306. Spring 2011. Shared via email correspondence.

"*U.S. News & World Report*" Rankings. Web. Accessed 18 June 2016. <http://colleges.usnews.rankingsandreviews.com/best-colleges>

Vinson, Jenna. "Spatial Shock: Place, Space, and the Politics of Representation." *Kairos: A Journal of Rhetoric, Technology, and Pedagogy* 16.3 (2012). Web. 14 July 2015. <http://kairos.technorhetoric.net/16.3/praxis/hea-et-al/vinson/index.html>.

Warner, Michael. *Publics and Counterpublics.* New York: Zone Books, 2005. Print.

Weisser, Christian R. *Moving Beyond Academic Discourse: Composition Studies and the Public Sphere.* Carbondale: Southern Illinois U P, 2002. Print.

Welch, Nancy. *Living Room: Teaching Public Writing in a Privatized World.* Portsmouth: Boynton/Cook, Heinemann, 2008. Print.

Wells, Jaclyn M. "Writing Program Administration and Community Engagement: A Bibliographic Essay." *Going Public: What Writing Programs Learn from Engagement.* Ed. Shirley K Rose and Irwin Weiser. Logan: Utah State U P, 2010. 237–55. Print.

Wells, Susan. "Claiming the Archive for Rhetoric and Composition." *Rhetoric and Composition as Intellectual Work.* Ed. Gary A. Olson. Carbondale: Southern Illinois State U P, 2002. 55–64. Print.

———. "Rogue Cops and Healthcare: What Do We Want from Public Writing?" *College Composition and Communication* 47.3 (1996): 325–41. *JSTOR.* Web. 6 Mar. 2010.

Wendler, Rachael. Personal Interview. 27 Apr. 2011.

Wharton-Michael, Patty, et al. "An Explication of Public Scholarship Objectives." *New Directions for Teaching and Learning* 105 (2006): 63–72. *Wiley InterScience.* Web. 1 Sept. 2011.

"Who We Are." Campus Compact. 3 Dec. 2011. Web. 2011. <http://www.compact.org/about/history-mission-vision/>.

Wiggins, Grant and Jay McTighe. *Understanding by Design*. Expanded 2nd ed. Alexandria: Association for Supervision and Curriculum Development, 2005. Print.

Wolf, Thia, Jill Swiencicki, and Chris Fosen. "Students, Faculty, and 'Sustainable' WPA Work." *Going Public: What Writing Programs Learn from Engagement*. Ed. Shirley K Rose and Irwin Weiser. Logan: Utah State U P, 2010. 140–59. Print.

Worsham, Lynn. "Going Postal: Pedagogic Violence and the Schooling of Emotion." *The Norton Book of Composition Studies*. Ed. Susan Miller. New York: Norton, 2009. 999–1031. Print.

"Writing Associates Program." *Department of Rhetoric and Composition*. Oberlin College. 23 Nov. 2011. Web. 2011. < http://new.oberlin.edu/arts-and-sciences/departments/rhetoric/writing-associates-program/>.

Yancey, Kathleen Blake. *Reflection in the Writing Classroom*. Logan: Utah State U P, 1998. Print.

INDEX

Note: throughout the index, Oberlin, Syracuse, and Arizona refer to Oberlin College, Syracuse University, and University of Arizona, respectively.

academic/public binary, 65–66
Ackerman, John M., ix, 20–21
Adler-Kassner, Linda, 98
administration and administrative methods. *See* writing program administration
affect and emotional responses
   Arizona business course example, 142–48
   Georgia State University Public Rhetorics of Social Change example, 152–55
   public vs. private and, 131
   reciprocal model of care, 149–56
   risks and rewards of going public and, 134–36, 141
   transformative learning theory and, 136–40
   trigger warnings and, 132–33, 152
   undertheorization of, 137
African American admissions, 118–20
Alexander, Robin, 10
Althusser, Louis, 102
Anson, Chris, 99, 107
Arbogast, Bo, 78–80, 172n7
Arizona, state of, 173n9
Arizona, University of. *See* University of Arizona
Ash, Sarah L., 174n3
assessment, 89, 93–94

Atkinson, Maxine P., 174n3
audience, 43, 55, 143–44
authority
   decentering, 26, 150–51, 152
   textual, 101

backwards design, 170n5(ch2)
Bakhtin, Mikhail, 101
Ball, Phyllis, 122, 173nn5–6
Barnard, John, 114–15
Bauman, H-Dirksen L., 134
Baumann, Roland M., 115, 119–20
Beaumont, Elizabeth, 67
Becker, Mark P., 128–29
Beere, Carole A., 67–68
Bergmann, Linda S., 80
Berlin, James, 12
binaries, 21–23, 65–67
Bjork, Olin, 158
Blodgett, Geoffrey, 101, 109, 112, 116–17, 118–19
blogging, 143–44
boundary crossing, 20–21, 34
Bousquet, Marc, 16
Boyer, Ernest L., 160
Broad, Bob, 94
Brown, Robert L., Jr., 99, 107
Burdick, Jake, 10–11, 19
Burkhardt, John C., 106
"business as usual" (BAU), 74

Campus Compact, 67, 70, 171nn2–4
Cantor, Nancy, 106, 130, 173n2
care, reciprocal model of, 149–56
Cella, Laurie JC, 65–66, 72–73, 76
Certeau, Michel de, x
Chambers, Tony C., 106
Chaput, Catherine, 101–2, 105
charity as religious value, 111–12
Chief Bill Orange mascot (Syracuse), 124–25
Christianity, 111–16, 117–18, 173n3
civic writing, 5–6, 13, 169n1
Civil War, 173n8
classroom space, traditional, importance of, 27–28
Claycomb, Ryan, 14
Clayton, Patti, 174n3
coeducation in institutional histories, 116–18
cognitive dissonance, 137
Colbert, Stephen, 12
Colby, Anne, 67
community-based vs. institutionalized models, in writing program administration, 67–71
Community Literacy and the Rhetoric of Local Publics (Long), 35–38
Conference on College Composition and Communication (CCCC), 1, 4
Connors, Robert J., 108, 128
Coogan, David J., 20–21, 127
Cooper, Jan, 34, 38, 39–44, 50, 51, 55, 57, 61–62, 134, 170n2
Corngold, Josh, 67
corporations, neoliberal, 11–17
counterpublics, 17–18, 37
course sequencing, 81–88
critical analysis, 5–6, 12
Crump, Adrienne, 92
cultural studies, 12, 14
"culture of changing," 74–75
curriculum design, allowing for morphing in, 71–75, 84–85

Cushman, Ellen, 23, 73, 79, 97, 139, 150, 172n6

DeGenaro, William, 137, 138–39
Dewey, John, 13, 19
digitality and mobile composition, 159
digital publics, 29–30
digital spaces and physical/local spaces, continuum of, 59–62
Di Leo, Jeffrey R., 18
disorienting dilemmas, 136–37, 139, 142–48, 153–55
Dobrin, Sidney I., 73
Donehower, Kim, 18

Elrich, Thomas, 67
Emmons, Challon, 23
emotions. *See* affect and emotional responses
engagement, student, 134–35
Engeström, Yrjö, 135
ethics, transformative learning and, 140

Fagerjord, Anders, 159
Fairchild, James H., 114
Feigenbaum, Paul, x, 69
Felten, Peter, 134
feminist historiography, 108–11
feminist pedagogies, 148–54
Festinger, Leon, 137
Finney, Charles, 114, 119
First-Year Writing Showcase (Arizona), 91–92
Fisher, Donald M., 125
Fletcher, Robert Samuel, 112
Flower, Linda, 2, 127, 152
Fodrey, Crystal, 34, 38, 50–57, 134
Fosen, Chris, 74
Foucault, Michel, 103
Fraser, Nancy, 17
Freeman, Elizabeth, 152

Gabriel, Trip, xi
Gaillet, Lynée Lewis, 64
Galpin, W. Freeman, 113
Garvin, Mary, 34, 38, 39–44, 50, 51, 55, 61–62, 170n2
Gee, James Paul, 57
geographies of writing, 19–20. *See also* relocation
George, Diana, 92
Georgia State University, 128–29, 152–55
Giberson, Greg A., 87
Ginzberg, Laurie D., 114, 116–17
Giroux, Henry A., viii, 5, 11–17, 29, 34–35, 44, 50, 56, 102, 156
Glenn, Cheryl, 109
Goggin, Peter, 73
Goldblatt, Eli, 2, 64, 86
Gorney, Jeffrey, 118
Grabill Jeffrey T., 29–30, 64
Green, Erik, 139
Guile, David, 135
Guilherme, Manuela, 156

Habermas, Jürgen, 17
Hall, Anne-Marie, 64, 73, 79, 88–94, 172nn8–9
Haraway, Donna, 109
Hart, Ann Weaver, 105–6
Hartzog, Carol P., 7, 8
Harvill, Richard A., 123, 126
Heilker, Paul, 23
Hesse, Doug, 99
histories, institutional
    African American admissions, 118–21
    coeducation, 116–18
    empowerment, contested agency, and, 127
    land-grant legacy, 121–24
    mission and vision statements, 100–107, 123–24, 126–30
    Native American relations, 124–27
    "onward and upward" and "Golden Age" approaches to, 101, 109
    religion and morality, historical values of, 111–16
    rhetorical power of constructing, 97–99, 107
    scholarship on, 97, 98–99
    speeches by leaders, 104–6, 107–8, 113, 123, 128–29
    storytelling, partiality, and feminist historiography, 107–11
    WPAs and use of, 98–99, 115–16, 120–21
HIV/AIDS issues, 45–50
Hogg, Charlotte, 18
Holland, Barbara A., 7–8, 175n5
Holmes, Ashley J., 17, 92, 151–52, 159, 170n5
hooks, bell, 151
Howard, Rebecca Moore, 87

ideographs, 102–3, 112
Illich, Ivan, 19
inequality analysis, 52–54
inquiry-driven pedagogies
    in Long's schema, 36, 37–38
    in Oberlin Field-Based Writing course, 41, 42–44
    in Syracuse Critical Research and Inquiry course, 46, 49
Institute for the Study of Literature, Literacy, and Culture, Temple University, 86
institutional histories. *See* histories, institutional
institutionalization, 67–71, 87–88
institutional pedagogies
    in Arizona spatial analysis composition courses, 52, 55
    in Long's schema, 36–37
    in Oberlin Field-Based Writing course, 41, 42
    in Syracuse Critical Research and Inquiry course, 46, 48–49
interpretive pedagogies

in Arizona spatial analysis
composition courses, 52, 54–55
in Long's schema, 35–36
in Oberlin Field-Based Writing
course, 40–42
in Syracuse Critical Research and
Inquiry course, 46–48

Jacobs, Walter R., 18
Jarratt, Susan, 109–10
Juarez, Marissa M., 92

Karpiak, Irene I., 140
Keep, John, 119
Keller, Christopher J., 56
Kezar, Adrianna, 106
Kimme Hea, Amy C., 88–89, 91–92, 158, 172n8
King, C. Richard, 173n9
Kirsch, Gesa E., 108–11
knowledge
academic vs. public, 5
excavating in everyday lives, 58
Long's institutional pedagogies and, 37
public and academic, reciprocal value of, 58
publication and, 54–55
risk and, 135
spatial analysis and public knowledge, 50–51
transformative learning and transfer of, 135
Krislov, Martin, 104
Kurtyka, Faith, 91–92, 141

land-grant institutional legacy, 121–24
Lasser, Carol, 117
learning, transformative. *See* transformative learning
learning and relocation, 18–19. *See also* public pedagogy; relocation
Lee, Amy, 18
L'Eplattenier, Barbara, 98
Lincoln, Abraham, 173n5

Living in the Vermilion Watershed (Cooper and Garvin), 40, 42–43
Long, Elenore, 35–38, 40, 43, 46, 49, 52, 54–56, 58–59, 62, 96, 170n1(ch2)
Løvlie, Anders Sundnes, 159
Luce, A. V., 34, 38, 44–50, 51, 57–58, 170nn3–4
Lutkewitte, Claire, 158
Lyons, Oren, 125

Mahan, Asa, 118–19
Mahoney, Kevin, 14, 33
Mansfeld, Jacob S., 122
Martin, Douglas D., 122
mascots, 124–27
Mastrangelo, Lisa, 98
Mathieu, Paula, x, 2, 20, 66–69, 72, 73, 76, 77, 79, 81, 88, 92
Mattingly, Justin, 130
Mauk, Johnathon, 19–20, 56
McAllister, Ken S., 57
McClennen, Sophia A., 12
McCombe, John H., 114
McDowell, George R., 123
McGee, Michael, 102
McGregor, Sue L. T., 137–38, 140, 149, 151
McTighe, Jay, 170n5
Medina, Jennifer, 132
Mezirow, Jack, 136–40, 142, 145, 174n1, 174n3, 175n6
Minnix, Christopher, 93
Mirtz, Ruth M., 98
mission statements, 100–107, 123–24, 126–27, 129–30, 161–65
mobile composition, 158–59
Moore, Jessie L., 90
Morgan, John, 118–19
Moriarty, Thomas A., 87
morphing
curriculum design for writing programs and, 71–75, 84–85
Oberlin Community-Based Writing Program and, 77–81

Syracuse Writing Program and, 84–85
Morrill, Justin Smith, 123
Morrill Act (1862), 122–23, 173n7
Mortensen, Peter, 1
Morton, Keith, 111–12
Mulhere, Kaitlin, 130
Myers, Nancy, 101

Native American relations, 124–27, 173n9–174n10
neoliberalism, viii–ix, 12–17, 50
"next step" course sequencing, 81–88
Ninde Scholars Program (Oberlin), 76, 78–81
North, Stephen M., 108
Nowotny-Young, Carol, 92

Oberlin College
  African American admissions, 118–20
  coeducational history, 116–18
  Community-Based Writing Program (CBWP) and Ninde Scholars Program, 76–81
  comparative data, 9
  Field-Based Writing: Ecology of the Vermilion River Watershed, 39–44, 61–62
  hate-related incidents and media coverage, xi
  mission statement, 100–101, 102–4, 161–62
  religious history, 112
  Writing Associates Program, 76–77, 172n7
observational skills, 39–41
O'Malley, Michael P., 10–11
oppositional public spheres, 16
OrangeAID (Syracuse), 45–50
Owens, Derek, 73

Parks, Steve, 64, 82–86, 93
partiality, 108, 109–10
Pérez-Peña, Richard, xi

performative pedagogies, 36, 38
personal-public intersections, 54
perspective transformation, 136, 139
Phelps, Louise Wetherbee, 107–8
Phillips, Richard L., 114
Piaget, Jean, 137
Pigg, Stacey, 158–59
Pisani, Elizabeth, 48
place and space
  aligning educational purposes with location, 59–62
  critical analysis and, 34–35
  Long and local publics, 58–59
  spatial analysis in Arizona composition courses, 50–56
  See also relocation
planning, pedagogical
  aligning location with educational purposes, 59–62
  backwards design, 170n5(ch2)
  morphing in curriculum design, allowing for, 71–75, 84–85
Portman-Daley, Joannah, 29
postmodern historiography, 109
Pratt, Mary Louise, 23
productive tensions
  administrative approach and, 63
  curriculum design and, 71–74, 76, 82, 84–85
  disorientation and, 148
  risk and safety, 135
  See also binaries
publication, 54–55. *See also* blogging
public pedagogy
  academic/public binary and, 65
  choice and, 134
  cultural critique and civic writing vs., 5–6
  definitions of, 4–5, 11–12
  educational purposes aligned with location, 59–62
  Giroux's critique of neoliberalism and, 12–17
  "going public" as phrase, 2
  history of term, 10–11

service learning, overlap with, 28
social media and, 29–30
terminologies of, 3–4
publics
   academic/real-world binary and boundary crossing, 20–23
   counterpublics and, 17–18
   digital, 29–30
   lens of, 28
   neoliberal, 12–17
   oppositional public spheres, 16
   personal-public intersections, 54
   risky, 23–28
   as umbrella concept, 4–5
   See also histories, institutional

reciprocal model of care, 149–56
reflection, 143, 174n3
Reid, Alex, 29
Reid, E. Shelley, 74–75, 94
relationship building, 41–42, 47–48
religious histories, 111–16
relocation
   going somewhere new, importance of, 40–42, 46–47
   Long's schema of pedagogical approaches for public action, 35–38
   mobile composition and, 158
   Oberlin Field-Based Writing Course, 39–44, 61–62
   public location and educational purposes, 56–62
   public pedagogy and, 6, 18–21
   spatial analysis in Arizona composition courses, 50–56
   Syracuse Critical Research and Inquiry course, 44–50
   unfamiliar places, importance of, 57–58
   writing program administration and, 64
Rensselaer Polytechnic Institute, 97
research methods pedagogy
   in Arizona spatial analysis composition courses, 51–52, 55
   in Oberlin Field-Based Writing course, 42–44
   in Syracuse Critical Research and Inquiry course, 48
Restaino, Jessica, 65–66, 69, 73, 76
Reynolds, Nedra, 19–23, 56
rhetoric
   institutional history and, 107–8
   relocation and, 20–21
   spatial analysis and rhetorical analysis, 51
Richards, Rebecca, 142–48, 174n2, 174n4
Riedner, Rachel, 14, 33
Rincon, Frank Legleu, 113
risks, 23–28, 37, 135–36
Ritter, Kelly, 64
Ropers-Huilman, Rebecca, 149–50, 152
Rose, Shirley K., 2, 64, 87, 98
Royster, Jacqueline Jones, 108–11
Ryder, Phyllis, 16–17

Safford, Anson P. K., 126
Sandlin, Jennifer A., 10–11, 19
Sandy, Marie, 175n5
Savage, Glenn C., 11, 15
Schell, Eileen E., 18, 83
Schmidt, Christopher, 159
Schneider, Barbara, 138
Schön, Donald, 24, 174n3
school administrators, valuable information from, 26–27
Schubert, William H., 19
Schultz, Brian D., 19
Schwartz, John Pedro, 158
Scott, Sue M., 137–38
sequencing of "next step" courses, 81–88
service learning
   affect in, 139
   institutional history and, 97
   institutionalization and, 68–71
   public pedagogy, overlap with, 28

sustainability in, 73
Syracuse Critical Research and
    Inquiry course, 44–50
Shipherd, John, 112–13, 118, 119
Smalley, Frank, 113
small groups, 48
social media
    blogging, 143–44
    digitality and mobile composition, 159
    public pedagogy and, 29–30
Soja, Edward, 53
Solomon, Barbara Miller, 118
Sonnichsen, C. L., 123
spatial analysis, 50–56. *See also* place and space
spatial shock, 24–25
Springwood, Charles Fruehling, 173n9
Stephens, C. C., 122
Stephens, Jason, 67
stereotypes, confronting, 41–42, 47–48
Stewart, Philo, 112–13
Stoecker, Randy, 175n5
Strickland, Michael, 90, 98
sustainability
    Oberlin Community-Based Writing Program and, 77–81
    service learning and, 73
    writing program administration and, 73–74
SVR2 event (Spatial and Visual Rhetorics 2), Arizona, 92–94, 172n10
"swampy lowlands," 24
Swiencicki, Jill, 74
Syracuse University
    African American admissions, 120
    as "anchor institution," 106, 173n1
    Chief Bill Orange mascot and Native American relations, 124–27
    comparative data, 9
    Critical Research and Inquiry course, 44–50
    "Fast Forward Syracuse," 129–30
    "next step" course sequencing, 81–88
    religious history, 113
    THE General Body and "Rewind Syracuse" movement, 130
    vision/mission statement, 100–103, 106, 126–27, 129–30, 163–64
Syverud, Kent, 106, 129, 173n2

tactical pedagogies
    in Long's schema, 36, 37
    in Syracuse Critical Research and Inquiry course, 48–49
Tappan, Arthur, 119
Tappan, Lewis, 119
Tempe Normal School, 173n6
Temple University, 85–86
textbooks, custom, 93
textual authority, 101
transformative learning
    affect and, 136–42
    Arizona business course example, 142–48
    cognitive dissonance, equilibrium, and, 137
    decentering authority, 150–51, 152
    disorienting dilemmas, 136–37, 139, 142–48, 153–55
    ethics and, 140
    feminist pedagogies and, 148–54
    Georgia State University Public Rhetorics of Social Change example, 152–55
    Mezirow's phases of transformation, 136–37, 139, 174n1
    perspective transformation, 139
    reciprocal model of care, 149–56
    risks and rewards of going public and, 134–36, 141
    tracking of, 175n6
    transformative education vs., 140
    transparency and, 151–52
transparency, 151–52

trigger warnings, 132–33, 152
Trubek, Anne, 72, 76–78, 80–81, 86, 172n7
Tryon, Elizabeth A., 175n5
Tuomi-Gröhn, Terttu, 135
tutoring, 76–81, 172n7

undergraduate writing majors, growth of, 87
United Methodist Church (UMC), 113, 173n3
University of Arizona
   business writing course and emotional responses, 142–48
   comparative data, 9
   First-Year Writing Showcase, 91–92
   land-grant institutional history, 121–24
   mission statement, 101, 102, 104–5, 123–24, 165–66
   Native American relations, 126–27, 174n10
   spatial analysis in composition courses, 50–56
   SVR2 event, 92–94, 172n10
   "Top 10 Facts About," 167–68
   Writing Program, 88–94, 172n8
Urban Rhythms project, 86

values, historical narratives of. *See* histories, institutional
Verzosa, Elise, 92
Vinson, Jenna, 24–25
Votruba, James C., 67–68

Warner, Michael, 17
Weiser, Irwin, 2, 64, 87
Weisser, Christian R., 2, 56, 73
Welch, Nancy, 2, 13, 131, 155, 157
Wells, Gail W., 67–68
Wells, Jaclyn M., 171n1
Wells, Susan, 98
Wendler, Rachael, 141–42

West, Cornel, 138
Wharton-Michael, Patty, 24
Wiggins, Grant, 170n5
Wolf, Thia, 74
women, historical admission of, 116–18
Worsham, Lynn, 137
Wright, Donald G., 114
Writing Associates Program (Oberlin), 76–77, 172n7
writing program administration
   binaries and, 65–67
   Community-Based Writing Program (Oberlin), 76–81
   curriculum design and morphing, 71–75, 84–85
   first-year writing curriculum (Arizona), 88–94
   going public and role of, 95
   institutional history and, 98–99
   institutionalized vs. community-based models, 67–71
   multiple hats, benefits of, 90
   "next step" course sequencing (Syracuse), 81–88
   relocation, impact of, 64
   undergraduate writing majors, growth of, 87
Writing Program Administrators (WPAs)
   curriculum design that allows for morphing and, 71–75
   follow-through and, 81
   institutional histories, use of, 98–99, 115–16, 120–21
   institutionalized models and, 70–71
   relocation and, 64, 95
   See also writing program administration
Writing Public Lives, 93

Yancey, Kathleen Blake, 174n3
Young, Michael, 135

AUTHOR

Ashley J. Holmes is assistant professor of English at Georgia State University where she teaches first-year composition and undergraduate and graduate courses in composition theory and pedagogy, public and visual rhetoric, and digital writing and production. She has published peer-reviewed essays in *English Journal, Community Literacy Journal, Reflections, Kairos,* and *Ubiquity,* as well as in three edited collections. She is currently an assistant editor with *Kairos*.

BOOKS IN THE CCCC STUDIES IN WRITING & RHETORIC SERIES

Public Pedagogy in Composition Studies
Ashley J. Holmes

From Boys to Men: Rhetorics of Emergent American Masculinity
Leigh Ann Jones

Freedom Writing: African American Civil Rights Literacy Activism, 1955–1967
Rhea Estelle Lathan

The Desire for Literacy: Writing in the Lives of Adult Learners
Lauren Rosenberg

On Multimodality: New Media in Composition Studies
Jonathan Alexander and Jacqueline Rhodes

Toward a New Rhetoric of Difference
Stephanie L. Kerschbaum

Rhetoric of Respect: Recognizing Change at a Community Writing Center
Tiffany Rousculp

After Pedagogy: The Experience of Teaching
Paul Lynch

Redesigning Composition for Multilingual Realities
Jay Jordan

Agency in the Age of Peer Production
Quentin D. Vieregge, Kyle D. Stedman, Taylor Joy Mitchell, and Joseph M. Moxley

Remixing Composition: A History of Multimodal Writing Pedagogy
Jason Palmeri

First Semester: Graduate Students, Teaching Writing, and the Challenge of Middle Ground
Jessica Restaino

Agents of Integration: Understanding Transfer as a Rhetorical Act
Rebecca S. Nowacek

Digital Griots: African American Rhetoric in a Multimedia Age
Adam J. Banks

The Managerial Unconscious in the History of Composition Studies
Donna Strickland

Everyday Genres: Writing Assignments across the Disciplines
Mary Soliday

The Community College Writer: Exceeding Expectations
Howard Tinberg and Jean-Paul Nadeau

A Taste for Language: Literacy, Class, and English Studies
James Ray Watkins

Before Shaughnessy: Basic Writing at Yale and Harvard, 1920–1960
Kelly Ritter

Writer's Block: The Cognitive Dimension
Mike Rose

Teaching/Writing in Thirdspaces: The Studio Approach
Rhonda C. Grego and Nancy S. Thompson

Rural Literacies
Kim Donehower, Charlotte Hogg, and Eileen E. Schell

Writing with Authority: Students' Roles as Writers in Cross-National Perspective
David Foster

Whistlin' and Crowin' Women of Appalachia: Literacy Practices since College
Katherine Kelleher Sohn

Sexuality and the Politics of Ethos in the Writing Classroom
Zan Meyer Gonçalves

African American Literacies Unleashed: Vernacular English and the Composition Classroom
Arnetha F. Ball and Ted Lardner

Revisionary Rhetoric, Feminist Pedagogy, and Multigenre Texts
Julie Jung

Archives of Instruction: Nineteenth-Century Rhetorics, Readers, and Composition Books in the United States
Jean Ferguson Carr, Stephen L. Carr, and Lucille M. Schultz

Response to Reform: Composition and the Professionalization of Teaching
Margaret J. Marshall

Multiliteracies for a Digital Age
Stuart A. Selber

Personally Speaking: Experience as Evidence in Academic Discourse
Candace Spigelman

Self-Development and College Writing
Nick Tingle

Minor Re/Visions: Asian American Literacy Narratives as a Rhetoric of Citizenship
Morris Young

A Communion of Friendship: Literacy, Spiritual Practice, and Women in Recovery
Beth Daniell

Embodied Literacies: Imageword and a Poetics of Teaching
Kristie S. Fleckenstein

Language Diversity in the Classroom: From Intention to Practice
edited by Geneva Smitherman and Victor Villanueva

Rehearsing New Roles: How College Students Develop as Writers
Lee Ann Carroll

Across Property Lines: Textual Ownership in Writing Groups
Candace Spigelman

Mutuality in the Rhetoric and Composition Classroom
David L. Wallace and Helen Rothschild Ewald

The Young Composers: Composition's Beginnings in Nineteenth-Century Schools
Lucille M. Schultz

Technology and Literacy in the Twenty-First Century: The Importance of Paying Attention
Cynthia L. Selfe

Women Writing the Academy: Audience, Authority, and Transformation
Gesa E. Kirsch

Gender Influences: Reading Student Texts
Donnalee Rubin

Something Old, Something New: College Writing Teachers and Classroom Change
Wendy Bishop

Dialogue, Dialectic, and Conversation: A Social Perspective on the Function of Writing
Gregory Clark

Audience Expectations and Teacher Demands
Robert Brooke and John Hendricks

Toward a Grammar of Passages
Richard M. Coe

Rhetoric and Reality: Writing Instruction in American Colleges, 1900–1985
James A. Berlin

Writing Groups: History, Theory, and Implications
Anne Ruggles Gere

Teaching Writing as a Second Language
Alice S. Horning

Invention as a Social Act
Karen Burke LeFevre

The Variables of Composition: Process and Product in a Business Setting
Glenn J. Broadhead and Richard C. Freed

Writing Instruction in Nineteenth-Century American Colleges
James A. Berlin

Computers & Composing: How the New Technologies Are Changing Writing
Jeanne W. Halpern and Sarah Liggett

A New Perspective on Cohesion in Expository Paragraphs
Robin Bell Markels

Evaluating College Writing Programs
Stephen P. Witte and Lester Faigley

This book was typeset in Garamond and Frutiger by Barbara Frazier.
Typefaces used on the cover include Adobe Garamond and Formata.
The book was printed on 55-lb. Natural Offset paper
by King Printing Company, Inc.

www.ingramcontent.com/pod-product-compliance
Lightning Source LLC
Chambersburg PA
CBHW070401240426
43661CB00056B/2485